OSHA 30-Hour
Construction

Student Workbook

Raúl Ross Pineda
compiler

OSHA Outreach Training Program Series

OSHA 30-Hour Construction; Student Workbook
© Raúl Ross Pineda
Chicago, Illinois, USA
V.1 September 2017
V.2 April 2018
ISBN-13: 978-1975997830
ISBN-10: 1975997832

OSHA 30-Hour Construction

Student Workbook

This book contains the handouts for the OSHA Outreach Training Program's 30-Hour Construction course. It includes the pamphlets that highlight the key points to be presented by the instructor, as well as the group activities to be performed and the questionnaires to be answered by the students in class.

This book is a compilation of the pamphlets provided by OSHA for the 13 classes of the OSHA 10-Hour course (as reviewed on April 2, 2018), plus my own selection of handouts to cover the remaining 11 classes of the OSHA 30-Hour course.

 Raúl Ross Pineda (mxsinfronteras@gmail.com) has worked for over 30 years in construction and general industry. He is an OSHA Authorized Trainer at the Latino Worker Safety Center (obrerolatino.org).

Content

Introduction to OSHA   1

Job safety and health it's the law. OSHA; 2015.   2

Employers must provide and pay for most PPE. OSHA.   3

Your rights as a whistleblower. Fact Sheet. OSHA; 2013.   5

We are OSHA, we can help. OSHA; 2015.   8

Activity: Ways to report workplace hazards. OSHA.   12

Workers rights practice worksheet; Crossword Puzzle. OSHA.   13

Safety and health programs   15

Core elements of the recommended practices for safety and health programs in construction. Recommended Practices for Safety & Health Programs in Construction. OSHA; 2016.   16

Prevention program checklist from the New Jersey Work Environment Council. Injury and Illness Prevention Programs. New Jersey Work Environment Council; 2012.   17

Personal protective and lifesaving equipment   21

Personal Protective Equipment. Fact Sheet. OSHA; 2006.   22

Knowledge Check: PPE. 10-hour Construction Outreach. OSHA; 2015.   24

Focus 4: Falls   27

Guardrail and safety net systems summary. Construction Safety and Health Fall Hazards. Central New York COSH; 2007.   28

Personal fall arrest systems summary. Construction Safety and Health Fall Hazards. Central New York COSH; 2007.   29

Preventing ladder falls: Construction Safety. CDC, NIOSH, CPWR, The Center for Construction Research and Training, Health and Society, Telemundo.   31

Scaffold work can be dangerous: Know the basics of scaffold safety. Construction Safety & Health Fall Hazards. Central New York COSH; 2007.   33

Ladder Safety: What's wrong with this picture? Construction Safety & Health Fall Hazards. Central New York COSH; 2007.   35

Personal fall arrest system checklist. Construction Safety & Health Fall Hazards. Central New York COSH; 2007.   40

Fall hazard recognition. OSHA.   41

Construction Focus Four: Fall Hazards Lesson Test. OSHA.   45

Focus 4: Electrocution   47

Electrocution, safety tips for workers. Construction Focus Four. OSHA; 2007.   48

What increases your risk of electrocution? Module 4, Electrocution Talk Number 1. IUOE National Training Fund.   50

What protective devices and procedures can you use to prevent electrocution? Module 4, Electrocution Talk Number 2. IUOE National Training Fund.   51

How can we prevent electrocutions while using power tools? Module 4, Electrocution Talk Number 3. IUOE National Training Fund.   52

Electrical Safety. Quick Card. OSHA.   53

Wet conditions / Ground Fault Circuit Interrupters. Activity option A. Central New York COSH.   54

Extension cords, copper and current. Activity option B. Central New York COSH.   57

Accident Summary #11. Fatal Facts. OSHA; 2001.   58

Accident Summary #17. Fatal Facts. OSHA; 2001.   59

Accident Summary #28. Fatal Facts. OSHA; 2001.   60

Accident Summary #30. Fatal Facts. OSHA; 2001.   61

Accident Summary #40. Fatal Facts. OSHA; 2001.   62

Accident Summary #49. Fatal Facts. OSHA; 2001.   63

Accident Summary #57. Fatal Facts. OSHA; 2001.   64

Accident Summary #60. Fatal Facts. OSHA.   65

Electrocution hazard recognition. OSHA.   66

Construction Focus Four: Electrocution hazards lesson test. OSHA.   72

Focus 4: Struck-by

   73

Nail Guns. Hazard Alert. CPWR; 2008.   74

Cranes and rigging. Focus 4. Construction Safety Council.   76

PPE for workers checklist. OSHA.   77

Option A: Focus Four Toolbox Talks 1. IUOE National Training Fund.   78

Option B: Focus Four Toolbox Talks 2. IUOE National Training Fund.   79

Accident Summary #2. Fatal Facts. OSHA.   80

Accident Summary #4. Fatal Facts. OSHA.   81

Accident Summary #8. Fatal Facts. OSHA.   82

Accident Summary #51. Fatal Facts. OSHA.   83

Struck-by hazard recognition. OSHA.   84

Construction Focus Four: Struck-by hazards lesson test. OSHA.   88

Focus 4: Caught-in or -between

   89

Accident Summary #5. Fatal Facts. OSHA.   90

Accident Summary #13. Fatal Facts. OSHA.   91

Accident Summary #15. Fatal Facts. OSHA.   92

Accident Summary #18. Fatal Facts. OSHA.   93

Accident Summary #22. Fatal Facts. OSHA.   94

Accident Summary #31. Fatal Facts. OSHA.   95

Accident Summary #38. Fatal Facts. OSHA.   96

Accident Summary #50. Fatal Facts. OSHA.   97

Accident Summary #61. Fatal Facts. OSHA.   98

Accident Summary #73. Fatal Facts. OSHA.   99

Caught-in or -between hazard recognition. OSHA.   100

Review Exercise. OSHA.   104

Construction Focus Four: Caught-in or -between hazards lesson test. OSHA.   105

Cranes   107

Subpart CC: Cranes and derricks in construction: assembly/disassembly. Fact Sheet. OSHA.   108

Subpart CC: Cranes and derricks in construction: wire rope inspection. Fact Sheet. OSHA; 2013.   110

Knowledge Check: Cranes. 10-hour Construction Outreach. OSHA; 2015.   113

Excavations   115

Trenching and excavation safety. Fact Sheet. OSHA; 2011.   116

Knowledge Check: Excavations. 10-hour Construction Outreach. OSHA; 2015.   118

Materials handling   119

Warehousing. Worker Safety Series. OSHA.   120

Knowledge Check: Materials Handling, Storage, Use, and Disposal. 10-hour Construction Outreach. OSHA; 2015.   123

Scaffolds   125

Tube and coupler scaffolds: Erection and use. Fact Sheet. OSHA; 2014.   126

Knowledge Check: Scaffolds. 10-hour Construction Outreach. OSHA; 2015.   129

Stairways and ladders   131

Reducing falls in construction: Safe use of extension ladders. Fact Sheet. OSHA; 2013.   132

Portable ladder safety. Quick Card. OSHA.   135

Reducing falls in construction: Safe use of stepladders. Fact Sheet. OSHA; 2013.   137

Reducing falls in construction: Safe use of job-made wooden ladders. Fact Sheet. OSHA; 2013.   139

Knowledge Check: Stairways and ladders. 10-hour Construction Outreach. OSHA; 2015.   141

Tools – hand and power   143

Amputations. Fact Sheet. OSHA; 2002.   144

Knowledge Check: Tools – hand and power. 10-hour Construction Outreach. OSHA; 2015.   146

Concrete and masonry construction   147

Concrete manufacturing. Pocket Guide. Worker Safety Series. OSHA; 2004.   148

Confined space entry 157

Confined spaces in residential construction. Fact Sheet. OSHA; 2017. 158

Lockout/tagout. Fact Sheet. OSHA; 2002. 161

Procedures for atmospheric testing in confined spaces. Fact Sheet. OSHA; 2005. 163

Is 911 your confined space rescue plan? Fact Sheet. OSHA; 2016. 165

Motor vehicles, mechanized equipment and marine operations; rollover protective structures and overhead protection; and signs, signals and barricades 169

Oil patch #1. Fatal Facts. OSHA; 2012. 170

Traffic lanes and personnel safety zones. Fact Sheet. OSHA; 2012. 171

Compactor rollover hazard. Safety and Health Information Bulletin. OSHA; 2008. 173

Work zone traffic safety. Fact Sheet. OSHA; 2005. 179

Powered industrial vehicles 181

Preventing injuries and deaths of workers who operate or work near forklifts. Alert. NIOSH; 2001. 182

Steel erection 191

Steel erection; Inspection Guide. eTool. OSHA. 192

Welding and cutting 201

Welding with Arc-Welding Equipment; Self-inspection checklist. NIOSH. 202

Controlling hazardous fume and gases during welding. Fact Sheet. OSHA; 2013. 206

Fire protection and prevention 209

Fire safety in the workplace. Fact Sheet. OSHA; 2002. 210

Oil patch #5. Fatal Facts. OSHA; 2012. 212

Ergonomics 215

Factsheet A: What are musculoskeletal disorders? Preventing Sprains, Strains, and Repetitive Motion Injuries. State Building and Construction Trades Council of California, AFL-CIO; and Labor Occupational Health Program, University of California, Berkeley; 2012. 216

Factsheet B: Risk factors for ergonomic injuries. Preventing Sprains, Strains, and Repetitive Motion Injuries. State Building and Construction Trades Council of California, AFL-CIO; and Labor Occupational Health Program, University of California, Berkeley; 2012. 218

Health hazards in construction 221

Protecting workers from asbestos hazards. Fact Sheet. OSHA; 2005. 222

Crystalline silica exposure; Health hazard information. Fact Sheet. OSHA; 2002. 224

Protecting workers from lead hazards. Fact Sheet. OSHA; 2005. 226

Knowledge Check: Health Hazards in Construction. 10-hour Construction Outreach. OSHA; 2015. 228

Managing safety and health   229

Introduction. Recommended Practices for Safety & Health Programs in Construction. OSHA; 2016.   230

Foundations for safety leadership   235

Management leadership. Recommended Practices for Safety & Health Programs in Construction. OSHA; 2016.   236

Worker participation. Recommended Practices for Safety & Health Programs in Construction. OSHA; 2016.   238

Leadership skills and action checklist. Foundations for Safety Leadership; Student Handout. CPWR; 2015.   242

Introduction to OSHA

Job Safety and Health
IT'S THE LAW!

All workers have the right to:

- A safe workplace.

- Raise a safety or health concern with your employer or OSHA, or report a work-related injury or illness, without being retaliated against.

- Receive information and training on job hazards, including all hazardous substances in your workplace.

- Request an OSHA inspection of your workplace if you believe there are unsafe or unhealthy conditions. OSHA will keep your name confidential. You have the right to have a representative contact OSHA on your behalf.

- Participate (or have your representative participate) in an OSHA inspection and speak in private to the inspector.

- File a complaint with OSHA within 30 days (by phone, online or by mail) if you have been retaliated against for using your rights.

- See any OSHA citations issued to your employer.

- Request copies of your medical records, tests that measure hazards in the workplace, and the workplace injury and illness log.

This poster is available free from OSHA.

Contact OSHA. We can help.

Employers must:

- Provide employees a workplace free from recognized hazards. It is illegal to retaliate against an employee for using any of their rights under the law, including raising a health and safety concern with you or with OSHA, or reporting a work-related injury or illness.

- Comply with all applicable OSHA standards.

- Report to OSHA all work-related fatalities within 8 hours, and all inpatient hospitalizations, amputations and losses of an eye within 24 hours.

- Provide required training to all workers in a language and vocabulary they can understand.

- Prominently display this poster in the workplace.

- Post OSHA citations at or near the place of the alleged violations.

FREE ASSISTANCE to identify and correct hazards is available to small and medium-sized employers, without citation or penalty, through OSHA-supported consultation programs in every state.

1-800-321-OSHA (6742) • TTY 1-877-889-5627 • **www.osha.gov**

2

Employers Must Provide and Pay for Most PPE

Personal Protective Equipment (PPE)

The Occupational Safety and Health Administration (OSHA) requires that employers protect you from workplace hazards that can cause injury or illness. Controlling a hazard at its source is the best way to protect workers. However, when engineering, work practice and administrative controls are not feasible or do not provide sufficient protection, employers must provide personal protective equipment (PPE) to you and ensure its use.

PPE is equipment worn to minimize exposure to a variety of hazards. Examples include items such as gloves, foot and eye protection, protective hearing protection (earplugs, muffs), hard hats and respirators.

Employer Obligations	Workers should:
✓ Performing a "hazard assessment" of the workplace to identify and control physical and health hazards.	✓ Properly wear PPE
	✓ Attend training sessions on PPE
✓ Identifying and providing appropriate PPE for employees.	✓ Care for, clean and maintain PPE, an
	✓ Inform a supervisor of the need to repair or replace PPE.
✓ Training employees in the use and care of the PPE.	
✓ Maintaining PPE, including replacing worn or damaged PPE.	
✓ Periodically reviewing, updating and evaluating the effectiveness of the PPE program.	

Employers Must Pay for Personal Protective Equipment (PPE)

On May 15, 2008, a new OSHA rule about employer payment for PPE went into effect. With few exceptions, OSHA now requires employers to pay for personal protective equipment used to comply with OSHA standards. The final rule does not create new requirements regarding what PPE employers must provide.

The standard makes clear that employers cannot require workers to provide their own PPE and the worker's use of PPE they already own must be completely voluntary. Even when a worker provides his or her own PPE, the employer must ensure that the equipment is adequate to protect the worker from hazards at the workplace.

Examples of PPE that Employers Must Pay for Include:

- Metatarsal foot protection
- Rubber boots with steel toes
- Non-prescription eye protection
- Prescription eyewear inserts/lenses for full face respirators
- Goggles and face shields

- Fire fighting PPE (helmet, gloves, boots, proximity suits, full gear)
- Hard hats
- Hearing protection
- Welding PPE

Employers Must Provide and Pay for Most PPE

Payment Exceptions under the OSHA Rule

Employers are not required to pay for some PPE in certain circumstances:

- Non-specialty safety-toe protective footwear (including steel-toe shoes or boots) and non-specialty prescription safety eyewear provided that the employer permits such items to be worn off the job site. (OSHA based this decision on the fact that this type of equipment is very personal, is often used outside the workplace, and that it is taken by workers from jobsite to jobsite and employer to employer.)
- Everyday clothing, such as long-sleeve shirts, long pants, street shoes, and normal work boots.
- Ordinary clothing, skin creams, or other items, used solely for protection from weather, such as winter coats, jackets, gloves, parkas, rubber boots, hats, raincoats, ordinary sunglasses, and sunscreen
- Items such as hair nets and gloves worn by food workers for consumer safety.
- Lifting belts because their value in protecting the back is questionable.
- When the employee has lost or intentionally damaged the PPE and it must be replaced.

OSHA Standards that Apply

OSHA General Industry PPE Standards

- 1910.132: General requirements and payment
- 1910.133: Eye and face protection
- 1910.134: Respiratory protection
- 1910.135: Head protection
- 1910.136: Foot protection
- 1910.137: Electrical protective devices
- 1910.138: Hand protection

OSHA Construction PPE Standards

- 1926.28: Personal protective equipment
- 1926.95: Criteria for personal protective equipment
- 1926.96: Occupational foot protection
- 1926.100: Head protection
- 1926.101: Hearing protection
- 1926.102: Eye and face protection
- 1926.103: Respiratory protection

There are also PPE requirements in shipyards and marine terminals and many standards on specific hazards, such as 1910.1030: Bloodborne pathogens and 1910.146: Permit-required confined spaces.

OSHA standards are online at www.osha.gov.

Sources:
- *Employers Must Provide and Pay for PPE, New Jersey Work Environment Council (WEC) Fact Sheet*
- *OSHA Standards, 1910.132(h) and 1926.95(d)*
- *Employer Payment for Personal Protective Equipment Final Rule, Federal Register: November 15, 2007 (Volume 72, Number 220)*

OSHA®FactSheet

Your Rights as a Whistleblower

You may file a complaint with OSHA if your employer retaliates against you by taking unfavorable personnel action because you engaged in protected activity relating to workplace safety or health, asbestos in schools, cargo containers, airline, commercial motor carrier, consumer product, environmental, financial reform, food safety, health insurance reform, motor vehicle safety, nuclear, pipeline, public transportation agency, railroad, maritime, and securities laws.

Whistleblower Laws Enforced by OSHA

Each law requires that complaints be filed within a certain number of days after the alleged retaliation.

- *Asbestos Hazard Emergency Response Act* (90 days)
- *Clean Air Act* (30 days)
- *Comprehensive Environmental Response, Compensation and Liability Act* (30 days)
- *Consumer Financial Protection Act of 2010* (180 days)
- *Consumer Product Safety Improvement Act* (180 days)
- *Energy Reorganization Act* (180 days)
- *Federal Railroad Safety Act* (180 days)
- *Federal Water Pollution Control Act* (30 days)
- *International Safe Container Act* (60 days)
- *Moving Ahead for Progress in the 21st Century Act* (motor vehicle safety) (180 days)
- *National Transit Systems Security Act* (180 days)
- *Occupational Safety and Health Act* (30 days)
- *Pipeline Safety Improvement Act* (180 days)
- *Safe Drinking Water Act* (30 days)
- *Sarbanes-Oxley Act* (180 days)
- *Seaman's Protection Act* (180 days)
- *Section 402 of the FDA Food Safety Modernization Act* (180 days)
- *Section 1558 of the Affordable Care Act* (180 days)
- *Solid Waste Disposal Act* (30 days)
- *Surface Transportation Assistance Act* (180 days)
- *Toxic Substances Control Act* (30 days)
- *Wendell H. Ford Aviation Investment and Reform Act for the 21st Century* (90 days)

Unfavorable Personnel Actions

Your employer may be found to have retaliated against you if your protected activity was a contributing or motivating factor in its decision to take unfavorable personnel action against you. Such actions may include:

- Applying or issuing a policy which provides for an unfavorable personnel action due to activity protected by a whistleblower law enforced by OSHA
- Blacklisting
- Demoting
- Denying overtime or promotion
- Disciplining
- Denying benefits
- Failing to hire or rehire
- Firing or laying off
- Intimidation
- Making threats
- Reassignment to a less desirable position, including one adversely affecting prospects for promotion
- Reducing pay or hours
- Suspension

Filing a Complaint

If you believe that your employer retaliated against you because you exercised your legal rights as an employee, contact OSHA as soon as possible because you must file your complaint within the legal time limits.

An employee can file a complaint with OSHA by visiting or calling the local OSHA office or sending a written complaint to the closest OSHA regional or area office. Written complaints may be filed by facsimile, electronic communication, hand delivery during business hours, U.S. mail (confirmation services recommended), or other third-party commercial carrier. The date of the postmark, facsimile, electronic communication, telephone call, hand delivery, delivery to a third-party commercial carrier, or in-person filing at an OSHA

5

office is considered the date filed. No particular form is required and complaints may be submitted in any language.

For OSHA area office contact information, please call 1-800-321-OSHA (6742) or visit www.osha.gov/html/RAmap.html.

Upon receipt of a complaint, OSHA will first review it to determine whether it is valid on its face. All complaints are investigated in accord with the statutory requirements.

With the exception of employees of the U.S. Postal Service, public sector employees (those employed as municipal, county, state, territorial or federal workers) are not covered by the *Occupational Safety and Health Act* (OSH Act). Non-federal public sector employees and, except in Connecticut, New York, New Jersey, the Virgin Islands, and Illinois, private sector employees are covered in states which operate their own occupational safety and health programs approved by Federal OSHA. For information on the 27 State Plan states, call 1-800-321-OSHA (6742), or visit www.osha.gov/dcsp/osp/index.html.

A federal employee who wishes to file a complaint alleging retaliation due to disclosure of a substantial and specific danger to public health or safety or involving occupational safety or health should contact the Office of Special Counsel (www.osc.gov) and OSHA's Office of Federal Agency Programs (www.osha.gov/dep/enforcement/dep_offices.html).

Coverage of public sector employees under the other statutes administered by OSHA varies by statute. If you are a public sector employee and you are unsure whether you are covered under a whistleblower protection statute, call 1-800-321-OSHA (6742) for assistance, or visit www.whistleblowers.gov.

How OSHA Determines Whether Retaliation Took Place

The investigation must reveal that:

- The employee engaged in protected activity;
- The employer knew about or suspected the protected activity;
- The employer took an adverse action; and
- The protected activity motivated or contributed to the adverse action.

If the evidence supports the employee's allegation and a settlement cannot be reached, OSHA will generally issue an order, which the employer may contest, requiring the employer to reinstate the employee, pay back wages, restore benefits, and other possible remedies to make the employee whole. Under some of the statutes the employer must comply with the reinstatement order immediately. In cases under the *Occupational Safety and Health Act*, *Asbestos Hazard Emergency Response Act*, and the *International Safe Container Act*, the Secretary of Labor will file suit in federal district court to obtain relief.

Partial List of Whistleblower Protections

Whistleblower Protections under the OSH Act

The OSH Act protects workers who complain to their employer, OSHA or other government agencies about unsafe or unhealthful working conditions in the workplace or environmental problems. You cannot be transferred, denied a raise, have your hours reduced, be fired, or punished in any other way because you used any right given to you under the OSH Act. Help is available from OSHA for whistleblowers.

If you have been punished or discriminated against for using your rights, you must file a complaint with OSHA within 30 days of the alleged reprisal for most complaints. No form is required, but you must send a letter or call the OSHA Area Office nearest you to report the discrimination (within 30 days of the alleged discrimination).

You have a limited right under the OSH Act to refuse to do a job because conditions are hazardous. You may do so under the OSH Act only when (1) you believe that you face death or serious injury (and the situation is so clearly hazardous that any reasonable person would believe the same thing); (2) you have tried, where possible, to get your employer to correct the condition, and been unable to obtain a correction and there is no other way to do the job safely; and (3) the situation is so urgent that you do not have time to eliminate the hazard through regulatory channels such as calling OSHA. For details, see www.osha.gov/as/opa/worker/refuse.html. OSHA cannot enforce union contracts or state laws that give employees the right to refuse to work.

Whistleblower Protections in the Transportation Industry

Employees whose jobs directly affect commercial motor vehicle safety or security are protected from retaliation by their employers for, among other things, reporting violations of federal or state commercial motor carrier safety or security regulations, or refusing to operate a vehicle because of violations of federal commercial motor vehicle safety or security regulations or because they have a reasonable apprehension of death or serious injury to themselves or the public and they have sought from the employer and been unable to obtain correction of the hazardous condition.

Similarly, employees of air carriers, their contractors or subcontractors who raise safety concerns or report violations of FAA rules and regulations are protected from retaliation, as are employees of owners and operators of pipelines, their contractors and subcontractors who report violations of pipeline safety rules and regulations. Employees involved in international shipping who report unsafe shipping containers are also protected. In addition, employees of railroad carriers or public transportation agencies, their contractors or subcontractors who report safety or security conditions or violations of federal rules and regulations relating to railroad or public transportation safety or security are protected from retaliation.

Whistleblower Protections for Voicing Environmental Concerns

A number of laws protect employees from retaliation because they report violations of environmental laws related to drinking water and water pollution, toxic substances, solid waste disposal, air quality and air pollution, asbestos in schools, and hazardous waste disposal sites. The *Energy Reorganization Act* protects employees from retaliation for raising safety concerns in the nuclear power industry and in nuclear medicine.

Whistleblower Protections When Reporting Corporate Fraud

Employees who work for publicly traded companies or companies required to file certain reports with the Securities and Exchange Commission are protected from retaliation for reporting alleged mail, wire, bank or securities fraud; violations of SEC rules or regulations of the SEC; or violations of federal laws relating to fraud against shareholders.

Whistleblower Protections for Voicing Consumer Product Concerns

Employees of consumer product manufacturers, importers, distributors, retailers, and private labelers are protected from retaliation for reporting reasonably perceived violations of any statute or regulation within the jurisdiction of the Consumer Product Safety Commission.

More Information

To obtain more information on whistleblower laws, go to www.whistleblowers.gov.

For assistance, contact us. We can help. It's confidential.

OSHA ® Occupational Safety and Health Administration

U.S. Department of Labor
www.osha.gov (800) 321-OSHA (6742)

DWP FS-3638 04/2013

We Are OSHA

We Can Help

Workers' rights under the OSH Act

Workers are entitled to working conditions that do not pose a risk of serious harm. To help assure a safe and healthful workplace, OSHA also provides workers with the right to:

* Ask OSHA to inspect their workplace;

* Use their rights under the law without retaliation;

* Receive information and training about hazards, methods to prevent harm, and the OSHA standards that apply to their workplace. The training must be in a language you can understand;

* Get copies of test results done to find hazards in the workplace;

* Review records of work-related injuries and illnesses; and

* Get copies of their medical records.

Occupational Safety and Health Administration
U.S. Department of Labor

Who OSHA covers

Private sector workers

Most employees in the nation come under OSHA's jurisdiction. OSHA covers private sector employers and employees in all 50 states, the District of Columbia, and other  U.S. jurisdictions either directly through Federal OSHA or through an OSHA-approved state program. State-run health and safety programs must be at least as effective as the Federal OSHA program. To find the contact information for the OSHA Federal or State Program office nearest you, call 1-800-321-OSHA (6742) or go to www.osha.gov.

State and local government workers

Employees who work for state and local governments are not covered by Federal OSHA, but have OSH Act protections if they work in those states that have an OSHA-approved state program. The following 22 states or territories have OSHA-approved programs:

Alaska	Arizona	California
Hawaii	Indiana	Iowa
Kentucky	Maryland	Michigan
Minnesota	Nevada	New Mexico
North Carolina	Oregon	South Carolina
Tennessee	Utah	Vermont
Virginia	Washington	Wyoming
Puerto Rico		

Five additional states and one U.S. territory have OSHA-approved plans that cover public sector workers only:

Connecticut	Illinois	Maine
New Jersey	New York	Virgin Islands

Private sector workers in these five states and the Virgin Islands are covered by Federal OSHA.

Federal government workers

Federal agencies must have a safety and health program that meets the same standards as private employers. Although OSHA does not fine federal agencies, it does monitor federal agencies and responds to workers' complaints. The United States Postal Service (USPS) is covered by OSHA.

Not covered under the OSH Act:

- Self-employed;
- Immediate family members of farm employers who do not employ outside employees;
- Workplace hazards regulated by another federal agency (for example, the Mine Safety and Health Administration, the Department of Energy, or Coast Guard).

OSHA standards: Protection on the job

OSHA standards are rules that describe the methods that employers must use to protect their employees from hazards. There are OSHA standards for Construction work, Agriculture, Maritime operations, and General Industry, which are the standards that apply to most worksites. These standards limit the amount of hazardous chemicals workers can be exposed to, require the use of certain safe practices and equipment, and require employers to monitor hazards and keep records of workplace injuries and illnesses.

Examples of OSHA standards include requirements to provide fall protection, prevent trenching cave-ins, prevent some infectious diseases, assure that workers safely enter confined spaces, prevent exposure to harmful substances like asbestos, put guards on machines, provide respirators or other safety equipment, and provide training for certain dangerous jobs.

Employers must also comply with the General Duty Clause of the OSH Act, which *requires employers to keep their workplace free of serious recognized hazards*. This clause is generally cited when no OSHA standard applies to the hazard.

Workers can ask OSHA to inspect their workplace

Workers, or their representatives, may file a complaint and ask OSHA to inspect their workplace if they believe there is a serious hazard or that their employer is not following OSHA standards. A worker can tell OSHA not to let their employer know who filed the complaint. **It is a violation of the OSH Act for an employer to fire, demote, transfer or retaliate in any way against a worker for filing a complaint or using other OSHA rights.**

Written complaints that are signed by a worker or their representative and submitted to the closest OSHA office are more likely to result in an on-site OSHA inspection. You can call 1-800-321-OSHA (6742) to request a complaint form from your local OSHA office or visit www.osha.gov/pls/osha7/eComplaintForm.html to submit the form online. Completed forms can also be faxed or mailed to the local OSHA office. Most complaints sent in online may be resolved informally over the phone with your employer.

When the OSHA inspector arrives, workers and their representatives have the right to:

* Go along on the inspection;
* Talk privately with the OSHA inspector; and
* Take part in meetings with the inspector and the employer before and after the inspection is conducted.

Where there is no union or employee representative, the OSHA inspector must talk confidentially with a reasonable number of workers during the course of the investigation.

When an inspector finds violations of OSHA standards or serious hazards, OSHA may issue citations and fines. A citation includes the methods an employer may use to fix a problem and the date by when the corrective actions must be completed. Workers only have the right to challenge the deadline for when a problem must be resolved. Employers, on the other hand, have the right to contest whether there is a violation or any other part of the citation. Workers or their representatives must notify OSHA that they want to be involved in the appeals process if the employer challenges a citation.

If you send in a complaint requesting an OSHA inspection, you have the right to find out the results of the OSHA inspection and request a review if OSHA does not issue citations.

Employer responsibilities

Employers have the responsibility to provide a safe workplace. **Employers MUST provide their employees with a workplace that does not have serious hazards and must follow all OSHA safety and health standards.** Employers must find and correct safety and health problems. OSHA further requires employers to try to eliminate or reduce hazards first by making changes in working conditions rather than just relying on masks, gloves, earplugs or other types of personal protective equipment. Switching to safer chemicals, implementing processes to trap harmful fumes, or using ventilation systems to clean the air are examples of effective ways to get rid of or minimize risks.

Employers **MUST** also:

* Prominently display the official OSHA *Job Safety and Health – It's the Law* poster that describes rights and responsibilities under the OSH Act. **This poster is free and can be downloaded from www.osha.gov**.

* Inform workers about chemical hazards through training, labels, alarms, color-coded systems, chemical information sheets and other methods.

* Provide safety training to workers in a language and vocabulary they can understand.

* Keep accurate records of work-related injuries and illnesses.

* Perform tests in the workplace, such as air sampling, required by some OSHA standards.

* Provide required personal protective equipment at no cost to workers.*

* Provide hearing exams or other medical tests required by OSHA standards.

- Post OSHA citations and injury and illness data where workers can see them.

- Notify OSHA within 8 hours of a workplace fatality or within 24 hours of any work-related inpatient hospitalization, amputation or loss of an eye (1-800-321-OSHA [6742]).

- Not retaliate against workers for using their rights under the law, including their right to report a work-related injury or illness.

* Employers must pay for most types of required personal protective equipment.

The law protects workers from retaliation when using their OSHA rights

The OSH Act protects workers who complain to their employer, OSHA or other government agencies about unsafe or unhealthful working conditions in the workplace or environmental problems. You cannot be transferred, denied a raise, have your hours reduced, be fired, or punished in any other way because you used any right given to you under the OSH Act. Help is available from OSHA for whistleblowers.

If you have been punished or retaliated against for using your rights, you must file a complaint with OSHA **within 30 days** from the date the retaliatory decision was both made and communicated to you. No form is needed, but you must call OSHA within 30 days of the alleged retaliation at 1-800-321-OSHA (6742) and ask to speak to the OSHA area office nearest you to report the retaliation.

You have the right to a safe workplace

The *Occupational Safety and Health Act of 1970* (OSH Act) was passed to prevent workers from being killed or seriously harmed at work. The law requires that employers provide their employees with working conditions that are free of known dangers. The Act created the Occupational Safety and Health Administration (OSHA), which sets and enforces protective workplace safety and health standards. OSHA also provides information, training and assistance to workers and employers. Workers may file a complaint to have OSHA inspect their workplace if they believe that their employer is not following OSHA standards or there are serious hazards.

Contact us if you have questions or want to file a complaint. We will keep your information confidential. We are here to help you. Call our toll-free number at 1-800-321-OSHA (6742) or go to www.osha.gov.

Occupational Safety and Health Administration

U.S. Department of Labor

1-800-321-OSHA (6742)   TTY 1-877-889-5627
www.osha.gov

OSHA 3334-09R 2015

11

Activity: Ways to Report Workplace Hazards

Instructions

Based on the following scenario, discuss how you would follow the *Ways to Report Workplace Hazards* to determine what reporting approach would be best. Read the questions listed below that when answered, provide the information important to reporting workplace hazards. Is any additional information needed?

Scenario

You are a construction worker for ABC, Inc., 1000 Sweet Road, Anytown, USA, 40001. ABC does non-residential plumbing, heating and air conditioning work. You have worked for ABC for 3 years. You, along with 7 co-workers, have been installing sheet metal ductwork in the lower level of the Anytown Shopping Mall, which is undergoing renovation, for the past few weeks. The site is located in the Northwest quadrant, in the basement of the anchor store, located at 555 Times Drive, in Anytown. One of your coworkers has been operating a 65-horsepower concrete cutting saw in the same area. The saw is being run in the propane mode. You and several coworkers get headaches from the fumes whenever the saw is used and have told your supervisor about the problem. The supervisor said that nothing could be done, because the General Contractor, CAB Management, has control over the site and this job will be complete in another month. You did some research and found out that exposure to propane in a confined, unventilated area can cause headaches, dizziness, difficulty breathing and unconsciousness. There is no ventilation or monitoring of the air in the area. After talking with coworkers, you decide to report the hazards.

Questions

- Has anyone been injured or made ill as a result of this problem?

- How many employees work at the site and how many are exposed to the hazard?

- How and when are workers exposed? On what shifts does the hazard exist?

- What work is performed in the unsafe or unhealthful area?

- What type of equipment is used? Is it in good condition?

- What materials and/or chemicals are used?

- Have employees been informed or trained regarding hazardous conditions?

- What process and/or operation is involved? What kinds of work are done nearby?

- How often and for how long do employees work at the task that leads to their exposure?

- How long (to your knowledge) has the condition existed?

- Have any attempts been made to correct the problem? Have there been any "near-miss" incidents?

Topic 4: Workers Rights Practice Worksheet
Crossword Puzzle

OSHA Provides Workers the Right to:

Across

      4. Hazard _____ and medical records

      6. Information about _____ and illnesses in your workplace

      7. A safe and _____ workplace

      8. Complain or request hazard _____ from employer

      9. Participate in an OSHA _____

Down

      1. Know about _____ conditions

      2. Be free from _____ for exercising safety and health rights

      3. _____ as provided in the OSHA standards

      5. File a complaint with _____

Safety and health programs

CORE ELEMENTS OF THE RECOMMENDED PRACTICES FOR SAFETY AND HEALTH PROGRAMS IN CONSTRUCTION

MANAGEMENT LEADERSHIP	• Top management demonstrates its commitment to eliminating hazards and to continuously improving workplace safety and health, communicates that commitment to workers, and sets program expectations and responsibilities. • Managers at all levels make safety and health a core organizational value, establish safety and health goals and objectives, provide adequate resources and support for the program, and set a good example.
WORKER PARTICIPATION	• Workers and their representatives are involved in all aspects of the program—including setting goals, identifying and reporting hazards, investigating incidents, and tracking progress. • All workers, including contractors and temporary workers, understand their roles and responsibilities under the program and what they need to do to effectively carry them out. • Workers are encouraged and have means to communicate openly with management and to report safety and health concerns or suggest improvements, without fear of retaliation. • Any potential barriers or obstacles to worker participation in the program (for example, language, lack of information, or disincentives) are removed or addressed.
HAZARD IDENTIFICATION AND ASSESSMENT	• Procedures are put in place to continually identify workplace hazards and evaluate risks. • Safety and health hazards from routine, nonroutine, and emergency situations are identified and assessed. • An initial assessment of existing hazards, exposures, and control measures is followed by periodic inspections and reassessments, to identify new hazards. • Any incidents are investigated with the goal of identifying the root causes. • Identified hazards are prioritized for control.
HAZARD PREVENTION AND CONTROL	• Employers and workers cooperate to identify and select methods for eliminating, preventing, or controlling workplace hazards. • Controls are selected according to a hierarchy that uses engineering solutions first, followed by safe work practices, administrative controls, and finally personal protective equipment (PPE). • A plan is developed that ensures controls are implemented, interim protection is provided, progress is tracked, and the effectiveness of controls is verified.
EDUCATION AND TRAINING	• All workers are trained to understand how the program works and how to carry out the responsibilities assigned to them under the program. • Employers, managers, and supervisors receive training on safety concepts and their responsibility for protecting workers' rights and responding to workers' reports and concerns. • All workers are trained to recognize workplace hazards and to understand the control measures that have been implemented.
PROGRAM EVALUATION AND IMPROVEMENT	• Control measures are periodically evaluated for effectiveness. • Processes are established to monitor program performance, verify program implementation, and identify program shortcomings and opportunities for improvement. • Necessary actions are taken to improve the program and overall safety and health performance.
COMMUNICATION AND COORDINATION FOR EMPLOYERS ON MULTIEMPLOYER WORKSITES	• General contractors, contractors, and staffing agencies commit to providing the same level of safety and health protection to all employees. • General contractors, contractors, subcontractors, and staffing agencies commmunicate the hazards present at the worksite and the hazards that work of contract workers may create on site. • General contractors establish specifications and qualifications for contractors and staffing agencies. • Prior to beginning work, general contractors, contractors, and staffing agencies coordinate on work planning and scheduling to identify and resolve any conflicts that could impact safety or health.

Prevention Program Checklist From the New Jersey Work Environment Council

Use this checklist to help evaluate the overall Injury and Illness Prevention Program in your workplace

Management Leadership

Does management...

___ Have a serious commitment to having an effective prevention program?

___ Provide appropriate financial, human, and organizational resources to protect workers' safety and health?

___ Institute policies that places safety and health on the level of importance as production?

___ Institute a communications system that encourages all workers to inform their supervisor and management about workplace hazards without fear of reprisal?

Worker participation

Are employees and their representatives...

___ Provided with timely information about hazards, including accident, illness, incident, and near-miss records and investigation results, as well as reports on employee exposure and hazard monitoring?

___ Included in planning, evaluation and implementation of hazard controls, including inspections and audits, worker surveys, recommendations for improvements, shutting down unsafe operations if necessary, developing an ongoing list of health and safety hazards, and tracking management follow-up?

___ Included in identifying and removing obstacles to participation, such as fear of reprisals for reporting hazards, injuries, or illnesses?

___ Included in a joint health and safety committee that operates with management and employee representatives as genuinely equal partners, sets deadlines for correcting hazards, investigates accidents and near misses, asks workers for their input about hazards, ensures access to all relevant information, and keeps records, track progress, and evaluates success?

(continued)

Hazard identification and assessment

____ Is the workplace designed so an error will not result in an injury or illness?

____ For each work process or material used, do employees (and their representatives) and management discuss whether there is a way to make it safer or reduce or eliminate exposure?

____ Are hazards identified by referring to state and federal laws, to records of injuries, illnesses and near misses, and to hazards typically faced in this industry?

____ Are hazards identified and controlled before new processes or materials are brought into the workplace?

____ Are employees who do the work consulted in purchasing decisions to ensure that the safest materials and processes are chosen?

____ Does identification of hazards cover the work of contractors?

Hazard prevention and control

____ Are hazards controlled first by eliminating them altogether, then by engineering controls, then by administrative controls, and only then by personal protective equipment?

____ Is equipment regularly and thoroughly maintained?

____ Is training provided on how to use and maintain personal protective equipment when it is the only alternative?

____ Do all employees understand and follow safe work procedures?

____ Is there a medical program tailored to your facility to help monitor and prevent workplace hazards and exposures?

____ Are there warning systems in place such as alarms, signs, and labels and do workers understand them?

____ Is there a plan in place and are employees trained to respond to an emergency such as a chemical leak, spill, fire, flood, or hurricane?

(continued)

Education and training

____ Are employees and their representatives involved in developing education and training about workplace hazards and how injuries and illnesses can be prevented, eliminated, or controlled?

____ Is the training…

- In language employees understand?
- On paid time?
- For all new employees?
- For all employees given new assignments?
- For contractors as well as employees?
- Whenever new substances, processes, or equipment are brought into the workplace?
- Whenever new hazards are recognized?
- Provided by competent trainers?
- Designed to include participation (discussions, questions, hands-on experiences, role playing), not just lectures or watching videos?
- Accessible to people with disabilities?

____ Does the training cover employees' right to information and right to report hazards, accidents, illnesses, and near-misses without facing reprisals?

Program evaluation and improvement

Is management's program for preventing illnesses and injuries evaluated in ways such as…

____ Workplace inspections?

____ Investigations of accidents, near-misses, injuries, and illnesses?

____ Records of hazards, showing when they are prevented, removed or controlled?

____ Employee participation in evaluating whether hazards are being prevented and controlled and in identifying improvements that are needed?

____ Compliance with federal and state laws?

Personal protective and lifesaving equipment

OSHA® FactSheet

Personal Protective Equipment

Personal protective equipment, or PPE, is designed to protect workers from serious workplace injuries or illnesses resulting from contact with chemical, radiological, physical, electrical, mechanical, or other workplace hazards. Besides face shields, safety glasses, hard hats, and safety shoes, protective equipment includes a variety of devices and garments such as goggles,coveralls, gloves, vests, earplugs, and respirators.

Employer Responsibilities

OSHA's primary personal protective equipment standards are in Title 29 of the Code of Federal Regulations (CFR), Part 1910 Subpart I, and equivalent regulations in states with OSHA-approved state plans, but you can find protective equipment requirements elsewhere in the General Industry Standards. For example, 29 CFR 1910.156, OSHA's Fire Brigades Standard, has requirements for firefighting gear. In addition, 29 CFR 1926.95-106 covers the construction industry. OSHA's general personal protective equipment requirements mandate that employers conduct a hazard assessment of their workplaces to determine what hazards are present that require the use of protective equipment, provide workers with appropriate protective equipment, and require them to use and maintain it in sanitary and reliable condition.

Using personal protective equipment is often essential, but it is generally the last line of defense after engineering controls, work practices, and administrative controls. Engineering controls involve physically changing a machine or work environment. Administrative controls involve changing how or when workers do their jobs, such as scheduling work and rotating workers to reduce exposures. Work practices involve training workers how to perform tasks in ways that reduce their exposure to workplace hazards.

As an employer, you must assess your workplace to determine if hazards are present that require the use of personal protective equipment. If such hazards are present, you must select protective equipment and require workers to use it, communicate your protective equipment selection decisions to your workers, and select personal protective equipment that properly fits your workers.

You must also train workers who are required to wear personal protective equipment on how to do the following:
- Use protective equipment properly,
- Be aware of when personal protective equipment is necessary,
- Know what kind of protective equipment is necessary,
- Understand the limitations of personal protective equipment in protecting workers from injury,
- Put on, adjust, wear, and take off personal protective equipment, and
- Maintain protective equipment properly.

Protection from Head Injuries

Hard hats can protect your workers from head impact, penetration injuries, and electrical injuries such as those caused by falling or flying objects, fixed objects, or contact with electrical conductors. Also, OSHA regulations require employers to ensure that workers cover and protect long hair to prevent it from getting caught in machine parts such as belts and chains.

Protection from Foot and Leg Injuries

In addition to foot guards and safety shoes, leggings (e.g., leather, aluminized rayon, or otherappropriate material) can help prevent injuries by protecting workers from hazards such as falling or rolling objects, sharp objects, wet and slippery surfaces, molten metals, hot surfaces, and electrical hazards.

Protection from Eye and Face Injuries

Besides spectacles and goggles, personal protective equipment such as special helmets or shields, spectacles with side shields, and faceshields can protect workers from the hazards of flying fragments, large chips, hot sparks, optical radiation, splashes from molten metals, as well as objects, particles, sand, dirt, mists, dusts, and glare.

Protection from Hearing Loss

Wearing earplugs or earmuffs can help prevent damage to hearing. Exposure to high noise levels can cause irreversible hearing loss or impairment as well as physical and psychological stress. Earplugs made from foam, waxed cotton, or fiberglass wool are self-forming and usually fit well. A professional should fit your workers individually for molded or preformed earplugs. Clean earplugs regularly, and replace those you cannot clean.

Protection from Hand Injuries

Workers exposed to harmful substances through skin absorption, severe cuts or lacerations, severe abrasions, chemical burns, thermal burns, and harmful temperatureextremes will benefit from hand protection.

Protection from Body Injury

In some cases workers must shield most or all of their bodies against hazards in the workplace, such as exposure to heat and radiation as well as hot metals, scalding liquids, body fluids, hazardous materials or waste, and other hazards. In addition to fire-retardant wool and fireretardant cotton, materials used in whole-body personal protective equipment include rubber, leather, synthetics, and plastic.

When to Wear Respiratory Protection

When engineering controls are not feasible, workers must use appropriate respirators to protect against adverse health effects caused by breathing air contaminated with harmful dusts, fogs, fumes, mists, gases, smokes, sprays, or vapors. Respirators generally cover the nose and mouth or the entire face or head and help prevent illness and injury. A proper fit is essential, however, for respirators to be effective. Required respirators must be NIOSH-approved and medical evaluation and training must be provided before use.

Additional Information

For additional information concerning protective equipment view the publication, Assessing the Need for Personal Protective Equipment: A Guide for Small Business Employers (OSHA 3151) available on OSHA's web site at www. osha. gov. For more information about personal protective equipment in the construction industry, visit www.osha-slc.gov/SLTC/construc-tionppe/ index.html.

Contacting OSHA

To report an emergency, file a complaint or seek OSHA advice, assistance or products, call (800) 321-OSHA or contact your nearest OSHA regional or area office.

This is one in a series of informational fact sheets highlighting OSHA programs, policies or standards. It does not impose any new compliance requirements. For a comprehensive list of compliance requirements of OSHA standards or regulations, refer to Title 29 of the Code of Federal Regulations. This information will be made available to sensory impaired individuals upon request. The voice phone is (202) 693-1999; teletypewriter (TTY) number: (877) 889-5627.

For more complete information:

OSHA® Occupational Safety and Health Administration

U.S. Department of Labor
www.osha.gov
(800) 321-OSHA

DOC 4/2006

Name: _____   Date: _____

Knowledge Check: PPE

1. Who is responsible for providing PPE?
   a. The employer
   b. The employee
   c. OSHA
   d. Workers' Compensation

2. Common causes of foot injuries include: crushing, penetration, molten metal, chemicals, slippery surfaces, and sharp objects.
   a. True
   b. False

3. Safety controls must meet the following order of priority:
   a. Substitution, PPE, workaround, and administrative
   b. Workaround, stop work, PPE, and engineering
   c. Stop work, PPE, engineering, and substitution
   d. Substitution, engineering, administrative, and PPE

4. Which type of hard hat would provide the most protection from electrical hazards?
   a. Class A
   b. Class C
   c. Class E
   d. Class G

5. The need for hearing protection is triggered at which decibel level?
   a. When it exceeds 80 decibels
   b. When it exceeds 90 decibels
   c. When it exceeds 100 decibels
   d. When it exceeds 110 decibels

6. Who is responsible for providing specialized work footwear?
   a. The employer
   b. The employee
   c. OSHA
   d. Insurance companies

7. Which of the following is considered approved eye protection?
   a. Sun glasses
   b. Prescription glasses
   c. Reading glasses
   d. Glasses meeting ANSI standard Z87

8. Which of the following is not considered PPE?
   a. Rubber gloves
   b. Glasses meeting ANSI Z87
   c. Sports shoes
   d. Hearing muffs

Focus 4: Falls

Guardrail and Safety Net Systems Summary

Guardrail and safety net systems are two ways to protect workers from falls on the job. If you are more than 6 feet above the lower surface, some type of fall protection must be used by your employer.

If your employer uses **guardrails:**

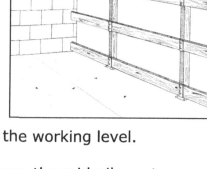

• Toprails must be at least ¼ inch thick to prevent cuts and lacerations; and they must be between 39 and 45 inches from the working surface;
• If wire rope is used, it must be flagged at least every six feet with highly visible materials;
• Midrails, screens or mesh must be installed when there are no walls at least 21 inches high. Screens and mesh must extend from the toprail to the working level.
• There can be no openings more than 19 inches;
• The toprail must withstand at least 200 lbs. of force; the midrail must withstand 150 lbs. of force;
• The system must be smooth enough to protect workers from cuts and getting their clothes snagged by the rail.
• If guardrails are used around holes at points of access, like a ladderway, a gate must be used to prevent someone from falling through the hole, or be offset so that a person cannot walk directly into the hole.

If your employer uses **safety nets**:

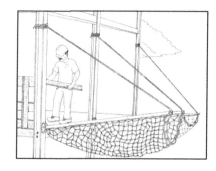

• The nets must be as close as practicable under the working surface, but never more than 30 feet below;
• The safety net must be inspected every week for damage;
• Each net must have a border rope with a minimum strength of 5,000 lbs.;
• The safety net must extend outward a sufficient distance, depending on how far the net is from the working surface (OSHA has a formula to follow);
• The safety net must absorb the force of a 400-pound bag of sand dropping on to the net ("the drop test");
• Items in the net that could be dangerous must be removed as soon as possible.

Personal Fall Arrest Systems Summary

Personal fall arrest systems are one way to protect workers from falls. In general, workers must have fall protection when they could fall 6 feet or more while they are working.

OSHA **requires** workers to wear a full-body harness, (one part of a *Personal Fall Arrest System*) when they are working on a *suspended scaffold* more than *10 feet* above the working surface, or when they are working in *bucket truck or aerial lift*. Employers may also choose to use a Personal Fall Arrest System, instead of a guardrail, when workers are working on a *supported scaffold* more than 10 feet above the working surface.

There are **three** major components of a Personal Fall Arrest System (PFAS):

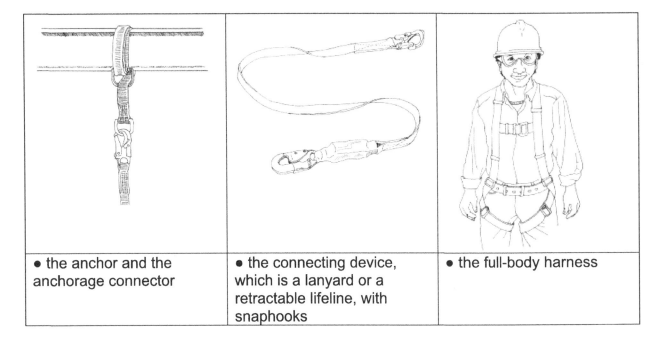

• the anchor and the anchorage connector	• the connecting device, which is a lanyard or a retractable lifeline, with snaphooks	• the full-body harness

The following are some things to remember about personal fall arrest systems:

1. A personal fall arrest system is made up of an **anchorage, connecting device, and a full-body harness**. The connecting device may be a lanyard with snaphooks, or a self-retracting lifeline. A lanyard could also include a deceleration device. Make sure you are using components from the same manufacturer to ensure that the system works as it should. If not, any substitution or change must be evaluated or tested by a competent person to ensure that it meets the standard.

2. **Body belts cannot be used** for fall arresting service. However, a body belt is allowed as part of a positioning system. A positioning system is one way to prevent falls from occurring. It involves equipment for keeping your body in a position where you are not able to fall. For all situations where you could actually fall, you need to wear a full-body harness.

3. Your personal fall arrest system must be **inspected for damage** each time before you wear it. [If there are defects, or if someone has taken a fall using the equipment, it must be removed from service.]

4. The **attachment location** of the body harness must be in the center of your back, near the shoulder level or above your head.

5. **Vertical lifelines or lanyards** must have a minimum breaking strength of 5,000 lbs., and be protected against being cut or abraded.

6. Each worker must be attached to a **separate vertical lifeline**. [There is a special exception when constructing elevator shafts.]

7. The **webbing**, which is the materials used for ropes and straps of lifelines, lanyard and harnesses, must be made of **synthetic** fibers.

8. **An anchorage** for workers' personal fall arrest equipment must be **independent of any anchorage** used to support or suspend platforms, and it must be able to support at least 5,000 lbs. per worker attached to it.

9. **Connectors** must be made from **steel or equivalent** materials, with a corrosion-resistant finish and the edges must be smooth.

10. **D-rings and snaphooks** must have a **minimum tensile strength** of 5,000 lbs.

11. **Snaphooks** must be a **locking-type** (they are generally double-locking) and designed to prevent the snaphook from opening and slipping off the connector.

12. **Snaphooks cannot be *directly connected*** to the webbing, rope or wire, to each other, to a D-ring to which another snaphook or other connector is attached, to a horizontal lifeline, or to any other object that could cause the snaphook to open.

Construction falls?

Here area few basic facts about falls in construction:
-- Every day, four construction workers die on the job.
-- Falls are the most common cause of fatal injuries to construction workers.

-- The consequences of a fall affect not only the worker, but also his or her family and community.
-- Construction falls can be prevented. Contractors and foreman can do many things to organize the worksite to be safer for their employees. But workers themselves can also make some inexpensive, simple changes to the way they work that can save their lives.
-- Ladders are one of the most common pieces of equipment on a construction site. But that doesn't mean they are safe. There are construction workers who are injured or killed falling from a height every day. Using ladders more safely is one way to start preventing falls at your work site.

Set an example at work

Your co-workers can learn a lot from you. At first, you might be the only one who is concerned with safety at your worksite. But over time, other workers will see that the foreman will give you the time you need to be safe. They will see how many little things add up to big effects on safety. And they will see how they, too, can help to make your worksite safer.

So, set an example. Don't worry about being the first—they'll thank you for it later.

How can I prevent a fall from a ladder?

There are many ways you can prevent a fall from a ladder—here are just three suggestions to get you started.

- **Choose the right ladder for the job.**
- **Tie the top and bottom of the ladder to fixed points when necessary.**
- **Don't carry tools or other materials in-hand while climbing the ladder.**

1. Choose the right ladder for the job.

- First you need to make sure that a ladder is the best equipment for what you need to do. Would scaffolding or a mechanical lift be better?
- Many times, the ladder is the only physical support you have while you are working. If it fails, you can fall. That's why it is so important to find the right ladder when you do need to use one. The three main types of ladders—step ladders, straight ladders, and extension ladders—are used in different situations for different tasks.
- Before you start using a ladder, ask yourself two questions.
- **Is the ladder long enough?** It should be long enough for you to set it at a stable angle and still extend at the top to give you something to hold on to when you get

on the ladder to descend. Setting the ladder at the right angle
balance on the ladder. It also helps keep the ladder from falling back.

- Make sure the ladder extends 3 feet (3 rungs; 0.9 meters) above the surface you will be working on.
- Make sure the ladder is placed at a stable angle. For every four feet (1.2 m) high the ladder is, the base should be 1 foot (.3 m) out from the wall
- For example, if you will be working on a 10 foot-high roof (3 m), you need a ladder that is at least 14 feet (4.25 m) long. The base should be 2 ½ feet (.75 m) from the wall.

– **Is the ladder in good working condition?** It shouldn't be missing pieces or be cracked or otherwise damaged. Check the duty rating on extension ladders – is it high enough for the weight you will be putting on it? Longer ladders don't always have higher duty ratings, so be sure to check. In construction, the most common ratings are:

- Heavy Duty (I) supports up to 250 pounds (113 kg).
- Extra heavy duty (IA) supports up to 300 pounds (136 kg).
- Special duty (IAA) supports up to 375 pounds (170 kg).

2. Tie the top and bottom of the ladder to fixed points when necessary: if it doesn't extend 3' above the landing, on slippery surfaces, and where it could be displaced by work activities or traffic.

– Tie both sides of the top of the ladder to a fixed point on the roof or other high surface near where you are working. The bottom should be tied to a fixed point on the ground. Securing the ladder in this way prevents the ladder from sliding side-to-side or falling backwards and prevents the base from sliding.
– Tying the ladder off at the beginning of the day and untying it at the end will only take you about 5 minutes. It can make all the difference for your safety. If you need to move the ladder around, allow extra time for this important step, or consider using something else, such as a scaffold.

3. Don't carry tools or other materials in-hand while climbing the ladder.

– Take precautions when you are going up or down a ladder. Instead of carrying tools, boards, or other materials in your hands, use a tool belt, install a rope and pulley system, or tie a rope around your materials and pull them up once you have reached the work surface. Ask for help if you need to use more than one hand to pull them up.
– Carrying tools or anything else in your hands as you climb the ladder can throw you off balance. When you climb a ladder, always use at least one hand to grasp the ladder when going up or down.

Scaffold Work Can Be Dangerous: Know the Basics of Scaffold Safety

There are thousands of scaffold-related injuries – and about 40 scaffold-related deaths – every year in the U.S. If you are doing work on scaffolds, know how to work on them safely – it could save your life!

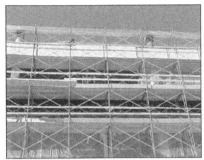

Here are some rules about scaffolds that must be followed if you want to work safely:

1. A **competent person** must be available to direct workers who are constructing or moving scaffolds. The competent person must also train workers, and **inspect** the scaffold and its components **before every work shift, and after any event that could affect the structural integrity of the scaffold**. The competent person must be able to identify unsafe conditions, and be authorized by the employer to take action to correct unsafe conditions, to make the workplace safe. And a **qualified person**, someone who has very specific knowledge or training, must actually design the scaffold and its rigging.

2. Every **supported** scaffold and its components must **support, without failure, its own weight and at least four times the intended load**. The intended load is the sum of the weights of all personnel, tools and materials that will be placed on the scaffold. Don't load the scaffold with more weight than it can safely handle.

3. On **supported** scaffolds, working platforms/decks must be planked close to the guardrails. Planks are to be overlapped on a support at least 6 inches, but not more than 12 inches.

4. Inspections of **supported** scaffolds must include:
   • Checking metal components for bends, cracks, holes, rust, welding splatter, pits, broken welds and non-compatible parts.
   • Covering and securing floor openings and labeling floor opening covers.

5. Each rope on a **suspended** scaffold must support the scaffold's weight and at least **six times** the intended load.

6. Scaffold **platforms** must be at least **18 inches wide, (there are some exceptions)**, and guardrails and/or personal fall arrest systems must be used for fall protection any time you are working 10 feet or more above ground level. **Guardrails** must be between 39 and 45 inches high, and **midrails** must be installed approximately halfway between the toprail and the platform surface.

7. OSHA standards require that workers have **fall protection when working on a scaffold 10 or more feet above the ground**. OSHA requires the following:

- The use of a **guardrail OR** a **personal fall arrest system** when working on a *supported scaffold*.
- **BOTH** a **guardrail AND** a **personal fall arrest system** when working on a *single-point or two-point suspended scaffold*.
- A **personal fall arrest system** when working on an *aerial lift*.

8. Your lifeline must be tied back to **a structural anchorage** capable of withstanding **5,000 lbs** of dead weight **per person** tied off to it. Attaching your lifeline to a guardrail, a standpipe or other piping systems will not meet the 5,000 lbs requirement and is not a safe move.

9. Wear hard hats, and make sure there are toeboards, screens and debris nets in place **to protect other people from falling objects**.

10. **Counterweights** for *suspended scaffolds* must be able to resist at least **four times the *tipping moment***, and they must be made of materials that cannot be easily dislocated (no sand, no water, no rolls of roofing, etc.). [This would be calculated by the *qualified person* who designs the scaffold.]

11. Your employer must provide safe access to the scaffold when a platform is more than two (2) feet above or below the point of access, or when you need to step across more than 14 inches to get on the platform. **Climbing on cross braces is not allowed!** Ladders, stair towers, ramps and walkways are some of the ways of providing safe access.

12. All workers must be **trained** on:
   - how to use the scaffold, and how to recognize hazards associated with the type of scaffold they are working on;
   - the maximum intended load and capacity;
   - how to recognize and report defects;
   - fall hazards, falling object hazards and any other hazards that may be encountered, including electrical hazards (such as overhead power lines); and,
   - having proper fall protection systems in place.

Read the following scenario; ask participants to take on the roles of Mike, Joe and the foreman. After reading the story, participants should identify all the **wrong** things that the workers did when working with ladders; discuss the RIGHT way to work safely on a ladder.

Roles: Mike and Joe, the workers and Mr. Smith, the foreman

INTRODUCTION:

Joe and Mike are excited; they just got the call to work on the new residential construction project in the area. They don't have much experience, but the pay is good, and they want to use this job as a stepping stone to bigger and better jobs. It's their first day on the job.

SCENE ONE: The foreman's office

Mr. Smith: So you know how to work on ladders, right guys?

Joe: Well, I haven't had a lot of experience, so maybe you could just go over the basics…

Mr. Smith: Well, I have to take this delivery, and I thought you told me you had lots of experience – where was your last job, anyway? We've got a deadline on this project, so….

Mike: Don't worry, Mr. Smith, I'll explain it all to him. I used ladders a lot on my last job.

Unsafe Work:
"What's wrong with this picture?"

Mr. Smith: Okay. First you need to paint the trim around the top of the building, and then, go inside and finish with the painting in the lobby. There are a couple of extension ladders out here, and a couple of step ladders inside. One of you should work out here, and the other start inside. Are you sure you know what to do? I asked them to find me some experienced guys, not rookies…

Mike: We're fine, Mr. Smith. We'll call you if we have any questions.

SCENE TWO: Mike and Joe are outside setting up.
Mike: So Joe, you work out here, and I'll do the inside work, okay?

Joe: Sure, but can you help me to set up here? Is this extension ladder okay, and how do I set it up?

Mike: Well, first you should inspect it. Of course the ladder needs to be long enough to reach the top, and it has to be able to hold you. So check the information on the ladder. It says it's a Type I – I'm not sure what that means, but I think it has something to do with your weight. How heavy are you?

Joe: About 260 pounds – I've been eating like a horse lately. I have to get back to the gym.

Mike: Well, that should be good enough. And how long is the ladder, and how high to the roof?

Unsafe Work:
"What's wrong with this picture?"

Joe: It says it's a 24-foot ladder, and the building is about 20 feet tall.

Mike: Okay, that should work. Just be careful if you're climbing onto the roof.

Joe: Am I supposed to check the ladder before using it?

Mike: Yeah, but this one looks fine to me.

Joe: Well, the step pads are ripped, and there is no pad on one of the feet – won't that make it uneven?

Mike: Just wrap some of this tape around it to even it off. I don't want to be asking for too much on our first day, you know?

Joe: This bolt seems a bit loose, and the pulley rope is a bit frayed. I wonder how that happened…and the steps feel like they have some kind of slippery stuff on them…

Mike: So just wipe them off. Listen, we need to get started here…

Joe: Okay, okay, let's just set up then. Where should I start?

LADDER SAFETY: What's Wrong with this Picture?

Mike: Start over by the doorway; it's early in the day, so not many people should be walking in and out. If you see anyone, just yell. And it's windy already, and it's supposed to get worse later on, so be careful.

Joe: Okay. The ground is pretty uneven here with all these rocks. And do I need to worry about those electrical wires? They seem like they are pretty close to the ladder.

Mike: Man, you ask a lot of questions, dude! Let's get this set up. Okay, you need to set this up at the right angle to make sure you don't fall. I remember that the ratio is 1 foot of length from the wall for every…every 5 feet of height, I think. So the building is 20 feet high, so put the ladder 4 feet from the wall.

Joe: That seems a little steep, doesn't it?

Mike: No, that's right. And remember that if we do well on this job, we get another one with this company, so we need to move fast. I will be inside, so don't keep calling me to help you. Carry the paint up with you – try to bring up a couple of cans the first time up to save time.

Joe: Should I try to tie the ladder to something so it doesn't move?

Mike: Don't worry about it moving at the top; just use this rope to tie the ladder to this bicycle stand.

Joe: And who left all these cans and plants around? Someone is going to trip on this stuff!

Mike: Yeah, yeah, don't worry about it; someone may be looking to use the stuff, so leave it there for now. I'm going inside to start on the lobby; I'll take one of these step ladders. See you later.

Joe: Yeah, see you.

Unsafe Work:
"What's wrong with this picture both inside and outside?

LADDER SAFETY: What's Wrong with this Picture?

SCENE THREE: Mike is inside, using the step ladder.

Mr. Smith: Hey Mike, how's it going?

Mike: Great, Mr. Smith, this is a great job.

Mr. Smith: Be careful, you should not be sitting on the ladder, and before I saw you standing on the top step.

Mike: Oh, don't worry, Mr. Smith, I can handle myself on a ladder – I've been working with my father for years doing this kind of work.

Mr. Smith: Okay, but try not to lean so far; just get down and walk the ladder closer, okay?

Mike: No problem, Mr. Smith, I'm a good worker, and I work fast. Suddenly, they hear Joe yelling from outside, and then they hear a "thud." They run outside to see what happened.

LADDER SAFETY: What's Wrong with this Picture?

Consider the Ladder Safety scenario to complete this worksheet.

1. Are there any problems with Joe's and Mike's ladder work?

_____

_____

_____

_____

_____

_____

_____

_____

_____

_____

_____

_____

_____

2. What could have been the reason for Joe's fall?

_____

_____

_____

_____

_____

_____

_____

_____

_____

_____

_____

_____

_____

3. Do you think Mike is working safely? Why or why not?

_____

_____

_____

_____

_____

_____

_____

_____

_____

_____

_____

_____

_____

Personal Fall Arrest System Checklist

Personal Fall Arrest Systems are one way to protect workers on construction sites where there are vertical drops of 6 or more feet. Systems must be set up so that a worker cannot fall more than 6 feet, nor come into contact with any lower level.

You should be able to answer **Yes** to each of the following.

1. Is your Personal Fall Arrest System made up of an anchorage, connecting device, and a full-body harness?

2. Are the components from the same manufacturer to ensure that the system works as it should? If not, has any substitution or change to a personal fall arrest system been fully evaluated or tested by a competent person to determine that it meets the standard?

3. Has your personal fall arrest system been inspected for damage each time before you wear it? [If there are defects, or if someone has taken a fall using the equipment, it must be removed from service.]

4. Is the attachment location of the body harness in the center of your back, near the shoulder level or above your head?

5. Do vertical lifelines or lanyards have a minimum breaking strength of 5,000 lbs? Are they protected against being cut or abraded?

6. Will each worker be attached to a separate vertical lifeline?

7. Is the webbing, [the materials used for ropes and straps of lifelines, lanyard and harnesses] made of synthetic fibers?

8. Is the anchorage for workers' personal fall arrest equipment independent of any anchorage used to support or suspend platforms? Is it able to support at least 5,000 lbs. per worker attached to it?

9. Are the connectors made from steel or equivalent materials, with a corrosion-resistant finish and smooth edges?

10. Do the D-rings and snaphooks have a minimum tensile strength of 5,000 lbs.?

11. Are snaphooks of a locking-type and designed to prevent the snaphook from opening and slipping off the connector?

12. Are the snaphooks not *directly connected* to the webbing, rope or wire, to each other, to a D-ring to which another snaphook or other connector is attached, to a horizontal lifeline, or to any other object that could cause the snaphook to open?

Is This a Fall Hazard?

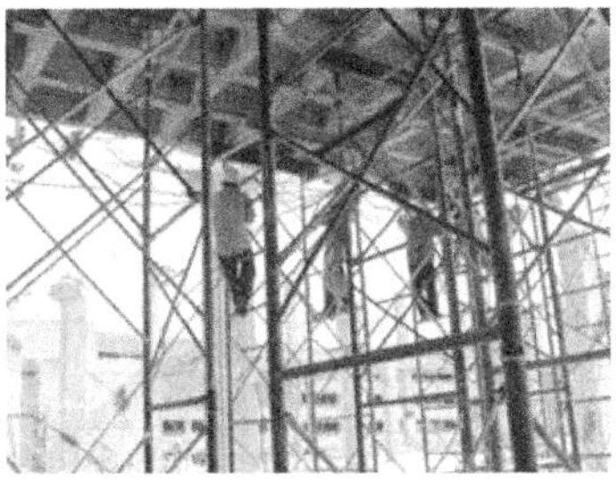

Photos in this presentation are from the OSHA Region 4 National Photo Archive and OSHA Region 5.

1

_____

_____

_____

_____

_____

_____

_____

Any Fall Hazard Here?

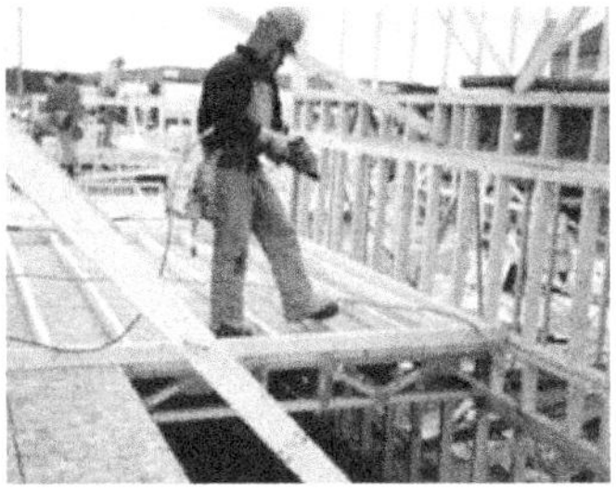

3

_____

_____

_____

_____

_____

_____

_____

Is This a Fall Hazard?

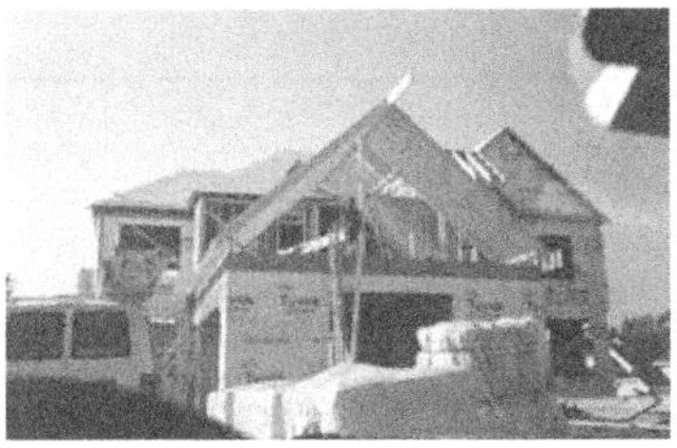

5

_____

_____

_____

_____

_____

_____

_____

41

Any Fall Hazard Here?

7

Is This a Fall Hazard?

9

Can You Identify the Fall Hazard?

11

Can You Identify the Fall Hazard?

13

Is This a Fall Hazard?

15

Can You Identify the Fall Hazards?

17

Any Fall Hazard Here?

19

Is This a Fall Hazard?

21

Is This a Fall Hazard?

23

Name: _____   Date: _____

1. In general, fall protection must be provided to construction workers who are
    working on surfaces with unprotected sides and edges which are _____ above the
    lower level:
    a. 3 feet
    b. 4 feet
    c. 6 feet

2. What are the ways an employer can protect workers from falls?
    a. Guardrails, safety net systems and safety belts
    b. Guardrails and safety nets
    c. Guardrails, safety net systems and personal fall arrest systems

3. For workers on scaffolds, fall protection must be provided if they are working
    _____ above a lower level.
    a. 4 feet
    b. 6 feet
    c. 10 feet

4. Guardrails are often used by employers to protect workers from falls. How high
    must the top guardrail (the toprail) be above the working surface?
    a. 24 inches, plus or minus 3 inches
    b. 42 inches, plus or minus 3 inches
    c. 60 inches, plus or minus 3 inches

5. A personal fall arrest system consists of:
    a. An anchorage and a body belt
    b. An anchorage, lanyard and connectors, and a body belt
    c. An anchorage, lanyard and connectors, and a full body harness

6. The top of a ladder must extend at least _____ above the surface you are
    climbing onto.
    a. 3 feet
    b. 4 feet
    c. 5 feet

46

Focus 4: Electrocution

General Rules for Construction

Electrical Safety

MAJOR PROTECTIVE METHODS FROM ELECTRICAL HAZARDS

Protection from electrical hazards generally includes the following methods:

1. **DISTANCE:** Commonly used with regard to power lines.

2. **ISOLATION AND GUARDING:** Restricting access, commonly used with high voltage power distribution equipment.

3. **ENCLOSURE OF ELECTRICAL PARTS:** A major concept of electrical wiring in general; e.g. all connections are made in a box.

4. **GROUNDING:** Required for all non-current carrying exposed metal parts, unless isolated or guarded as above. (However, corded tools may be either *grounded* OR be *double-insulated*.)

5. **INSULATION:** Intact insulation allows safe handling of everyday electrical equipment, including corded tools. Category also includes insulated mats and sleeves.

6. **DE-ENERGIZING AND GROUNDING:** Protective method used by electrical utilities and also in conjunction with electrical lockout/tagout.

7. **PERSONAL PROTECTIVE EQUIPMENT (PPE):** Using insulated gloves and other apparel to work on energized equipment, limited to qualified and trained personnel working under very limited circumstances.

Effects of Electric Current in the Human Body

Current / Reaction
(1,000 milliampere = 1 amp; therefore, 15,000 milliampere = 15 amp circuit)
Below 1 milliampere Generally not perceptible
1 milliampere Faint tingle
5 milliampere Slight shock felt; not painful but disturbing. Average individual can let go. Strong involuntary reactions can lead to other injuries.
6-25 milliamperes (women) Painful shock, loss of muscular control
9-30 milliamperes (men) The freezing current or "let-go" range. Individual cannot let go, but can be thrown away from the circuit if extensor muscles are stimulated.
50-150 milliamperes Extreme pain, respiratory arrest, severe muscular contractions. Death is possible.
1,000 - 4,300 milliamperes Rhythmic pumping action of the heart ceases. Muscular contraction and nerve damage occur; death likely.
10,000 milliamperes Cardiac arrest, severe burns; death probable

Construction Focus Four: Electrocution
Directorate of Training and Education
2020 S. Arlington Heights Rd.
Arlington Heights, IL 60005

Some content adapted from: Central New York COSH, 2007. Construction Safety & Health Electrocution hazards Grantee module, Grant Number SH-16586-07-06-F-36 from OSHA

OSHA®

www.osha.gov

Construction Focus Four™: Electrocution

Safety Tips for Workers

Contents:

- Electrical Safety Overview
- General Rules for Electrical Work
- Condensed Electrical Glossary
- General Rules for Construction Electrical Safety
- Effects of Electric Current in the Human Body

AMPERE OR AMP: The unit of electrical current (flow of electrons). • One milliamp (mA) = 1/1,000 of 1 Amp.

CONDUCTORS: Materials, such as metals, in which electrical current can flow.

ELECTRICAL HAZARDS can result in various effects on the body, including: • SHOCK – The physical effects caused by electric current flowing in the body • ELECTROCUTION – Electrical shock or related electrical effects resulting in death • BURNS – Often occurring on the hands, thermal damage to tissue can be caused by the flow of current in the body, by overheating of improper or damaged electrical components, or by an arc flash • FALLS – A common effect, sometimes caused by the body's reaction to an electrical current. A non-fatal shock may sometimes result in a fatal fall when a person is working on an elevated surface.

EXPOSED LIVE PARTS: Energized electrical components not properly enclosed in a box or otherwise isolated, such that workers can touch them and be shocked or killed. Some of the common hazards include: missing knockouts, unused openings in cabinet and missing covers. Covers must not be removed from wiring or breaker boxes. Any missing covers must be replaced with approved covers.

INSULATORS: Materials with high electrical resistance, so electrical current can't flow.

LOCKOUT/TAGOUT: The common name for an OSHA standard. *The control of hazardous energy (lockout/tagout). Lockout* is a means of controlling energy during repairs and maintenance of equipment, whereby energy sources are de-energized and then locked out to prevent possible start-up of equipment which would endanger workers. *Lockout* includes – but is not limited to – the control of electrical energy. *Tagout* means the placing of warning tags to alert other workers about the presence of equipment that has been locked out. Tags alone DO NOT LOCK OUT equipment. *Tagout is most effective when done in addition to lockout.*

OHM or Ω: The unit of *electrical resistance* (opposition to current flow).

OHM'S LAW: A mathematical expression of the relationship among *voltage* (volts), *current* (amps) and *resistance* (ohms). This is often expressed as: $E = I \times R$ in this case, E = volts, I = amp and R = ohms. (The equation, Amps = Volts/Ohms, is used in this curriculum, is one form of Ohm's Law.)

VOLT: The unit of *electromotive force* (emf) caused by a *difference in electrical charge or electrical potential between one point and another point*. The presence of voltage is necessary before current can flow in a circuit (in which current flows from a source to a *load* – the equipment using the electricity – and then back to its source).

WET CONDITIONS: Rain, sweat, standing in a puddle – all will decrease the skin's electrical resistance and increase current flow through the body in the event of a shock. Have a qualified electrician inspect any electrical equipment that has gotten wet before energizing it.

* Non-conductive PPE is essential for electricians. NO METAL PPE! Class B hard hats provide the highest level of protection against electrical hazards, with high-voltage shock and burn protection (up to 20,000 volts). Electrical hazard, safety-toe shoes are nonconductive and will prevent the wearer's feet from completing an electrical circuit to the ground.

* Be alert to electrical hazards, especially when working with ladders, scaffolds and other platforms.

* Never bypass electrical protective systems or devices.

* Disconnect cord tools when not in use and when changing cord blades, bits or other accessories.

* Inspect all tools before use.

* Use only grounded extension cords.

* Remove damaged tools and damaged extension cords from use.

* Keep working spaces and walkways clear of electrical cords.

RULES FOR TEMPORARY WIRING AND LIGHTING

* Use Ground Fault Circuit Interrupters (GFCIs) on all 15-Amp and 20-Amp temporary wiring circuits.

* Protect temporary lights from contact and damage.

* Don't suspend temporary lights by cords, unless the temporary light is so designed.

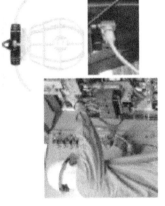

1. CORD AND PLUG OPERATED electric tools with exposed metal parts must have a three-prong grounding plug – AND be grounded – or else be double-insulated.

2. EQUIPMENT GROUNDING only works when there is a permanent and continuous electrical connection between the metal shell of a tool and the earth.

3. PROPER POLARITY IN ELECTRICAL WIRING IS IMPORTANT. hot to hot, neutral to neutral, equipment ground to equipment ground. Polarized plugs have a wider neutral blank so maintain correct polarity. Reversed polarity can kill.

4. CIRCUITS MUST BE EQUIPPED WITH FUSES OR CIRCUIT BREAKERS to protect against dangerous overloads. Fuses melt, while circuit breakers trip to turn off current like a switch. Overcurrent protection devices protect wiring and equipment from overheating and fires. They save or may not protect you.

5. MOST 120 VOLT CIRCUITS are wired to deliver up to 15 or 20 amps of current. Currents of 50 – 100 milliamperes can kill you. (1 mA = 1/1000 of 1 Amp.)

6. WET CONDITIONS LOWER SKIN RESISTANCE, allowing more current to flow through your body. Currents above 75 milliamps can cause ventricular fibrillation, which may be fatal. Severity of a shock depends on: path of current, amount of current, duration of current, voltage level, moisture and your general health.

7. A GROUND FAULT CIRCUIT INTERRUPTER (GFCI) protects from a ground-fault, the most common electrical hazard! GFCIs detect differences in current flow between hot and neutral. They trip when there is current leakage – such as through a person – of about 5 milliamperes and they act within 1/40 of a second! Test a GFCI every time you use it. It must "Trip" and it must "Reset."

8. EXTENSION CORD WIRES MUST BE HEAVY ENOUGH for the amount of current they will carry. For construction, they must be UL approved, have a strain relief and a 3-prong grounding plug, be durable, and be rated for hard or worn-hard usage.

9. OVERHEAD POWER LINES CAN KILL. The three major methods of protection are: maintaining a safe distance, de-energizing AND grounding lines, having the power company install insulating sleeves. Have a power company rep on the site.

10. UNDERGROUND POWER LINES CAN KILL. Call before you dig to locate all underground cables. Hand dig within three feet of cable location!

49

Focus Four [Electrocution] Toolbox Talks 1:
What increases your risk of electrocution?

[Ask the following questions and give time for answers.]

What are the hazards? Bodily contact with electricity

What are the results? Shock, fire, burns, falls or death

What should we look for? Damaged equipment, faulty wiring, improper cord use, no GFCIs, wet conditions, reverse polarity, potential arc flash areas, lack of assured equipment grounding conductor program

[Relate this incident or, better, one you know.]

Actual Incident: A 40-year-old male plumber died after lying on his work light while installing plumbing under a house being remodeled. The victim was crawling under the house carrying the work light with him. The wire inside the work light's conduit became bare and energized the light's housing. Investigation of the incident showed a damaged work light was used with no GFCI. Also, the home's electrical system was not properly grounded.

[Ask the following question and ensure every item is covered.]

How do we prevent these results?

- □ Inspect all electrical equipment before use.
- □ Use GFCI with all power tools.
- □ Use intact and properly rated cords (i.e. correct AWG).
- □ Do not use damaged equipment - take it out of service.
- □ Institute an assured equipment grounding conductor program.
- □ Do not work in wet conditions with electricity.

[Ask the following questions about this site and ensure every item is covered.]

Let's talk about this site now.

- □ What factors increase your chance of being electrocuted?
- □ Can someone demonstrate how to inspect this tool for electrical safety? (If possible, provide a tool)
- □ What are some areas on the site that could use attention pertaining to electrical hazards?

What are the hazards show in these photos?

[Record questions below that you want to ask about this site.]

Focus Four [Electrocution] Toolbox Talks 2:

What protective devices and procedures can you use to prevent electrocution?

[Ask the following questions and give time for answers.]

What are the hazards? Bodily contact with electricity due to faulty equipment, ungrounded or damaged equipment, wet conditions, etc.

What are the results? Shock, fire, burns, falls or death

What should we look for? Proper training in using engineering controls (e.g. GFCIs, proper cords), assured equipment grounding conductor written program, electrical testing meters

[Relate this incident or, better, one you know.]

Actual Incident: A 29-year- old male welder was electrocuted and died when he contacted an energized receptacle end of an extension cord. It was found that the welding unit and cord were incompatible; however, both the welding cord and extension cord were damaged allowing them to be used together. The result was an ungrounded system that killed a worker.

American Wire Gauge (AWG)	
Cord Size	Handles Up To
#10 AWG	30 amps
#12 AWG	25 amps
#14 AWG	18 amps
#16 AWG	13 amps

[Ask the following question and ensure every item is covered.]

How do we prevent these results?

- ☐ Inspect all electrical equipment before use.
- ☐ Use GFCI with all power tools.
- ☐ Use intact and properly-rated cords (i.e. correct AWG).
- ☐ Do not use damaged equipment - take it out of service.
- ☐ Institute an assured equipment grounding conductor program.
- ☐ Use testing meters, where appropriate, if you are trained to do so.

[Ask the following questions about this site and ensure every item is covered.]

Let's talk about this site now.

- ☐ Can someone explain how a GFCI works? (If possible, provide a GFCI to use).

- ☐ Who has read this site's assured equipment grounding conductor program?
- ☐ What are some of the requirements?

[Record questions below that you want to ask about this site.]

Focus Four [Electrocution] Toolbox Talks 3:

How can we prevent electrocutions while using power tools?

[Ask the following questions and give time for answers.]

What are the hazards? Bodily contact with electricity

What are the results? Shock, fire, burns, falls or death

What should we look for? Tools that aren't double-insulated, damaged tools and cords, incorrect cords, wet conditions, tools used improperly

[Relate this incident or, better, one you know.]

Actual Incident: A 45-year-old male electrician was electrocuted when he contacted an energized 1/2" electric drill casing. The victim was working in wet conditions and using a single insulated drill attached to damaged extensions cords run through water.

[Ask the following question and ensure every item is covered.]

How do we prevent these results?

☐ Get proper training on manufacturers' tool use and specs.

☐ Inspect tool before each use according to manufacturers' instructions.

☐ Do not use damaged tools, remove them from service.

☐ Use only battery-powered tools in wet conditions.

☐ Use with GFCI.

☐ Use with properly sized and intact cords.

[Ask the following questions about this site and ensure every item is covered.]

Let's talk about this site now.

☐ What can lead to an electrocution while using power tools? *Non double-insulated tools, damaged cord, wet conditions*

☐ Have you seen or used any defective power tool?

☐ What should you do if you find a defective power tool?

[Record questions below that you want to ask about this site.]

Electrical Safety

Electrical hazards can cause burns, shocks and electrocution (death).

Safety Tips

- Assume that all overhead wires are energized at lethal voltages. Never assume that a wire is safe to touch even if it is down or appears to be insulated.

- Never touch a fallen overhead power line. Call the electric utility company to report fallen electrical lines.

- Stay at least 10 feet (3 meters) away from overhead wires during cleanup and other activities. If working at heights or handling long objects, survey the area before starting work for the presence of overhead wires.

- If an overhead wire falls across your vehicle while you are driving, stay inside the vehicle and continue to drive away from the line. If the engine stalls, do not leave your vehicle. Warn people not to touch the vehicle or the wire. Call or ask someone to call the local electric utility company and emergency services.

- Never operate electrical equipment while you are standing in water.

- Never repair electrical cords or equipment unless qualified and authorized.

- Have a qualified electrician inspect electrical equipment that has gotten wet before energizing it.

- If working in damp locations, inspect electric cords and equipment to ensure that they are in good condition and free of defects, and use a ground-fault circuit interrupter (GFCI).

- Always use caution when working near electricity.

For more complete information:

OSHA Occupational
Safety and Health
Administration
U.S. Department of Labor
www.osha.gov   (800) 321-OSHA

ACTIVITY OPTION A
Wet Conditions / Ground Fault Circuit Interrupters

Student Copy

Source: Central New York (COSH) Susan Harwood Training Grant #SH-16586-07-06-F-36

In your small group, read fact sheets A1 and A2, and the following scenario. Then answer the questions that follow.

- You're an experienced worker in building maintenance, helping a new worker to learn the job. The task involves cleaning up a flooded basement. The new worker has started setting up electrical cords and tools for the job. You tell her, "Hold on a minute, let's check out the wiring first." Then you say, "No, we can't do this without GFCI protection. I'll tell you why."

1. What would you tell your new co-worker?

2. What can you do to correct this problem for now?

3. What is the best way to deal with this in the future?

4. What work practices help protect you against electrical hazards?

_____

_____

_____

_____

_____

_____

_____

_____

_____

_____

_____

_____

Examples of accidents related to wet conditions/ground fault circuit interrupters

A journeyman HVAC worker was installing metal duct work using a double-insulated drill connected to a drop light cord. Power was supplied through two extension cords from a nearby residence. The individual's perspiration-soaked clothing/body contacted bare exposed conductors on one of the cords, causing an electrocution. No GFCI's were used. Additionally, the ground prongs were missing from the two cords.

Factsheet A1 – Using Electrical Equipment in Wet Locations

Using electrical tools or equipment in wet areas can be a hazard. If your skin is dry, it has quite a lot of _resistance_ (measured in _ohms_ or Ω). However, if your skin is wet for any reason (rain, sweat, standing in a puddle of water), the skin's electrical resistance drops dramatically. The amount of electrical **current**, in _amps,_ that flows through your body **goes up when resistance** in _ohms_ **goes down. Amps = Volts/Ohms.**

The Current in **Amps** = Voltage in **Volts** DIVIDED BY Resistance in **Ohms**.
HIGHER VOLTAGE = more current (if resistance remains the same).
LOWER RESISTANCE = more current (if voltage remains the same).
HOW MUCH CURRENT DOES IT TAKE TO KILL ME?

It doesn't take much, especially if it passes through your heart. Currents above about _75 milliamps(mA)_ can cause a condition called _ventricular fibrillation_. (A milliamp is 1/1,000 of 1 amp.) If your heart goes into fibrillation, it beats very rapidly – but it doesn't pump any blood – because it's not beating in its normal rhythm. If your blood can't carry oxygen to your brain, you'll experience brain
death in 3 to 4 minutes. The way to get you back involves another electric shock, from a _defibrillator._

If your skin is wet and you get your body across 120 volts of electricity, it's very likely that you'll have a current of 100 mA or more flowing through your heart. **Currents ABOVE 10 mA** can cause _muscle paralysis._ You may not be able to let go of energized tools or equipment. **Shocks that are longer in duration are more severe.**

Electrical systems must be wired with either *fuses* or *circuit breakers.* These devices are known as *overcurrent protection* and they are rated in amps. Most common household circuits are wired for 15 amps or 20 amps. **Overcurrent protection devices protect wiring and equipment from overheating and fires.** They may – or may not – protect you from electrical shock. If the current isn't high enough, the fuse won't blow or the circuit breaker won't trip. You could be shocked or killed without ever blowing a fuse or tripping a circuit breaker.

Factsheet A2 – GFCIs to the Rescue

A great breakthrough in electrical safety came with the invention of the *ground fault circuit interrupter (GFCI).* A *ground fault* occurs when electrical current flows on a path where it's not supposed to be. Under normal conditions, current flows in a circuit, traveling from the source, through the device it operates, called the *load,* and then back to the source. [See Activity 2 for more about wiring of electrical circuits.]

Current (amps) flows out to the load from the "hot" side (which is generally at 120 volts AC) and returns on the "neutral" side (which is at zero volts). Under normal conditions, these two currents (hot and neutral) are equal. If they are not equal, because of *current leakage* (current returning on a different path than the neutral conductor), we get a ground fault. This can occur if current flows through your body and returns to the source through a path to ground. **Electricity will take ANY available path to return to its source.** We want it to return only on the neutral.

The ground fault circuit interrupter (GFCI) works by using the above principles. It measures total current on the hot side and total current on the neutral side of the circuit. They are supposed to be equal. If these two currents differ from each other by *more than 5 milliamps* (plus or minus 1 mA), the GFCI acts as a fast-acting circuit breaker and shuts off the electricity within 1/40 of 1 second. You can still feel this small amount of current, but it will quickly shut off.

GFCIs are manufactured in many forms. The most common one is the GFCI outlet. However, there are also GFCI circuit breakers, plug-in GFCI outlets and GFCI extension cords, as well as GFCIs hard-wired into devices such as hair dryers. All types have **"Test"** and **"Reset"** functions. **The GFCI must trip when you press the "Test" button. It must also energize the circuit when you press "Reset." If either test fails, you must replace the GFCI in order to be protected!**

In your small group, read fact sheets B1 and B2, and the following scenario.
Then answer the questions that follow.

SCENARIO:
You're at work one day and a co-worker starts screaming: It
looks like his saw is smoking, it smells like it's burning and his
extension cord is getting hot enough to burn his hand. You
walk over, take one look at the scene and start shaking
your head. "Well, I know what your problem is, and I'll explain
if you stop shouting," you tell him.

1. What is your explanation to the worker?

_____

_____

_____

_____

_____

_____

_____

_____

2. What are some steps to deal with this issue?

_____

_____

_____

_____

_____

_____

_____

_____

_____

_____

3. What is the best way to correct the problem?

_____

_____

_____

_____

_____

_____

_____

_____

_____

_____

Factsheet B1 – Wire Size and Ampacity

In terms of conducting electrical current, size matters: the size of the electrical conductor. Take a look at the following table regarding *ampacity,* the current carrying capacity of a conductor in amps. You'll notice two things: the **amount of current** a wire can safely carry **increases** as the **diameter** (and area) of the wire increases and as the number of the **wire size decreases**. Welcome to the American Wire Gauge (AWG).

AWG Copper Wire Table

Copper Wire Size (AWG)	Diameter (mils)	Area (Circular mils)	Ampacity in free air	Ampacity as part of 3-conductor cable
14 AWG	64.1	4109	20 Amps	15 Amps
12 AWG	80.8	6529	25 Amps	20 Amps
10 AWG	101.9	10,384	40 Amps	30 Amps
8 AWG	128.5	16,512	70 Amps	50 Amps

BUT I DON'T WANT TO BE AN ENGINEER...

Hey, neither do I, but this stuff is important. Notice that a #8 wire is *twice the diameter,* but *four times the area* of a #14 wire. There are a couple of practical applications here. For one thing, the gauge of the wire determines the rating of a fuse or circuit breaker in amps. A circuit wired with #14 copper will get a 15 amp circuit breaker. A circuit with #12 copper can get a 20 amp breaker; #10 copper can be 30 amps, and so on.

The second thing to consider is that it's possible to create a fire hazard by *overloading an extension cord.* This occurs when too much current is fl owing in a conductor that's not heavy enough for the electrical load in amps. The circuit can be properly wired and its circuit breaker correctly rated, but if too much current flows through an extension cord whose wires are too small, the cord will heat up. Sometimes there is also a *voltage drop* over a longer extension cord, which could damage your tools.

Factsheet B2 – Extension Cord Facts

With the wide use of power tools on construction sites, flexible extension cords often are necessary. Because they are exposed, flexible, and unsecured, they are more susceptible to damage than is fixed wiring. Hazards are created when cords, cord connectors, receptacles, and cord- and plug connected equipment are improperly used and maintained. **Here are some factors on extension cord safety noted by OSHA.**

Strain Relief

- To reduce hazards, flexible cords must connect to devices and to fittings in ways that prevent tension at joints and terminal screws. Flexible cords are finely stranded for flexibility, so straining a cord can cause the strands of one conductor to loosen from under terminal screws and touch another conductor.

Cord Damage

- A flexible cord may be damaged by door or window edges, by staples and fastenings, by abrasion from adjacent materials, or simply by aging. If the electrical conductors become exposed, there is a danger of shocks, burns, or fire. Replace frayed or damaged cords. Avoid running cords over sharp corners and edges.

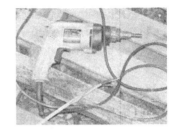

Durability

- The OSHA construction standard requires flexible cords to be rated for hard or extra-hard usage. These ratings are derived from the National Electrical Code, and are required to be indelibly marked approximately every foot along the length of the cord. Examples of these codes are: S, ST, SO, and STO for hard service, and SJ, SJO, SJT, and SJTO for junior hard service.

Grounding

- Extension cords must be 3-wire type so they may be grounded, and to permit grounding of any tools or equipment connected to them.

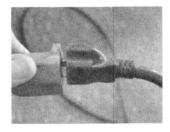

Wet Conditions

When a cord connector is wet, electric current can leak to the equipment grounding conductor, and to anyone who picks up that connectors if they provide a path to ground. Such leakage can occur not just on the face of the conductor, but at any wetter portion. Limit exposure of connectors and tools to excessive moisture by using watertight or sealable connectors.

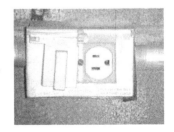

ACCIDENT REPORT

ACCIDENT SUMMARY No. 11

Accident Type:	Electrocution
Weather Conditions:	Wet Ground
Type of Operation:	Remodeling
Size of Work Crew:	2
Collective Bargaining	No
Competent Safety Monitor on Site:	Yes
Safety and Health Program in Effect:	No
Was the Worksite Inspected Regularly:	Yes
Training and Education Provided:	No
Employee Job Title:	Carpenter
Age & Sex:	33-Male
Experience at this Type of Work:	30 Days
Time on Project:	3 Days

BRIEF DESCRIPTION OF ACCIDENT

Two employees were installing aluminum siding on a farmhouse when it became necessary to remove a 36-foot high metal pole CB antenna. One employee stood on a metal pick board between two ladders and unfastened the antenna at the top of the house. The other employee, who was standing on the ground, took the antenna to lay it down in the yard. The antenna made electrical contact with a 7200-volt power transmission tine 30 feet 10 inches from the house and 23 feet 9 inches above the ground. The employee handling the antenna received a fatal shock and the other employee a minor shock.

INSPECTION RESULTS

Following its investigation, OSHA issued one citation for two alleged serious violations of its construction standards. Had these standards been adhered to, the fatality might have been prevented.

ACCIDENT PREVENTION RECOMMENDATIONS

_____
_____
_____
_____
_____
_____
_____
_____
_____
_____
_____
_____

NOTE: The Fatal Facts were selected as being representative of fatalities caused by improper work practices. No special emphasis or priority is implied nor is the case necessarily a recent occurrence. The legal aspects of the incident have been resolved, and the case is now closed. Current as of: 11/01/2001.

ACCIDENT REPORT
FATAL FACTS

ACCIDENT SUMMARY No. 17

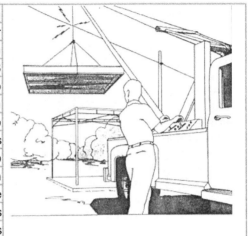

Accident Type:	Electrocution
Weather Conditions:	Sunny, Clear
Type of Operation:	Steel Erection
Size of Work Crew:	3
Collective Bargaining	No
Competent Safety Monitor on Site:	Yes - Victim
Safety and Health Program in Effect:	No
Was the Worksite Inspected Regularly:	Yes
Training and Education Provided:	No
Employee Job Title:	Steel Erector Foreman
Age & Sex:	43-Male
Experience at this Type of Work:	4 months
Time on Project:	4 Hours

BRIEF DESCRIPTION OF ACCIDENT

Employees were moving a steel canopy structure using a "boom crane" truck. The boom cable made contact with a 7200 volt electrical power distribution line electrocuting the operator of the crane; he was the foreman at the site.

INSPECTION RESULTS

As a result of its investigation. OSHA issued citations for four serious violations of its construction standards dealing with training, protective equipment, and working too close to power lines. OSHA's construction safety standards include several requirements which, If they had been followed here. might have prevented this fatality.

ACCIDENT PREVENTION RECOMMENDATIONS

_____
_____
_____
_____
_____
_____
_____
_____
_____
_____
_____
_____
_____

NOTE: The Fatal Facts were selected as being representative of fatalities caused by improper work practices. No special emphasis or priority is implied nor is the case necessarily a recent occurrence. The legal aspects of the incident have been resolved, and the case is now closed. Current as of: 11/01/2001.

ACCIDENT SUMMARY No. 28

Accident Type:	Electrocution
Weather Conditions:	Clear
Type of Operation:	Power Line Work
Size of Work Crew:	2
Collective Bargaining	Yes
Competent Safety Monitor on Site:	Yes
Safety and Health Program in Effect:	No
Was the Worksite Inspected Regularly:	No
Training and Education Provided:	No
Employee Job Title:	Lineman
Age & Sex:	44-Male
Experience at this Type of Work:	11 Months
Time on Project:	6 Weeks

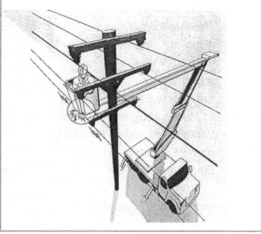

BRIEF DESCRIPTION OF ACCIDENT

A lineman was electrocuted while working on grounded de-energized lines. He was working from a defective basket on an articulated boom aerial lift when the basket contacted energized lines which ran beneath the de-energized lines. The defective basket permitted current to pass through a drain hole cut into the body of the basket, then through the employee, and to ground via the de-energized line.

INSPECTION RESULTS

OSHA cited the company for two serious violations and one other than serious violation of its construction standards. Had barriers been erected to prevent contact with adjacent energized lines, the electrical shock might have been prevented.

ACCIDENT PREVENTION RECOMMENDATIONS

_____
_____
_____
_____
_____
_____
_____
_____
_____
_____
_____
_____

NOTE: _The Fatal Facts were selected as being representative of fatalities caused by improper work practices. No special emphasis or priority is implied nor is the case necessarily a recent occurrence. The legal aspects of the incident have been resolved, and the case is now closed. Current as of: 11/01/2001._

ACCIDENT SUMMARY No. 30

Accident Type:	Electrocution
Weather Conditions:	Raining
Type of Operation:	Electrical Contractor
Size of Work Crew:	2
Collective Bargaining	No
Competent Safety Monitor on Site:	Yes
Safety and Health Program in Effect:	Inadequate
Was the Worksite Inspected Regularly:	Yes
Training and Education Provided:	No
Employee Job Title:	Journeyman Electrician
Age & Sex:	39-Male
Experience at this Type of Work:	16 Years
Time on Project:	1 Day

BRIEF DESCRIPTION OF ACCIDENT

An electrician was removing metal fish tape from a hole at the base of a metal light pole. The fish tape became energized, electrocuting him.

INSPECTION RESULTS

As a result of its inspection, OSHA issued a citation for three serious violations of the agency's construction standards. Had requirements for de-energizing energy sources been followed, the electrocution might have been prevented.

ACCIDENT PREVENTION RECOMMENDATIONS

_____
_____
_____
_____
_____
_____
_____
_____
_____
_____
_____
_____
_____
_____

NOTE: The Fatal Facts were selected as being representative of fatalities caused by improper work practices. No special emphasis or priority is implied nor is the case necessarily a recent occurrence. The legal aspects of the incident have been resolved, and the case is now closed. Current as of: 11/01/2001.

ACCIDENT SUMMARY No. 40

Accident Type:	Electrocution
Weather Conditions:	Sunny/Clear
Type of Operation:	Fence Construction
Size of Work Crew:	5
Collective Bargaining	No
Competent Safety Monitor on Site:	No
Safety and Health Program in Effect:	Yes
Was the Worksite Inspected Regularly:	No
Training and Education Provided:	No
Employee Job Title:	Laborer
Age & Sex:	25-Male
Experience at this Type of Work:	3 Months
Time on Project:	1 Day

BRIEF DESCRIPTION OF ACCIDENT

Five employees were constructing a chain link fence in front of a house and directly below a 7200-volt energized power line. They were installing 21-foot sections of metal top rail on the fence. One employee picked up a 21-foot section of top rail and held it up vertically. The top rail contacted the 7200-volt line, and the employee was electrocuted.

INSPECTION RESULTS

Following its inspection, OSHA determined that the employee who was killed had never received any safety training from his employer nor any specific instruction in avoiding the hazards posed by overhead power lines. The agency issued two serious citations for the training deficiencies.

ACCIDENT PREVENTION RECOMMENDATIONS

_____
_____
_____
_____
_____
_____
_____
_____
_____
_____
_____
_____
_____

NOTE: The Fatal Facts were selected as being representative of fatalities caused by improper work practices. No special emphasis or priority is implied nor is the case necessarily a recent occurrence. The legal aspects of the incident have been resolved, and the case is now closed. Current as of: 11/01/2001.

ACCIDENT SUMMARY No. 49

Accident Type:	Electrical Shock
Weather Conditions:	Clear/Hot
Type of Operation:	Masonry Contractor
Size of Work Crew:	6
Collective Bargaining	No
Competent Safety Monitor on Site:	No
Safety and Health Program in Effect:	Inadequate
Was the Worksite Inspected Regularly:	Yes
Training and Education Provided:	No
Employee Job Title:	Cement Finisher
Age & Sex:	34-Male
Experience at this Type of Work:	10 Years
Time on Project:	1 Day

BRIEF DESCRIPTION OF ACCIDENT

Two employees were spreading concrete as it was being delivered by 1 concrete pumper truck boom. The truck was parked across the street from the worksite. Overhead power lines ran perpendicular to the boom on the pumper truck. One employee was moving the hose (elephant trunk) to pour the concrete when the boom of the pumper truck came in contact with the overhead rover line carrying 7,620 volts. Employee received a fatal electric shock and fell on the other employee who was assisting him. The second employee received massive electrical shock and burns. * Safety training requirement was not being carried out at time of accident.

INSPECTION RESULTS

OSHA cited the employer for not instructing each employee to recognize and avoid unsafe conditions which apply to the work and work areas. Employer was also cited for operating equipment within ten feet of an energized electrical, ungrounded transmission lines rated 50 kV or less and not erecting insulating barriers.

ACCIDENT PREVENTION RECOMMENDATIONS

_____
_____
_____
_____
_____
_____
_____
_____
_____
_____
_____
_____
_____

NOTE: _The Fatal Facts were selected as being representative of fatalities caused by improper work practices. No special emphasis or priority is implied nor is the case necessarily a recent occurrence. The legal aspects of the incident have been resolved, and the case is now closed. Current as of: 11/01/2001._

ACCIDENT SUMMARY No. 57

Accident Type:	Electrocution
Weather Conditions:	Clear/Hot/Humid
Type of Operation:	Window Shutter Installers
Size of Work Crew:	2
Collective Bargaining	N/A
Competent Safety Monitor on Site:	No
Safety and Health Program in Effect:	Partial
Was the Worksite Inspected Regularly:	No
Training and Education Provided:	Some
Employee Job Title:	Helper
Age & Sex:	17-Male
Experience at this Type of Work:	One Month
Time on Project:	One Month

BRIEF DESCRIPTION OF ACCIDENT

One employee was climbing a metal ladder to hand an electric drill to the journeyman installer on a scaffold about five feet above him. When the victim reached the third rung from the bottom of the ladder he received an electric shock that killed him. The investigation revealed that the extension cord had a missing grounding prong and that a conductor on the green grounding wire was making intermittent contact with the energizing black wire thereby energizing the entire length of the grounding wire and the drill's frame. The drill was not double insulated.

INSPECTION RESULTS

As a result of its investigation, OSHA issued citations for violations of construction standards.

ACCIDENT PREVENTION RECOMMENDATIONS

_____
_____
_____
_____
_____
_____
_____
_____
_____
_____
_____
_____

NOTE: The Fatal Facts were selected as being representative of fatalities caused by improper work practices. No special emphasis or priority is implied nor is the case necessarily a recent occurrence. The legal aspects of the incident have been resolved, and the case is now closed. Current as of: 11/01/2001.

ACCIDENT SUMMARY No. 60

Accident Type:	Electrocution
Weather Conditions:	Indoor Work
Type of Operation:	Installing and Trouble-shooting overhead lamps
Size of Work Crew:	15
Competent Safety Monitor on Site:	Yes
Safety and Health Program in Effect:	Inadequate
Was the Worksite Inspected Regularly:	Yes
Training and Education Provided:	No
Employee Job Title:	Electrician
Age & Sex:	53-Male
Experience at this Type of Work:	Journeyman
Time on Project:	1 Month

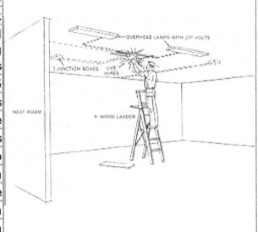

BRIEF DESCRIPTION OF ACCIDENT

The employee was attempting to correct an electrical problem involving two non-operational lamps. He proceeded to the area where he thought the problem was. He had not shut off the power at the circuit breaker panel nor had he tested the wires to see if they were live. He was electrocuted when he grabbed the two live wires with his left hand and then fell from the ladder.

INSPECTION RESULTS

As a result of its investigation, OSHA Issued citations alleging three serious violations. OSHA's construction standards include several requirements which, if they had been followed here, might have prevented this fatality.

ACCIDENT PREVENTION RECOMMENDATIONS

_____
_____
_____
_____
_____
_____
_____
_____
_____
_____
_____
_____

NOTE: _The case here described was selected as being representative of fatalities caused by improper work practices. No special emphasis or priority is implied nor is the case necessarily a recent occurrence. The legal aspects of the incident have been resolved, and the case is now closed._

Recognize Any Hazard(s)?

Recognize Any Hazard(s)?

Recognize Any Hazard(s)?

Recognize Any Hazard(s)?

_____

_____

_____

_____

_____

_____

_____

Recognize Any Hazard(s)?

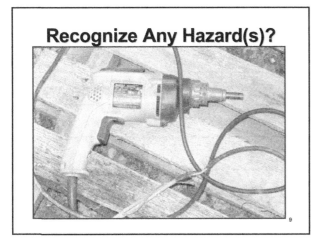

_____

_____

_____

_____

_____

_____

_____

_____

Recognize Any Hazard(s)?

_____

_____

_____

_____

_____

_____

_____

_____

Recognize Any Hazard(s)?

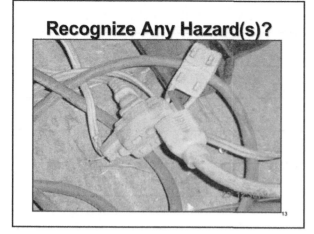

_____
_____
_____
_____
_____
_____
_____

Recognize Any Hazard(s)?

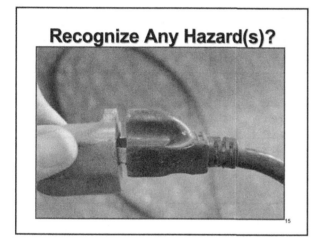

_____
_____
_____
_____
_____
_____
_____

Recognize Any Hazard(s)?

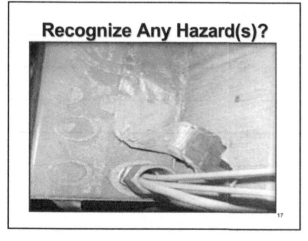

_____
_____
_____
_____
_____
_____
_____

Recognize Any Hazard(s)?

_____

_____

_____

_____

_____

_____

_____

71

Construction Focus Four: Electrocution Hazards Lesson Test

NAME: _____   DATE: ___/___/___

1. "BE SAFE" reminds workers that burns, electrocution, shock, arc flash/arc blast, fire and explosions are all:
   a. Electrical hazards workers are exposed to when working around cranes and power lines.
   b. Serious workplace hazards that workers are exposed to when working in and/or around electrical power sources.
   c. Electrical hazards workers are exposed to when working with flammables.

2. A ground fault circuit interrupter (GFCI):
   a. Detects ground faults and interrupts the flow of electric current, and is designed to protect the worker by limiting the duration of an electrical shock.
   b. Detects ground faults and interrupts the electric source thus, it disables the equipment that is attached; however, the worker is still exposed to electrocution.
   c. A tool used to determine if a power system is properly grounded.

3. To protect yourself from being electrocuted by contact with overhead power lines, you should always assume overhead lines are energized and keep yourself and equipment at least _____ away from power lines up to 50kV.
   a. 5 feet
   b. 8 feet
   c. 10 feet

4. Which of the following is a safe work practice to protect you from electrocution hazards?
   a. Use GFCI only when using double insulated power tools
   b. Do not operate electrical equipment when working in wet conditions
   c. Attach ungrounded, two-prong adapter plugs to three-prong cords and tools

5. Some requirements employers must do to protect workers from electrocution hazards are: ensure overhead power lines safety; supply GFCIs; isolate electrical parts; ensure proper grounding, and:
   1. Provide training
   2. Ensure power tools are maintained in a safe condition
   3. Ensure proper use of flexible cords
   4. Report worker jobsite complaints to OSHA

   a. 1, 2, and 3
   b. 2, 3, and 4
   c. 1, 3 and 4

6. When a power system is properly grounded workers need to be aware that:
   a. It is a safe system and can not change from safe to hazardous; therefore working with electrical equipment is always safe.
   b. Electrical equipment can instantly change from safe to hazardous because of extreme conditions and rough treatment.
   c. The system will remain safe and will not be impacted by changing worksite conditions or electrical equipment.

Focus 4: Struck-by

How to prevent injury

◆ Ask for a nail gun with a sequential trigger mechanism.

◆ NEVER shoot towards yourself or a co-worker.

◆ Do not press the trigger unless the nose of the gun (contact element) is firmly pressed against the work material.

◆ NEVER walk around with your finger on the trigger.

◆ NEVER clean or clear jams or adjust a nail gun when it is connected to the air supply.

◆ Avoid nailing into knots and metal; nails are more likely to ricochet. Dense materials, like laminated beams, are also difficult to nail.

◆ NEVER remove or bypass safety devices, triggers, or contact springs.

◆ NEVER use a defective tool. If a tool is malfunctioning, it needs to be tagged and taken out of service.

To read stories about nail gun injuries and see photos, visit
www.cpwr.com/nailguns

To learn more about CPWR, visit
www.cpwr.com

For more safety and health information, visit
www.elcosh.org

CPWR
8484 Georgia Ave, Suite 100
Silver Spring, MD 20910
301-578-8500

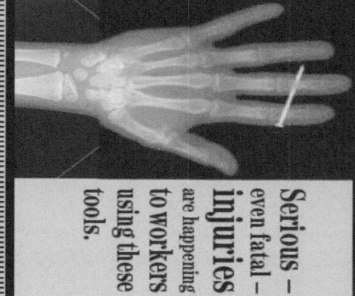

HAZARD ALERT

Nail Guns

Serious – even fatal – injuries are happening to workers using these tools.

What's the problem?

Nail guns are popular for a reason. They get the job done in a blink of an eye.

But that rapid-fire action can work against you. In a split second, a nail can enter your finger, your hand, or worse.

Nail gun injuries are much more common than people think. Most injuries involve puncture wounds to hands or fingers, but serious, even fatal, injuries are also associated with the use of these tools.

How most nail gun injuries happen

◆ Accidental or unintended firing, often associated with recoil of the tool after firing

◆ Ricocheting nails

◆ Nail going through work surface

◆ Airborne nails

◆ By-passed safety features

◆ Unsafe work practices

◆ Holding finger on contact trigger

Basic information about nail guns

Although there are many types of nail guns (framing, finishing, flooring, etc.), there are two common triggers:

Contact trip trigger mechanisms allow the tool to fire anytime the trigger and the nose of the gun (contact element) are both depressed. Trigger can be held down to allow bump or bounce nailing.

Sequential triggers require the nose of gun (contact element) to be depressed before the trigger is pulled. That avoids inadvertent discharge of nails.

WARNING:

The two triggers look exactly alike. You will not be able to tell the difference!

If you can "bump nail" by holding the trigger down, and bouncing the nose against a nailing surface, that is a contact trigger gun. Use extreme caution.

Why it's important:

1) The contact trip trigger mechanism carries twice the risk of the sequential trigger, even after considering experience and training.

2) Accidental firings are most common following recoil of tools with contact trip triggers.

3) If you are not trained in using either of these tools, you are at high risk of injury.

"Faster" trigger does not increase productivity

A recent study measuring productivity in construction found that the contact trip trigger showed no significant difference (less than 1 percent) in productivity than the sequential trigger. Also, there was no significant difference between the two tools in nail count and placement.

The study, which involved journeymen carpenters with an average of 13 years in the trade, found that the difference in productivity was the worker, not the tool.

Cranes and rigging

Properly securing any load with appropriate rigging is crucial to any lifting being done by machinery on the job-site. If the rigging fails the results can cause serious injury and even death. Before any load is lifted all components of the rigging hardware should be evaluated to ensure they can withstand the forces of the load.

Follow these safe work practices

1. Guard all exposed gears, rotating shafts, pulleys, sprockets or other moving parts to prevent contact with employees.

2. Guard or block the swing radius of the crane to restrict and prevent employees from entering into and being struck by the machine.

3. Inspect all rigging equipment prior to each lift, this should include all slings, chains, ropes, and like materials used to support and lift materials.

4. Remove from service any defective equipment immediately.

5. Be sure to inspect all hooks, clamps, and other lifting accessories for their rated load.

6. Clearly communicate to all employees on site that no one is permitted to work under loads.

7. Be sure the person responsible for signaling the crane operator stays in visual contact with the operator and has been trained to use the correct signals.

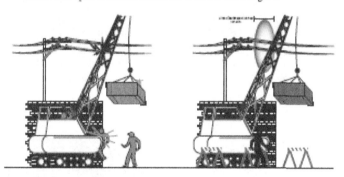

WRONG WAY   RIGHT WAY

76

PPE for Workers Checklist

Protection	TYPICAL OPERATIONS OF CONCERN	YES	NO
EYE	Sawing, cutting, drilling, sanding, grinding, hammering, chopping, abrasive blasting, punch press operations, etc.		
	Pouring, mixing, painting, cleaning, siphoning, dip tank operations, dental and health care services, etc.		
	Battery charging, installing fiberglass insulation, compressed air or gas operations, etc.		
	Welding, cutting, laser operations, etc.		
FACE	Pouring, mixing, painting, cleaning, siphoning, dip tank operations, etc.		
	Welding, pouring molten metal, smithing, baking, cooking, drying, etc.		
	Cutting, sanding, grinding, hammering, chopping, pouring, mixing, painting, cleaning, siphoning, etc.		
HEAD	Work stations or traffic routes located under catwalks or conveyor belts, construction, trenching, utility work, etc.		
	Construction, confined space operations, building maintenance, etc.		
	Building maintenance; utility work; construction; wiring; work on or near communications, computer, or other high tech equipment; arc or resistance welding; etc.		
FEET	Construction, plumbing, smithing, building maintenance, trenching, utility work, grass cutting, etc.		
	Building maintenance; utility work; construction; wiring; work on or near communications, computer, or other high tech equipment; arc or resistance welding; etc.		
	Welding, foundry work, casting, smithing, etc.		
	Demolition, explosives manufacturing, grain milling, spray painting, abrasive blasting, work with highly flammable materials, etc.		
HANDS	Grinding, sanding, sawing, hammering, material handling, etc.		
	Pouring, mixing, painting, cleaning, siphoning, dip tank operations, health care and dental services, etc.		
	Welding, pouring molten metal, smithing, baking, cooking, drying, etc.		
	Building maintenance; utility work; construction; wiring; work on or near communications, computer, or other high tech equipment; arc or resistance welding; etc.		
BODY	Pouring, mixing, painting, cleaning, siphoning, dip tank operations, machining, sawing, battery charging, installing fiberglass insulation, compressed air or gas operations, etc.		
	Cutting, grinding, sanding, sawing, glazing, material handling, etc.		
	Welding, pouring molten metal, smithing, baking, cooking, drying, etc.		
	Pouring, mixing, painting, cleaning, siphoning, dip tank operations, etc.		
HEARING	Machining, grinding, sanding, work near conveyors, pneumatic equipment, generators, ventilation fans, motors, punch and brake presses, etc. Samples shown are: ear muffs (left) and earplugs (right)		

NOTE: Pictures of PPE are intended to provide a small sample of what the protection gear may look like. They are not to scale nor are they inclusive of all protection gear required and/or that is available.

OPTION A: Focus Four Toolbox Talks 1 [Student copy]

Actual Incident:
A 36-year-old construction inspector for the county died when an asphalt dump truck backed over him. The inspector was wearing an orange reflective vest and hard-hat and the dump truck had a backup alarm that was functioning. The truck traveled approximately 770 feet in reverse.

How do we prevent these results?

_____
_____
_____
_____
_____
_____
_____
_____
_____
_____
_____
_____
_____
_____
_____
_____
_____
_____
_____
_____
_____
_____
_____

Additional discussion notes:

_____
_____
_____
_____

OPTION B: Focus Four Toolbox Talks 2 [Student copy]

Actual Incident:
A 56-year-old truck driver was crushed when a crane tipped over and the crane's boom landed on the cab of the dump truck in which he was sitting. The crane had been lowering an empty 4-yard concrete bucket, while booming out.

How do we prevent these results?

_____
_____
_____
_____
_____
_____
_____
_____
_____
_____
_____
_____
_____
_____
_____
_____
_____
_____
_____
_____
_____
_____
_____
_____

Additional discussion notes:

_____
_____
_____
_____

ACCIDENT SUMMARY No. 2

Accident Type:	Struck by Nail
Weather Conditions:	N/A
Type of Company:	General Contractors
Size of Work Crew:	17
Union or Non-union:	Union
Worksite Inspection?:	No
Designated Competent Person on Site?:	No
Employer Safety and Health Program?:	No
Training and Education for Employees?:	No
Craft of Deceased Employee(s):	Carpenter
Age; Sex	22; Male
Time of the Job:	3:00 p.m.
Time at the Task	Unknown

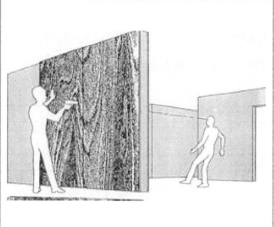

BRIEF DESCRIPTION OF ACCIDENT

A carpenter apprentice was killed when he was struck in the head by a nail that was fired from a powder actuated tool. The tool operator, while attempting to anchor a plywood form in preparation for pouring a concrete wall, fired the gun causing the nail to pass through the hollow wall. The nail travelled some twenty-seven feet before striking the victim. The tool operator had never received training in the proper use of the tool, and none of the employees in the area were wearing personal protective equipment.

INSPECTION RESULTS

Section not listed on original

ACCIDENT PREVENTION RECOMMENDATIONS

_____
_____
_____
_____
_____
_____
_____
_____
_____
_____
_____
_____
_____

NOTE: _The case here described was selected as being representative of fatalities caused by improper work practices. No special emphasis or priority is implied nor is the case necessarily a recent occurrence. The legal aspects of the incident have been resolved, and the case is now closed._

ACCIDENT SUMMARY No. 4

Accident Type:	Struck by Collapsing Crane Boom
Weather Conditions:	Clear
Type of Company:	General Contractor
Size of Work Crew:	9
Union or Non-union:	Union
Worksite Inspections Conducted:	Yes
Designated Competent Person on Site (1926.20(b)(2)):	Yes
Employer Safety Health Program:	Yes
Training and Education for Employees:	Yes
Craft of Deceased Employee(s):	3. Iron Worker 4. Management Trainee
Age & Sex	3. Ironworker-35; male 4. Management Trainee-26; male
Time on the Job:	1 hour
Time on Task:	1 hour

BRIEF DESCRIPTION OF ACCIDENT

A crew of ironworkers and a crane operator were unloading a 20-ton steel slab from a low-boy trailer using a 50-ton crawler crane with 90-foot lattice boom. The operator was inexperienced on this crane and did not know the length of the boom. Further, no one had determined the load radius. During lifting, the load moved forward and to the right, placing a twisting force on the boom. The boom twisted under the load, swinging down, under and to the right. Two employees standing 30 feet away apparently saw the boom begin to swing and ran. The boom struck one of the employees - an ironworker - on the head, causing instant death. Wire rope struck the other -- a management trainee -- causing internal injuries. He died two hours later at a local hospital.

INSPECTION RESULTS

Section not listed on original

ACCIDENT PREVENTION RECOMMENDATIONS

_____

_____

_____

_____

NOTE: The case here described was selected as being representative of fatalities caused by improper work practices. No special emphasis or priority is implied nor is the case necessarily a recent occurrence. The legal aspects of the incident have been resolved, and the case is now closed.

ACCIDENT SUMMARY No. 8

Accident Type:	Struck by Falling Object
Weather Conditions:	Clear
Type of Operation:	Transmission Tower Construction
Size of Work Crew:	4
Union or Non-union	Union
Competent Safety Monitor on Site:	Yes
Safety and Health Program in Effect:	Yes
Was the Worksite Inspected Regularly:	Yes
Training and Education Provided:	No
Employee Job Title:	Groundman (Framer)
Age & Sex:	24-Male
Experience at this Type of Work:	2 Years
Time on Project:	3 Days

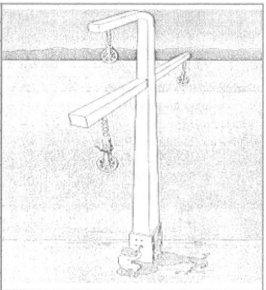

BRIEF DESCRIPTION OF ACCIDENT

Ball and socket connectors are used to attach conductor stringing blocks to insulators on the arms of 90 foot metal towers of electrical transmission lines. Normally stainless steel cotter keys secure the ball and socket connector in place. In this case, however, black electrical tape was wrapped around the socket to keep the ball in place rather than a cotter key. The tape apparently stretched and the ball came loose, dropping the stringing block approximately 90 feet onto the head of an employee below, one of a four-man erection crew.

INSPECTION RESULTS

As result of the its investigation, OSHA issued citations alleging three serious and two other-than-serious violations.

OSHA's construction safety standards include several requirements which, if they had been followed here, might have prevented this fatality.

ACCIDENT PREVENTION RECOMMENDATIONS

_____
_____
_____
_____
_____
_____

NOTE: _The case here described was selected as being representative of fatalities caused by improper work practices. No special emphasis or priority is implied nor is the case necessarily a recent occurrence. The legal aspects of the incident have been resolved, and the case is now closed._

ACCIDENT SUMMARY No. 51

Accident Type:	Struck By	
Weather Conditions:	Clear/Cool/Windy	
Type of Operation:	Construction Maintainence	
Size of Work Crew:	3	
Collective Bargaining	Yes	
Competent Safety Monitor on Site:	No	
Safety and Health Program in Effect:	No	
Was the Worksite Inspected Regularly:	Inadequate*	
Training and Education Provided:	No	
Employee Job Title:	Laborer	
Age & Sex:	33-Male	
Experience at this Type of Work:	18 Weeks	
Time on Project:	1 Day	

BRIEF DESCRIPTION OF ACCIDENT

Employees were dismantling grain spouts at a grain elevator. Sections of the spout were connected by collars. A ten foot section of a spout weighing 600 pounds was being pulled through a vent hole by a 5-ton winch. As the spout was being pulled through the opening to the outside, the spout became wedged at the point where the collar was to pass through. Several employees used pry bars to free the collar which was under tension. The spout popped out of the vent striking and killing an employee who was standing beside the spout. * Employer provided but did not require use of hard hats.

INSPECTION RESULTS

As a result of its investigation, OSHA issued two citations alleging serious violations. The employee should have been able to recognize that this situation was hazardous. Additionally, the investigation revealed that this employee was not wearing personal protective equipment in this hazardous situation. Had he been wearing a hard hat this death might have been prevented.

ACCIDENT PREVENTION RECOMMENDATIONS

_____
_____
_____
_____
_____
_____

NOTE: The case here described was selected as being representative of fatalities caused by improper work practices. No special emphasis or priority is implied nor is the case necessarily a recent occurrence. The legal aspects of the incident have been resolved, and the case is now closed.

Recognize Any Hazard(s)?

Source: OTI Course #3030

1

_____

_____

_____

_____

_____

_____

_____

Recognize Any Hazard(s)?

Source: Susan Harwood Grant Number SH-17792-08-60-F-48 by Compacion Foundation

3

_____

_____

_____

_____

_____

_____

_____

Recognize Any Hazard(s)?

Source: Construction Safety Council

5

_____

_____

_____

_____

_____

_____

_____

_____

Recognize Any Hazard(s)?

Source: National Photo Archive ID #3295

7

Recognize Any Hazard(s)?

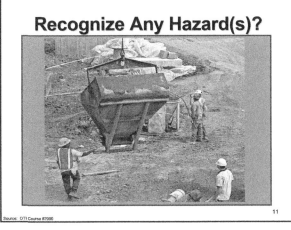

Source: National Photo Archive ID #1470

9

Recognize Any Hazard(s)?

Source: OTI Course #2000

11

Recognize Any Hazard(s)?

Source: National Photo Archive ID #3466

13

Recognize Any Hazard(s)?

Source: National Photo Archive ID #1860

15

Recognize Any Hazard(s)?

Source: OTI Course #2080

17

Recognize Any Hazard(s)?

Construction Focus Four: Struck-By Hazards Lesson Test

NAME: _____ DATE: ___/___/___

1. Struck-by injuries are produced by forcible contact or impact between the injured person and a/n _____.
   a. High voltage power line or other energy source
   b. Object or piece of equipment
   c. Co-worker or employer

2. The following are examples of struck-by hazards. Which one is an example of a struck-by <u>flying</u> hazard?
   a. Hit by a nail from a nail gun
   b. Hit by a load dropped from a crane
   c. Run over by a vehicle in a roadway work zone

3. As a load is mechanically lifted, the materials _____.
   a. May strike workers if the load swings, twists or turns
   b. Will not be affected by windy conditions or bad weather
   c. Can weigh any amount without causing a problem with the equipment

4. Among the list of ways workers can protect themselves when working on or near any construction zone, is to _____.
   a. Direct traffic in and out of the work zone
   b. Work behind moving vehicles
   c. Wear high-visibility reflective clothing

5. A struck-by hazard can be described as anytime a worker _____.
   a. Falls from a height of greater than ten feet
   b. Is hit by a falling, swinging, flying or rolling object
   c. Can get any part of his/her body caught in or in between objects

6. Employers must protect workers from struck-by hazards by _____.
   a. Providing PPE such as hard hats and safety glasses
   b. Establishing guidelines that allow only contractors access in the crane work zone
   c. Ensuring guards on tools and equipment are removed when it is absolutely necessary to get the job done

Focus 4: Caught-in or -between

ACCIDENT SUMMARY No. 5

Accident Type:	Caught in or Between	
Weather Conditions:	Clear	
Type of Company:	Street Paving Contractor	
Size of Work Crew:	1	
Union or Non-union:	Non-Union	
Worksite Inspections Conducted (1926.20(b)(2)):	Yes	
Designated Competent Person on Site (1926.20(b)(2)):	Yes	
Employer Safety Health Program:	Yes	
Training and Education for Employees (1926.21(b)):	Yes	
Craft of Deceased Employee(s):	Ironworker	
Age & Sex:	22-Male	
Time on the Job:	1 day	
Time on Task:	3 Hours	

BRIEF DESCRIPTION OF ACCIDENT

A laborer was steam cleaning a scraper. The bowl apron had been left in the raised position. The hydraulically controlled apron had not been blocked to prevent it from accidently falling. The apron did fall unexpectedly and the employee was caught between the apron and the cutting edge of the scraper bowl. The apron weighted approximately 2500 pounds.

ACCIDENT PREVENTION RECOMMENDATIONS

_____
_____
_____
_____
_____
_____
_____
_____
_____

ACCIDENT SUMMARY No. 13

Accident Type:	Collapse of Shoring
Weather Conditions:	Clear
Type of Operation:	Boring and Pipe Jacking Excavation
Size of Work Crew:	4
Collective Bargaining	Yes
Competent Safety Monitor on Site:	Yes
Safety and Health Program in Effect:	No
Was the Worksite Inspected Regularly:	Yes
Training and Education Provided:	Yes
Employee Job Title:	Pipe Welder
Age & Sex:	62-Male
Experience at this Type of Work:	18 years
Time on Project:	2½

BRIEF DESCRIPTION OF ACCIDENT

Four employees were boring a hole and pushing a 20-inch pipe casing under a road. The employees were in an excavation approximately 9 feet wide, 32 feet long and 7 feet deep. Steel plates 8' × 15' × ¾", being used as shoring, were placed vertically against the north and south walls of the excavation at approximately a 30 degree angle. There were no horizontal braces between the steel plates. The steel plate on the south wall tipped over, pinning an employee (who was killed) between the steel plate and the pipe casing. At the time the plate tipped over, a backhoe was being operated adjacent to the excavation.

ACCIDENT PREVENTION RECOMMENDATIONS

_____

_____

_____

_____

_____

_____

_____

_____

_____

_____

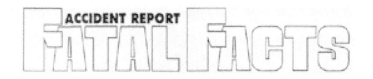

ACCIDENT SUMMARY No. 15

Accident Type:	Crushed by Dump Truck Body	
Weather Conditions:	Clear, Warm	
Type of Operation:	General Contractor	
Size of Work Crew:	N/A	
Collective Bargaining	Yes	
Competent Safety Monitor on Site:	Yes	
Safety and Health Program in Effect:	Yes	
Was the Worksite Inspected Regularly:	Yes	
Training and Education Provided:	No	
Employee Job Title:	Truck Driver	
Age & Sex:	25-Male	
Experience at this Type of Work:	2 Months	
Time on Project:	2 Weeks at Site	

BRIEF DESCRIPTION OF ACCIDENT

A truck driver was crushed and killed between the frame and dump box of a dump truck. Apparently a safety "over-travel" cable attached between the truck frame and the dump box malfunctioned by catching on a protruding nut of an air brake cylinder. This prevented the dump box from being fully raised, halting its progress at a point where about 20 inches of space remained between it and the truck frame. The employee, apparently assuming that releasing the cable would allow the dump box to continue up-ward, reached between the rear dual wheels and over the frame, and disengaged the cable with his right hand. The dump box then dropped suddenly, crushing his head. The employee had not received training or instruction in proper operating procedures and was not made aware of all potential hazards in his work.

ACCIDENT PREVENTION RECOMMENDATIONS

ACCIDENT SUMMARY No. 18

Accident Type:	Caught by Rotating Part	
Weather Conditions:	Clear	
Type of Operation:	Telephone Line Installation	
Size of Work Crew:	3	
Collective Bargaining	No	
Competent Safety Monitor on Site:	Yes - Victim	
Safety and Health Program in Effect:	Yes	
Was the Worksite Inspected Regularly:	Yes	
Training and Education Provided:	No	
Employee Job Title:	Boring Machine Operator	
Age & Sex:	56-Male	
Experience at this Type of Work:	10 Years	
Time on Project:	5 Days	

BRIEF DESCRIPTION OF ACCIDENT

A three-man crew was installing an underground telephone cable in a residential area. They had just completed a bore hole under a driveway using a horizontal boring machine. The bore hole rod had been removed from the hole. While the rod was still rotating, the operator straddled it and stooped over to pick it up. His trouser leg became entangled in the rotating rod and he was flipped over. He struck tools and materials, sustaining fatal injuries.

ACCIDENT PREVENTION RECOMMENDATIONS

_____
_____
_____
_____
_____
_____
_____
_____
_____
_____
_____

ACCIDENT SUMMARY No. 22

		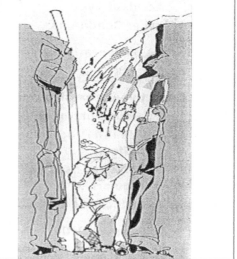
Accident Type:	Cave-in	
Weather Conditions:	Warm, Clear	
Type of Operation:	Excavator	
Size of Work Crew:	2	
Collective Bargaining	No	
Competent Safety Monitor on Site:	Yes	
Safety and Health Program in Effect:	No	
Was the Worksite Inspected Regularly:	Yes	
Training and Education Provided:	No	
Employee Job Title:	Laborer	
Age & Sex:	37-Male	
Experience at this Type of Work:	3 Years	
Time on Project:	2 Days	

BRIEF DESCRIPTION OF ACCIDENT

An employee was installing a small diameter pipe in a trench 3 feet wide, 12-15 feet deep and 90 feet long. The trench was not shored or sloped nor was there a box or shield to protect the employee. Further, there was evidence of a previous cave-in. The employee apparently reentered the trench, and a second cave-in occurred, burying him. He was found face down m the bottom of the trench.

ACCIDENT PREVENTION RECOMMENDATIONS

_____
_____
_____
_____
_____
_____
_____
_____
- -
- -
- -
- -
- -
- -
- -
- -

ACCIDENT SUMMARY No. 31

Accident Type:	Cave-in	
Weather Conditions:	Cloudy and Dry	
Type of Operation:	Trenching and excavation	
Size of Work Crew:	4	
Collective Bargaining:	No	
Competent Safety Monitor on Site:	Yes	
Safety and Health Program in Effect:	Yes	
Was the Worksite Inspected Regularly:	Yes	
Training and Education Provided:	No	
Employee Job Title:	Pipe Layer	
Age & Sex:	32-Male	
Experience at this Type of Work:	9 Months	
Time on Project:	2 Weeks	

BRIEF DESCRIPTION OF ACCIDENT

Employees were laying sewer pipe in a trench 15 feet deep. The sides of the trench, 4 feet wide at the bottom and 15 feet wide at the top, were not shored or protected to prevent a cave-in. Soil in the lower portion of the trench was mostly sand and gravel and the upper portion was clay and loam*. The trench was not protected from vibration caused by heavy vehicle traffic on the road nearby. To leave the trench, employees had to exit by climbing over the backfill. As they attempted to leave the trench, there was a small cave-in covering one employee to his ankles. When the other employee went to his co-worker's aid another cave-in occurred covering him to his waist. The first employee died of a rupture of the right ventricle of his heart at the scene of the cave-in. The other employee suffered a hip injury.

ACCIDENT PREVENTION RECOMMENDATIONS

----

* Clay and loam are terms not used any longer; Soil condition is now described using A, B, or C

ACCIDENT SUMMARY No. 38

Accident Type:	Caught in or between
Weather Conditions:	Clear, dry
Type of Operation:	Highway, street construction
Size of Work Crew:	4
Collective Bargaining	Yes
Competent Safety Monitor on Site:	Yes
Safety and Health Program in Effect:	Yes
Was the Worksite Inspected Regularly:	Yes
Training and Education Provided:	No
Employee Job Title:	Equipment Operator
Age & Sex:	38-Male
Experience at this Type of Work:	11 Months
Time on Project:	1 Hour

BRIEF DESCRIPTION OF ACCIDENT

An employee was driving a front-end loader up a dirt ramp onto a lowboy trailer. The tractor tread began to slide off the trailer. As the tractor began to tip, the operator, who was not wearing a seat belt, jumped from the cab. As he hit the ground, the tractor's rollover protective structure fell on top of him, crushing him.

ACCIDENT PREVENTION RECOMMENDATIONS

ACCIDENT SUMMARY No. 50

Accident Type:	Caught between Backhoe Superstructure and Concrete Wall
Weather Conditions:	Clear/Cool
Type of Operation:	Excavation Contractor
Size of Work Crew:	9
Collective Bargaining	Yes
Competent Safety Monitor on Site:	No
Safety and Health Program in Effect:	No
Was the Worksite Inspected Regularly:	No
Training and Education Provided:	No
Employee Job Title:	Truck Driver
Age & Sex:	34-Male
Experience at this Type of Work:	Unknown
Time on Project:	4 Days

Picture used may not be representative of a backhoe as indicated in the report

BRIEF DESCRIPTION OF ACCIDENT

The contractor was operating a backhoe when an employee attempted to walk between the swinging superstructure of the backhoe and a concrete wall. As the employee approached the backhoe from the operator's blind side, the superstructure hit the victim crushing him against the wall.

ACCIDENT PREVENTION RECOMMENDATIONS

ACCIDENT REPORT FATAL FACTS

ACCIDENT SUMMARY No. 61

Accident Type:	Trench Collapse
Weather Conditions:	Fair
Type of Operation:	Excavation Work
Size of Work Crew:	2
Competent Safety Monitor on Site:	No
Safety and Health Program in Effect:	No
Was the Worksite Inspected Regularly:	No
Training and Education Provided:	Inadequate
Employee Job Title:	Laborer
Age & Sex:	51-Male
Experience at this Type of Work:	6 Months
Time on Project:	2 Days

BRIEF DESCRIPTION OF ACCIDENT

An employee was working in a trench 4 feet wide and 7 feet deep. About 30 feet away a backhoe was straddling the trench when the backhoe operator noticed a large chunk of dirt falling from the side wall behind the worker in the trench, he called out a warning. Before the worker could climb out, 6 to 8 feet of the trench wall had collapsed on him and covered his body up to his neck. He suffocated before the backhoe operator could dig him out. There were no exit ladders. No sloping, shoring or other protective system had been used in the trench.

ACCIDENT PREVENTION RECOMMENDATIONS

ACCIDENT SUMMARY No. 73

Accident Type:	Struck by/Caught between	
Weather Conditions:	Clear/warm	
Type of Operation:	Stacking Structural Steel	
Size of Work Crew:	6	
Competent Person on Site:	No	
Safety and Health Program in Effect:	No	
Was the Worksite Inspected Regularly by the Employer:	No	
Training and Education Provided:	No	
Employee Job Title:	Laborer	
Age & Sex:	28-Male	
Experience at this Type of Work:	4 Years	
Time on Project:	5 Weeks	

BRIEF DESCRIPTION OF ACCIDENT

Two laborers and a fork lift driver were staking 40-foot-long I-beams in preparation for structural steel erection. One laborer was placing a 2 X 4 inch wooden spacer on the last I-beam on the stack. The fork lift driver drove up to the stack with another I-beam that was not secured or blocked on the fork lift tines. The I-beam fell from the tines, pining the laborer between the fallen I beam and the stack of beams.

ACCIDENT PREVENTION RECOMMENDATIONS

Caught-In or –Between Hazard Recognition
Student Copy
Take notes and record the details of the hazards that may be present

Recognize Any Hazard(s)?

Source: Southwest Safety Training Alliance   1

_____

_____

_____

_____

_____

_____

_____

Recognize Any Hazard(s)?

Source: Compacion Foundation (HCAdetejas.org)   3

_____

_____

_____

_____

_____

_____

_____

_____

Recognize Any Hazard(s)?

Source: OSHA Region IV National Photo Archive   5

_____

_____

_____

_____

_____

_____

_____

_____

Recognize Any Hazard(s)?

Source: Compacion Foundation (HCAdetajas.org)

7

Recognize Any Hazard(s)?

Source: OSHA Directorate of Construction

9

Recognize Any Hazard(s)?

Source: Indian River Community (now State) College

11

Recognize Any Hazard(s)?

Source: Indian River Community (now State) College

Recognize Any Hazard(s)?

Source: Indian River Community (now State) College

Recognize Any Hazard(s)?

Source: Construction Safety Council

Recognize Any Hazard(s)?

14 11:16

19

Source: OSHA Region IV National Photo Archive

103

NAME: _____ DATE: ___/___/___

Review Exercise – Student Copy

Complete the following sentences using words from the word bank.

WORD BANK		
Safety guard	Identifying	5 feet
Cave-in	Stacked	Corrective	Secured
Equipment	Immovable	Seatbelt

Each word will be used once.

1. To protect yourself from hazardous moving parts of power tools and equipment, always use a/n _____ when using the equipment.

2. To avoid being caught in a/n _____, do not work in an unprotected trench that is _____ deep or more.

3. Wear a/n _____, if required, to avoid being thrown from a vehicle and then crushed by the vehicle as it tips over.

4. Make sure all loads carried by equipment are stable and _____.

5. Never place yourself between moving materials and a/n _____ structure, vehicle, or _____ materials.

6. Your employer must train you on how to use any provided _____ safely.

7. A competent person is capable of _____ hazards in the work environment and is authorized to take _____ measures.

NAME: _____ DATE: ___/___/___

1. Caught in or -between hazards are related with excavations [trenches]; therefore, the hazard considered to be the greatest risk is:
   a. Cave-ins
   b. Severing of underground utilities
   c. Equipment falling into trenches

2. One who is capable of identifying existing and predictable hazards in the surroundings, or working conditions which are unsanitary, hazardous, or dangerous to employees, and who has authorization to take prompt corrective measures to eliminate them is a/n _____:
   a. Competent person
   b. OSHA Compliance Officer
   c. Qualified person

3. To protect against caught-in or –between hazards, a worker should not only avoid wearing loose clothing or jewelry, but also a worker should avoid:
   a. Operating equipment/machinery while wearing a seatbelt
   b. Working with equipment/machinery that has not been locked-out
   c. Using equipment/machinery that is guarded

4. Providing worker training on the safe use of the equipment being operated is the responsibility of the:
   a. Employer
   b. Worker
   c. State OSHA consultation

5. Workers should not work in an unprotected trench that is 5 feet deep or more. The type of protection installed may be sloping or benching; trench box or shield; and _____.
   a. Stabilizing
   b. Steadying
   c. Shoring

6. To prevent being pinned between equipment or other objects, workers should avoid _____.
   a. Using a trench box or shield during excavation work
   b. Placing themselves between moving vehicles and an immovable structure, vehicle, or staked materials
   c. Removing a safety guard when a tool such as, a circular saw or power drill, is being used.

Cranes

OSHA FactSheet

Subpart CC – Cranes and Derricks in Construction: Assembly/Disassembly

This fact sheet explains the assembly and disassembly requirements of subpart CC – Cranes and Derricks in Construction, as specified in 29 CFR 1926.1403-1926.1406 and 192.1412. These provisions are effective November 8, 2010.

Procedures

Under this standard, employers must comply with all manufacturer prohibitions regarding assembly and disassembly. However, the standard generally allows employers to choose between the manufacturer's procedures or their own (see exception below for synthetic slings procedures). Employer procedures must be developed by a "qualified person" and must satisfy a number of specified requirements, such as providing adequate support and stability for all parts of the equipment, and positioning employees involved to minimize exposure to any unintended movement or collapse.

Assembly/Disassembly responsibilities

- The rule requires the work to be directed by an A/D (Assembly/Disassembly) director. The A/D director must meet the criteria for both a "competent person" and a "qualified person," which are defined terms in this rule, or must be a "competent person" assisted by a "qualified person."
- The A/D director must understand the applicable procedures.
- The A/D director must review the procedures immediately prior to beginning work unless he or she understands the procedures and has

used them before for that equipment type and configuration.
- The A/D director must ensure that each member of the crew understands his or her tasks, the hazards of the tasks, and any hazardous positions or locations to avoid.
- The A/D director must verify all capacities of any equipment used, including rigging, lifting lugs, etc.
- The A/D director must also address hazards associated with the operation, including 12 specified areas of concern: site and ground conditions, blocking material, proper location of blocking, verifying assist crane loads, boom & jib pick points, center of gravity, stability upon pin removal, snagging, struck by counterweights, boom hoist brake failure, loss of backward stability, and wind speed and weather.

Inspection

- Upon completion of assembly, but before use, the equipment must be inspected by a "qualified person" to ensure that it is configured in accordance with the manufacturer equipment criteria. If these criteria are unavailable, the employer's "qualified person," with the assistance of a registered professional engineer if necessary, must develop the appropriate configuration criteria and ensure that these criteria are met.

For more complete information:

OSHA Occupational Safety and Health Administration

U.S. Department of Labor
www.osha.gov
(800) 321-OSHA

Page 1 of 2

Assembly/Disassembly, continued.

General requirements

- A crew member who moves out of the operator's view to a location where the crew member could be injured by movement of the equipment (or load) MUST inform the operator before going to that location. The operator must not move the equipment until that crew member informs the operator that he or she has relocated to a safe position.
- Employees must never be under the boom or jib when pins (or similar devices) are being removed, unless it is required by site constraints and the A/D director has implemented procedures that minimize the risk of unintended movement and the duration and extent of exposure under the boom.
- Component weights must be readily available for all components to be assembled.
- All rigging must be done by a "qualified rigger."
- Pins may not be removed during disassembly when the pendants are in tension.
- Booms supported only by cantilevering must not exceed manufacturer limitations or RPE limitations, as applicable.
- Component selection and equipment configuration that affects the capacity or safe operation of the equipment must be in accordance with manufacturer requirements and limits or RPE requirements and limits, as applicable.

Synthetic slings

- The employer must follow manufacturer procedures when using synthetic slings during assembly or disassembly rigging (even when the employer has developed its own A/D procedure as an alternative to the manufacturer's other procedures.)
- Synthetic slings must be protected from abrasive, sharp or acute edges, and configurations that might reduce the sling's rated capacity.

Outriggers and stabilizers

When outriggers or stabilizers are used or are necessary in light of the load to be handled and the operating radius:

- Outriggers and stabilizers must be fully extended or, if permitted by manufacturer procedures, deployed as specified in the load chart.
- Outriggers must be set to remove equipment weight from the wheels, except for locomotive cranes.
- Outrigger floats, if used, must be attached to the outriggers; stabilizer floats, if used, must be attached to the stabilizers.
- Each outrigger or stabilizer must be visible to the operator or to a signal person during extension and setting.
- Outrigger and stabilizer blocking must be placed under the float/pad of the jack or, if there is no jack, under the outer bearing surface of the outrigger or stabilizer beam. Blocking must also be sufficient to sustain the loads and maintain stability and must be properly placed.

Tower cranes

- Tower cranes are subject to additional requirements for erecting, climbing and dismantling, including a pre-erection inspection (29 CFR 1926.1435).

For more complete information:

OSHA® Occupational Safety and Health Administration

U.S. Department of Labor
www.osha.gov
(800) 321-OSHA

OSHA FactSheet

Subpart CC – Cranes and Derricks in Construction: Wire Rope – Inspection

This fact sheet describes the inspection requirements of subpart CC – Cranes and Derricks in Construction, as specified in 29 CFR 1926.1413. These provisions are effective November 8, 2010. This document is intended to assist wire rope inspectors and supervisors.

Inspection Trigger	Inspection Details	Performed by	Documentation
Each shift	See list below, visual inspection must begin prior to each shift in which the equipment is used.	Competent Person	Not required
Monthly	See details below.	Competent Person	Required. Must be signed by the person who conducted the inspection and retained for a minimum of 3 months.
Annual	See details below.	Qualified Person	Required. Must be signed by the person who conducted the inspection and retained for a minimum of 12 months.

- The annual/comprehensive and monthly inspections must be documented according to 1926.1412(f)(7) and 1916.1412(e)(3), respectively.
- Rope lubricants of the type that hinder inspection must not be used.
- All documents produced under this section must be available, during the applicable document retention period, to all persons who conduct inspections under this section.

Shift Inspection

Shift inspections are visual inspections that a competent person must begin prior to each shift during which the equipment is used. Shift inspections do not require untwisting (opening) of wire ropes or booming down. The inspection must consist of observation of wire ropes (running and standing) that are likely to be in use during the shift for apparent deficiencies, including the following:

Apparent Deficiencies – Category I	Removal from Service Criteria
• Significant distortion of the wire rope structure such as kinking, crushing, unstranding, birdcaging, signs of core failure, or steel core protrusion between the outer strands. • Significant corrosion. • Electric arc damage (from a source other than power lines) or heat damage. • Improperly applied end connections. • Significantly corroded, cracked, bent, or worn end connections (such as from severe service).	If a Category I deficiency is identified, the competent person must immediately determine whether it constitutes a safety hazard. If the deficiency is determined to be a safety hazard, all operations involving use of the wire rope in question must be prohibited until: • The wire rope is replaced. (See 1926.1417), or • If the deficiency is localized, the problem is corrected by severing the wire rope in two; the undamaged portion may continue to be used. Joining lengths of wire rope by splicing is prohibited. If a rope is shortened under this paragraph, the employer must ensure that the drum will still have two wraps of wire when the load and/or boom is in its lowest position.

Apparent Deficiencies – Category II	Removal from Service Criteria

• Visible broken wires:
  ○ In running wire ropes: six randomly distributed broken wires in one rope lay or three broken wires in one strand in one rope lay, where a rope lay is the length along the rope in which one strand makes a complete revolution around the rope.
  ○ In rotation-resistant ropes: two randomly distributed broken wires in six rope diameters or four randomly distributed broken wires in 30 rope diameters.
  ○ In pendants or standing wire ropes: more than two broken wires in one rope lay located in rope beyond end connections and/or more than one broken wire in a rope lay located at an end connection.
• A diameter reduction of more than 5% from nominal diameter.
	If a Category II deficiency is identified, operations involving use of the wire rope in question must be prohibited until:
	• Employer complies with the wire rope manufacturer's established criterion for removal from service, or with a different criterion that the wire rope manufacturer has approved in writing for that specific wire rope. (See 1926.1417).
	• The wire rope is replaced. (See 1926.1417), or
	• If the deficiency is localized, the problem is corrected by severing the wire rope in two; the undamaged portion may continue to be used. Joining lengths of wire rope by splicing is prohibited. If a rope is shortened under this paragraph, the employer must ensure that the drum will still have two wraps of wire when the load and/or boom is in its lowest position.

Apparent Deficiencies – Category III	Removal from Service Criteria
• In rotation-resistant wire rope, core protrusion or other distortion indicating core failure. • Prior electrical contact with a power line. • A broken strand.	If a Category III deficiency is identified, operations involving use of the wire rope in question must be prohibited until: • The wire rope is replaced. (See 1926.1417), or • If the deficiency (other than power line contact) is localized, the problem is corrected by severing the wire rope in two; the undamaged portion may continue to be used. Joining lengths of wire rope by splicing is prohibited. Repair of wire rope that contacted an energized power line is also prohibited. If a rope is shortened under this paragraph, the employer must ensure that the drum will still have two wraps of wire when the load and/or boom is in its lowest position.

Where a wire rope is required to be removed from service under this section, either the equipment (as a whole), or the hoist with that wire rope must be tagged-out, in accord with 1926.1417(f)(1), until the wire rope is repaired or replaced.

Critical Review Items

Particular attention must be given to all of the following:

• Rotation-resistant wire rope in use.
• Wire rope being used for boom hoists and luffing hoists, particularly at reverse bends.
• Wire rope at flange points, crossover points, and repetitive pickup points on drums.
• Wire rope at or near terminal ends.
• Wire rope in contact with saddles, equalizer sheaves or other sheaves where rope travel is limited.

Monthly Inspection

Each month an inspection must be conducted as stated under "Shift Inspection" above.

In addition to the criteria for shift inspection, monthly inspections require that:

• The inspection must include any deficiencies that the qualified person who conducts the annual inspection determines under 1926.1413(c)(3)(ii) must be monitored.
• Wire ropes on equipment must not be used until an inspection under this paragraph demonstrates that no corrective action under 1926.1413(a)(4) is required.
• The inspection must be documented according to 1926.1412(e)(3) (monthly inspection documentation).

Annual/Comprehensive Inspection

At least every 12 months, wire ropes in use on equipment must be inspected by a qualified person as stated under "Shift Inspection" above.

In addition to the criteria for shift inspection, annual inspections require that –

- The inspection must be complete and thorough, covering the surface of the entire length of the wire ropes, with particular attention given to all of the following:
  - Critical review items from 1926.1413(a)(3)–(see "Critical Review Items" above).
  - Those sections that are normally hidden during shift and monthly inspections.
  - Wire rope subject to reverse bends.
  - Wire rope passing over sheaves.

Exception

In the event an annual inspection under 1926.1413(c)(2) is not feasible due to existing set-up and configuration of the equipment (such as where an assist crane is needed) or due to site conditions (such as a dense urban setting), such inspections must be conducted as soon as it becomes feasible, but no longer than an additional 6 months for running ropes and, for standing ropes, at the time of disassembly.

- If a deficiency is determined to constitute a safety hazard, operations involving use of the wire rope in question must be prohibited until:
  - The wire rope is replaced (see 1926.1417), or
  - If the deficiency is localized, the problem is corrected by severing the wire rope in two; the undamaged portion may continue to be used. Joining wire rope by splicing is prohibited. If a rope is shortened under this paragraph, the employer must ensure that the drum will still have two wraps of wire when the load and/or boom is in its lowest position.
- If a deficiency is identified and the qualified person determines that, though not presently a safety hazard, the deficiency needs to be monitored, the employer must ensure that the deficiency is checked in the monthly inspections.

Additionally

- The inspection must be documented according to 1926.1412(f)(7).
- Rope lubricants of the type that hinder inspection must not be used.
- All documents produced under this section must be available, during the applicable document retention period, to all persons who conduct inspections under this section.

For assistance, contact us. We can help. It's confidential.

OSHA ® Occupational Safety and Health Administration

U.S. Department of Labor
www.osha.gov (800) 321-OSHA (6742)

DOC FS-3635   01/2013

Name: _____   Date: _____

Knowledge Check: Cranes

1. Nearly 45% of crane accidents are the result of the boom or crane making contact with ___.
   a. other cranes
   b. work zone barricades
   c. energized power lines
   d. workers on the ground

2. Before beginning equipment operations, the employer must ___.
   a. identify the work zone and determine proximity to power lines
   b. notify utility company of lift and estimate voltage of power lines
   c. locate the fall zone and test load by lifting it at least 20 feet off the ground
   d. remove hazard area barriers and observe weather conditions

3. A broken window that distorts the operator's visibility of the task is acceptable for operation.
   a. True
   b. False

4. Which of the following must be readily available to the crane operator for use at all times?
   a. Load charts and recommended operating speeds
   b. Special hazard warnings
   c. Instructions and operator's manual
   d. All of the above

5. Who is responsible for inspecting all machinery and equipment prior to each use and during use, to make sure it is in safe operating condition.
   a. Certified person
   b. Qualified person
   c. Proficient person
   d. Competent person

Excavations

OSHA® FactSheet

Trenching and Excavation Safety

Two workers are killed every month in trench collapses. The employer must provide a workplace free of recognized hazards that may cause serious injury or death. The employer must comply with the trenching and excavation requirements of 29 CFR 1926.651 and 1926.652 or comparable OSHA-approved state plan requirements.

An excavation is any man-made cut, cavity, trench, or depression in an earth surface formed by earth removal.

Trench (Trench excavation) means a narrow excavation (in relation to its length) made below the surface of the ground. In general, the depth is greater than the width, but the width of a trench (measured at the bottom) is not greater than 15 feet (4.6 meters).

Dangers of Trenching and Excavation
Cave-ins pose the greatest risk and are much more likely than other excavation-related accidents to result in worker fatalities. Other potential hazards include falls, falling loads, hazardous atmospheres, and incidents involving mobile equipment. One cubic yard of soil can weigh as much as a car. An unprotected trench is an early grave. Do not enter an unprotected trench.

Trench Safety Measures
Trenches 5 feet (1.5 meters) deep or greater require a protective system unless the excavation is made entirely in stable rock. If less than 5 feet deep, a competent person may determine that a protective system is not required.

Trenches 20 feet (6.1 meters) deep or greater require that the protective system be designed by a registered professional engineer or be based on tabulated data prepared and/or approved by a registered professional engineer in accordance with 1926.652(b) and (c).

Competent Person
OSHA standards require that employers inspect trenches daily and as conditions change by a competent person before worker entry to ensure elimination of excavation hazards. A competent person is an individual who is capable of identifying existing and predictable hazards or working conditions that are hazardous, unsanitary, or dangerous to workers, soil types and protective systems required, and who is authorized to take prompt corrective measures to eliminate these hazards and conditions.

Access and Egress
OSHA standards require safe access and egress to all excavations, including ladders, steps, ramps, or other safe means of exit for employees working in trench excavations 4 feet (1.22 meters) or deeper. These devices must be located within 25 feet (7.6 meters) of all workers.

General Trenching and Excavation Rules
- Keep heavy equipment away from trench edges.
- Identify other sources that might affect trench stability.
- Keep excavated soil (spoils) and other materials at least 2 feet (0.6 meters) from trench edges.
- Know where underground utilities are located before digging.
- Test for atmospheric hazards such as low oxygen, hazardous fumes and toxic gases when > 4 feet deep.
- Inspect trenches at the start of each shift.
- Inspect trenches following a rainstorm or other water intrusion.
- Do not work under suspended or raised loads and materials.
- Inspect trenches after any occurrence that could have changed conditions in the trench.
- Ensure that personnel wear high visibility or other suitable clothing when exposed to vehicular traffic.

Protective Systems
There are different types of protective systems.

Benching means a method of protecting workers from cave-ins by excavating the sides of an excavation to form one or a series of horizontal levels or steps, usually with vertical or near-vertical surfaces between levels. *Benching cannot be done in Type C soil.*

Sloping involves cutting back the trench wall at an angle inclined away from the excavation.

Shoring requires installing aluminum hydraulic or other types of supports to prevent soil movement and cave-ins.

Shielding protects workers by using trench boxes or other types of supports to prevent soil cave-ins. Designing a protective system can be complex because you must consider many factors: soil classification, depth of cut, water content of soil, changes caused by weather or climate, surcharge loads (e.g., spoil, other materials to be used in the trench) and other operations in the vicinity.

Additional Information

Visit OSHA's Safety and Health Topics web page on trenching and excavation at
www.osha.gov/SLTC/trenchingexcavation/index.html
www.osha.gov/dcsp/statestandard.html

This is one in a series of informational fact sheets highlighting OSHA programs, policies or standards. It does not impose any new compliance requirements. For a comprehensive list of compliance requirements of OSHA standards or regulations, refer to Title 29 of the Code of Federal Regulations. This information will be made available to sensory-impaired individuals upon request. The voice phone is (202) 693-1999; teletypewriter (TTY) number: (877) 889-5627.

For assistance, contact us. We can help. It's confidential.

U.S. Department of Labor
www.osha.gov   (800) 321-OSHA (6742)

DOC FS-3476 9/2011

Name: _____   Date: _____

Knowledge Check: Excavations

1. What is the minimum distance that excavation materials, tools, and other supplies be kept back from the excavation's edge?
   a. 1 foot
   b. 2 feet
   c. 7.5 feet
   d. 25 feet

2. At what depth must a ladder, ramp, steps, or runway be present for quick worker exit?
   a. 4 feet
   b. 5 feet
   c. 10 feet
   d. It is never required

3. What is the greatest hazard facing a worker while working in a trench?
   a. Hazardous atmospheres
   b. Falls
   c. Cave-ins
   d. Falling objects

4. Unless made in entirely stable rock, at what depth is a protective system required for a trench?
   a. Any depth if the competent person says so
   b. 5 feet and greater
   c. Only at depths greater than 10 feet
   d. Both a and b

Materials handling

Worker Safety Series
Warehousing

Think Safety

- More than 145,000 people work in over 7,000 warehouses.
- The fatal injury rate for the warehousing industry is higher than the national average for all industries.
- Potential hazards for workers in warehousing:
  - Unsafe use of forklifts;
  - Improper stacking of products;
  - Failure to use proper personal protective equipment;
  - Failure to follow proper lockout/tagout procedures;
  - Inadequate fire safety provisions; or
  - Repetitive motion injuries.

Think Safety Checklists

The following checklists may help you take steps to avoid hazards that cause injuries, illnesses and fatalities. As always, be cautious and seek help if you are concerned about a potential hazard.

General Safety

- Exposed or open loading dock doors and other areas that employees could fall 4 feet or more or walk off should be chained off, roped off or otherwise blocked.
- Floors and aisles are clear of clutter, electrical cords, hoses, spills and other hazards that could cause employees to slip, trip or fall.
- Proper work practices are factored into determining the time requirements for an employee to perform a task.
- Employees performing physical work have adequate periodic rest breaks to avoid fatigue levels that could result in greater risk of accidents and reduced quality of work.
- Newly-hired employees receive general ergonomics training and task-specific training.
- The warehouse is well ventilated.
- Employees are instructed on how to avoid heat stress in hot, humid environments.
- Employees are instructed on how to work in cold environments.
- The facility has lockout/tagout procedures.

Materials Handling Safety

- There are appropriately marked and sufficiently safe clearances for aisles and at loading docks or passageways where mechanical handling equipment is used.
- Loose/unboxed materials which might fall from a pile are properly stacked by blocking, interlocking or limiting the height of the pile to prevent falling hazards.

- Bags, containers, bundles, etc. are stored in tiers that are stacked, blocked, interlocked and limited in height so that they are stable and secure to prevent sliding or collapse.
- Storage areas are kept free from accumulation of materials that could lead to tripping, fire, explosion or pest infestations.
- Excessive vegetation is removed from building entrances, work or traffic areas to prevent possible trip or fall hazards due to visual obstructions.
- Derail and/or bumper blocks are provided on spur railroad tracks where a rolling car could contact other cars being worked on and at entrances to buildings, work or traffic areas.
- Covers and/or guardrails are provided to protect personnel from the hazards of stair openings in floors, meter or equipment pits and similar hazards.
- Personnel use proper lifting techniques.
- Elevators and hoists for lifting materials/ containers are properly used with adequate safe clearances, no obstructions, appropriate signals and directional warning signs.

Hazard Communication Safety

- All hazardous materials containers are properly labeled, indicating the chemical's identity, the manufacturer's name and address, and appropriate hazard warnings.
- There is an updated list of hazardous chemicals.
- The facility has a written program that covers hazard determination, including Material Safety Data Sheets (MSDSs), labeling and training.
- There is a system to check that each incoming chemical is accompanied by a MSDS.
- All employees are trained in the requirements of the hazard communication standard, the chemical hazards to which they are exposed, how to read and understand a MSDS and chemical labels, and on what precautions to take to prevent exposure.
- All employee training is documented.
- All outside contractors are given a complete list of chemical products, hazards and precautions.
- Procedures have been established to maintain and evaluate the effectiveness of the current program.
- Employees use proper personal protective equipment when handling chemicals.
- All chemicals are stored according to the manufacturer's recommendations and local or national fire codes.

Forklift Safety

- Powered industrial trucks (forklifts) meet the design and construction requirements established in American National Standard for Powered Industrial Trucks, Part II ANSI B56.1-1969.
- Written approval from the truck manufacturer has been obtained for any modifications or additions that affect the capacity and safe operation of the vehicle.
- Capacity, operation and maintenance instruction plates, tags or decals are changed to specify any modifications or additions to the vehicle.
- Nameplates and markings are in place and maintained in a legible condition.
- Forklifts that are used in hazardous locations are appropriately marked/approved for such use.
- Battery charging is conducted only in designated areas.
- Appropriate facilities are provided for flushing and neutralizing spilled electrolytes, for fire extinguishing, for protecting charging apparatus from damage by trucks and for adequate ventilation to disperse fumes from gassing batteries.
- Conveyors, overhead hoists or equivalent materials handling equipment are provided for handling batteries.
- Reinstalled batteries are properly positioned and secured.

- Carboy tilters or siphons are used for handling electrolytes.
- Forklifts are properly positioned and brakes applied before workers start to change or charge batteries.
- Vent caps are properly functioning.
- Precautions are taken to prevent smoking, open flames, sparks or electric arcs in battery charging areas and during storage/changing of propane fuel tanks.
- Tools and other metallic objects are kept away from the top of uncovered batteries.
- Concentrations of noxious gases and fumes are kept below acceptable levels.
- Forklift operators are competent to operate a vehicle safely as demonstrated by successful completion of training and evaluation conducted and certified by persons with the knowledge, training and experience to train operators and evaluate their performance.
- The training program content includes all truck-related topics, workplace related topics and the requirements of 29 CFR 1910.178 for safe truck operation.
- Refresher training and evaluation is conducted whenever an operator has been observed operating the vehicle in an unsafe manner or has been involved in an accident or a near-miss incident.
- Refresher training and evaluation is conducted whenever an operator is assigned to drive a different type of truck or whenever a condition in the workplace changes in a manner that could affect safe operation of the truck.
- Evaluations of each operator's performance are conducted at least once every three years.
- Load engaging means are fully lowered, with controls neutralized, power shut off and brakes set when a forklift is left unattended.
- Operators maintain a safe distance from the edge of ramps or platforms while using forklifts on any elevated dock, platform or freight car.
- There is sufficient headroom for the forklift and operator under overhead installations, lights, pipes, sprinkler systems, etc.
- Overhead guards are provided in good condition to protect forklift operators from falling objects.
- Operators observe all traffic regulations, including authorized plant speed limits.
- Drivers are required to look in the direction of and keep a clear view of the path of travel.
- Operators run their trucks at a speed that will permit the vehicle to stop in a safe manner.
- Dock boards (bridge plates) are properly secured when loading or unloading from dock to truck.
- Stunt driving and horseplay are prohibited.
- All loads are stable, safely arranged and fit within the rated capacity of the truck.
- Operators fill fuel tanks only when the engine is not running.
- Replacement parts of trucks are equivalent in terms of safety with those used in the original design.
- Trucks are examined for safety before being placed into service and unsafe or defective trucks are removed from service.

Name: _____   Date: _____

Knowledge Check: Materials Handling, Storage, Use, and Disposal

1. How old do you have to be to operate a forklift, regardless of training?
   a. 16 years old
   b. 18 years old
   c. 21 years old
   d. 25 years old

2. One good way to prevent materials handling hazards is to _____.
   a. refuse to allow personnel to ride equipment without a seat and seatbelt
   b. report all damaged equipment immediately
   c. operate within manufacturer's specifications
   d. All of these

3. Which of the following is a method for eliminating or reducing crane operation hazards?
   a. Operators should know how much they are lifting as well as the rated capacity of the crane.
   b. A competent person should visually inspect the crane once a year.
   c. Never exceed the load limit by more than 10%.
   d. All of these.

4. Employers must comply with OSHA standards related to materials handling, including training and _____.
   a. equipment
   b. operations
   c. inspection
   d. All of these

Scaffolds

OSHA FactSheet

Tube and Coupler Scaffolds — Erection and Use

Workers building scaffolds risk serious injury from falls and tip-overs, being struck by falling tools and other hazards, and electrocution from energized power lines. Before starting any scaffold project, the employer should conduct a hazard assessment to ensure the safety of workers.

A tube and coupler scaffold has a platform(s) supported by tubing, and is erected with coupling devices connecting uprights, braces, bearers, and runners (see Fig. 1). Due to their strength, these scaffolds are frequently used where heavy loads need to be carried, or where multiple platforms must reach several stories high. These scaffolds can be assembled in multiple directions, making them the preferred option for work surfaces with irregular dimensions and/or contours.

When Erecting a Scaffold

- Use footings that are level, sound, rigid and capable of supporting the load without settlement or displacement.
- Plumb and brace poles, legs, posts, frames, and uprights to prevent swaying and displacement.
- Position the first level of bracing as close to the base as possible.
- Plumb and level the scaffold as it is being erected.
- Fasten all couplers and/or connections securely before assembling the next level.
- Install guys, ties, and braces according to the manufacturer's recommendations.
- Do not intermix scaffold components from different manufacturers, unless you can do so while maintaining the scaffold's structural integrity.
- When platform units are abutted together to create a long platform, each abutted end must rest on a separate support surface.
- Once erected, provide toeboards on all railed sides to prevent falling object hazards.

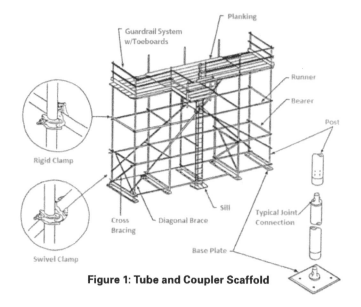

Figure 1: Tube and Coupler Scaffold

When Using a Scaffold

- Make sure that a competent person inspects the scaffold before each work shift.
- If during the inspection a defect or damage to the scaffold is discovered, the scaffold must be tagged out and not used until repairs are made. Attach tags at the access point to the scaffold.

One common tagging system uses the following tags:

Red tag indicates: unsafe, do not use.
Green tag indicates: ready to use.

- Use scaffolds according to the manufacturer's instructions.
- Never load a scaffold beyond its maximum intended load or rated capacity.
- Do not use makeshift methods to increase the working height of the scaffold platform, such as with ladders, buckets or blocks.

126

- Employees must not work on platforms covered with snow, ice, or other slippery material.
- The employer must provide suitable access to and between scaffolds, such as portable ladders, hook-on ladders, attachable ladders and stairway-type ladders.

When Dismantling a Scaffold

Check to ensure that the scaffold has not been structurally altered in a way which would make it unsafe. Before beginning dismantling procedures, reconstruct and/or stabilize the scaffold as necessary.

Training Workers

Only trained and authorized persons should be allowed to use a scaffold. This training must be provided by a qualified person who understands the hazards associated with the type of scaffold being used and who knows the procedures to control or minimize those hazards. Training must include how to safely:

- Use the scaffold, handle materials on the scaffold and determine the maximum load limits when handling materials.
- Recognize and avoid scaffolding hazards such as electric shock, falls from heights, and being hit by falling objects.
- Erect, maintain and disassemble fall and falling object protection systems.

Erectors and dismantlers of tube and coupler scaffolds are at particular risk because their work starts before ladders, guardrails and platforms are completely installed. These workers must also be trained to:

- Recognize scaffold hazards.
- Properly erect, move, operate, repair, inspect, maintain and disassemble the scaffold;
- Identify the maximum load-carrying capacity and intended use of the scaffold.

Employers should train workers on the following safety factors:

- The shape and structure of the building to be scaffolded.

- Distinctive site conditions and any special features of the building structure in relation to the scaffold (i.e., overhead electric power lines or storage tanks). Also consider the proximity and condition of surrounding buildings.
- Weather and environmental conditions.
- Fall protection requirements for workers using scaffolds, such as guardrail systems or personal fall arrest systems.
- The type and amount of scaffold equipment needed to access all areas to be worked on.
- Proper storage and transporting of scaffolding components, materials and equipment.
- How to access the scaffold, (i.e., via ladders, stair rail systems, etc.).

Workers building scaffolds risk serious injury from falls and tip-overs, being struck by falling tools and other hazards, and electrocution from energized power lines.

To avoid scaffold hazards, employers must:

- Ensure that a competent person supervises and directs workers erecting, moving, dismantling, or altering a scaffold.
- Provide a safe means of access for each worker erecting or dismantling the scaffold. As early as possible, install hook-on or attachable ladders.
- Ensure that workers do not climb diagonal braces to reach the scaffold platform.
- Provide fall protection for workers erecting or dismantling the scaffold.
- Secure scaffolds to the structure during erection and dismantling.

For more information on scaffolding, see OSHA's Safety and Health Topics page at www.osha.gov/SLTC/scaffolding.

Contact OSHA

For more information, to report an emergency, fatality or catastrophe, to order publications, to file a confidential complaint, or to request OSHA's free on-site consultation service, contact your nearest OSHA office, visit www.osha.gov, or call OSHA at 1-800-321-OSHA (6742), TTY 1-877-889-5627.

Worker Rights

Workers have the right to:

- Working conditions that do not pose a risk of serious harm.
- Receive information and training (in a language and vocabulary the worker understands) about workplace hazards, methods to prevent them, and the OSHA standards that apply to their workplace.
- Review records of work-related injuries and illnesses.

- File a complaint asking OSHA to inspect their workplace if they believe there is a serious hazard or that their employer is not following OSHA's rules. OSHA will keep all identities confidential.
- Exercise their rights under the law without retaliation, including reporting an injury or raising health and safety concerns with their employer or OSHA. If a worker has been retaliated against for using their rights, they must file a complaint with OSHA as soon as possible, but no later than 30 days.

For more information, see OSHA's Workers page.

This is one in a series of informational fact sheets highlighting OSHA programs, policies or standards. It does not impose any new compliance requirements. For a comprehensive list of compliance requirements of OSHA standards or regulations, refer to Title 29 of the Code of Federal Regulations. This information will be made available to sensory-impaired individuals upon request. The voice phone is (202) 693-1999; teletypewriter (TTY) number: 1-877-889-5627.

For assistance, contact us. We can help. It's confidential.

www.osha.gov (800) 321-OSHA (6742)

U.S. Department of Labor

DOC FS-3759 11/2014

128

Name: _____   Date: _____

Knowledge Check: Scaffolds

1. Who trains employees that work on scaffolds?
    a. Employees do not need training
    b. Employees are responsible for their own training
    c. Fellow employees who have experience
    d. Employer-designated competent person

2. Scaffold plans must be developed by a _____.
    a. competent person
    b. construction site manager
    c. qualified person
    d. experience scaffold worker

3. Which of the following is NOT an example of proper access?
    a. Ladders
    b. Crossbraces
    c. Stair towers
    d. Walkways

Stairways and ladders

OSHA® FactSheet

Reducing Falls in Construction:
Safe Use of Extension Ladders

Workers who use extension ladders risk permanent injury or death from falls and electrocutions. These hazards can be eliminated or substantially reduced by following good safety practices. This fact sheet examines some of the hazards workers may encounter while working on **extension ladders** and explains what employers and workers can do to reduce injuries. OSHA's requirements for extension ladders are in Subpart X—Stairways and Ladders of OSHA's Construction standards.

What is an Extension Ladder?

Also known as "portable ladders," extension ladders usually have two sections that operate in brackets or guides allowing for adjustable lengths. (See Figure 1, below.) Because extension ladders are not self-supporting they require a stable structure that can withstand the intended load.

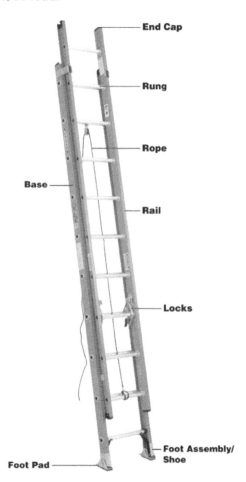

Figure 1: Extension Ladder

(Labels on figure: End Cap, Rung, Rope, Base, Rail, Locks, Foot Assembly/Shoe, Foot Pad)

PLAN Ahead to Get the Job Done Safely.

- Use a ladder that can sustain at least four times the maximum intended load, except that each extra-heavy duty type 1A metal or plastic ladder shall sustain at least 3.3 times the maximum intended load. Also acceptable are ladders that meet the requirements set forth in Appendix A of Subpart X. Follow the manufacturer's instructions and labels on the ladder. To determine the correct ladder, consider your weight plus the weight of your load. Do not exceed the load rating and always include the weight of all tools, materials and equipment.

- A competent person must visually inspect all extension ladders before use for any defects such as: missing rungs, bolts, cleats, screws and loose components. Where a ladder has these or other defects, it must be immediately marked as defective or tagged with "Do Not Use" or similar language.

- Allow sufficient room to step off the ladder safely. Keep the area around the bottom and the top of the ladder clear of equipment, materials and tools. If access is obstructed, secure the top of the ladder to a rigid support that will not deflect, and add a grasping device to allow workers safe access.

- Set the ladder at the proper angle. When a ladder is leaned against a wall, the bottom of the ladder should be one-quarter of the ladder's working length away from the wall. For access to an elevated work surface, extend the top of the ladder three feet above that surface or secure the ladder at its top.

- Before starting work, survey the area for potential hazards, such as energized overhead power lines. Ladders shall have nonconductive side rails if they are used where the worker or the ladder could contact exposed energized electrical equipment. Keep all ladders and other tools at least 10 feet away from any power lines.

- Set the base of the ladder so that the bottom sits securely and so both side rails are evenly supported. The ladder rails should be square to the structure against which it is leaning with both footpads placed securely on a stable and level surface.
- Secure the ladder's dogs or pawls before climbing.
- When using a ladder in a high-activity area, secure it to prevent movement and use a barrier to redirect workers and equipment. If the ladder is placed in front of a door, always block off the door.

Figure 2: Ladder extending three feet above the landing area.

PROVIDE the Right Extension Ladder for the Job with the Proper Load Capacity.

Select a ladder based on the expected load capacity (duty rating), the type of work to be done and the correct height. There are five categories of ladder duty ratings.

Type	Duty Rating	Use	Load
IAA*	Special Duty	Rugged	375 lbs.
IA	Extra Duty	Industrial	300 lbs.
I	Heavy Duty	Industrial	250 lbs.
II	Medium Duty	Commercial	225 lbs.
III	Light Duty	Household	200 lbs.

Source for Types IA, I, II, III: Subpart X—Stairways and Ladders, Appendix A (American National Standards Institute (ANSI)) 14.1, 14.2, 14.5 (1982)) of OSHA's Construction standards. Source for Type IAA: ANSI 14.1, 14.2, 14.5 (2009), which are non-mandatory guidelines.

TRAIN Workers to Use Extension Ladders Safely.

Employers must train each worker to recognize and minimize ladder-related hazards.

PLAN.
PROVIDE.
TRAIN.
Three simple steps to prevent falls.

Safe Ladder Use—DO:

- Maintain a 3-point contact (two hands and a foot, or two feet and a hand) when climbing/descending a ladder.
- Face the ladder when climbing up or descending.
- Keep the body inside the side rails.
- Use extra care when getting on or off the ladder at the top or bottom. Avoid tipping the ladder over sideways or causing the ladder base to slide out.
- Carry tools in a tool belt or raise tools up using a hand line. Never carry tools in your hands while climbing up/down a ladder.
- Extend the top of the ladder three feet above the landing. (See Figure 2.)
- Keep ladders free of any slippery materials.

Safe Ladder Use—DO NOT:

- Place a ladder on boxes, barrels, or unstable bases.
- Use a ladder on soft ground or unstable footing.
- Exceed the ladder's maximum load rating.
- Tie two ladders together to make them longer.
- Ignore nearby overhead power lines.
- Move or shift a ladder with a person or equipment on the ladder.
- Lean out beyond the ladder's side rails.
- Use an extension ladder horizontally like a platform.

OSHA standard: **29 CFR 1926 Subpart X**—Stairways and Ladders

American National Standards Institute standard: **ANSI A14.1, A14.2, A14.5—Ladder Safety Requirements**
(Not an OSHA standard, included to be used as guidance to meet OSHA's requirements)

Employers using extension ladders must follow the ladder requirements set forth in 29 CFR 1926 Subpart X. Per Appendix A to Subpart X of Part 1926—Ladders, ladders designed in accordance with the following ANSI standards will be considered in accordance with 29 CFR 1926.1053(a)(1): ANSI A14.1-1982—American National Standard for Ladders—Portable Wood—Safety Requirements, ANSI A14.2-1982—American National Standard for Ladders—Portable Metal—Safety Requirements, and ANSI A14.5-1982—American National Standard for Ladders—Portable Reinforced Plastic—Safety Requirements.

State plan guidance: States with OSHA-approved state plans may have additional requirements for avoiding falls from ladders. For more information on these requirements, please visit: www.osha.gov/dcsp/ osp/statesstandards.html.

Most OSHA offices have compliance assistance specialists to help employers and workers comply with OSHA standards. For details call 1-800-321-OSHA (6742) or visit: www.osha.gov/htm/RAmap.html.

For assistance, contact us. We can help. It's confidential.

U.S. Department of Labor
www.osha.gov (800) 321-OSHA (6742)

DOC FS-3660 05/2013

OSHA® QUICK CARD™

Portable Ladder Safety

Falls from portable ladders (step, straight, combination and extension) are one of the leading causes of occupational fatalities and injuries.

• Read and follow all labels/markings on the ladder.

• Avoid electrical hazards! – Look for overhead power lines before handling a ladder. Avoid using a metal ladder near power lines or exposed energized electrical equipment.

• Always inspect the ladder prior to using it. If the ladder is damaged, it must be removed from service and tagged until repaired or discarded.

3-Point Contact

• Always maintain a 3-point (two hands and a foot, or two feet and a hand) contact on the ladder when climbing. Keep your body near the middle of the step and always face the ladder while climbing (see diagram).

• Only use ladders and appropriate accessories (ladder levelers, jacks or hooks) for their designed purposes.

• Ladders must be free of any slippery material on the rungs, steps or feet.

• Do not use a self-supporting ladder (e.g., step ladder) as a single ladder or in a partially closed position.

• Do not use the top step/rung of a ladder as a step/rung unless it was designed for that purpose.

(continued on reverse)

- Use a ladder only on a stable and level surface, unless it has been secured (top or bottom) to prevent displacement.

- Do not place a ladder on boxes, barrels or other unstable bases to obtain additional height.

- Do not move or shift a ladder while a person or equipment is on the ladder.

- An extension or straight ladder used to access an elevated surface must extend at least 3 feet above the point of support (see diagram). Do not stand on the three top rungs of a straight, single or extension ladder.

- The proper angle for setting up a ladder is to place its base a quarter of the working length of the ladder from the wall or other vertical surface (see diagram).

- A ladder placed in any location where it can be displaced by other work activities must be secured to prevent displacement or a barricade must be erected to keep traffic away from the ladder.

- Be sure that all locks on an extension ladder are properly engaged.

- Do not exceed the maximum load rating of a ladder. Be aware of the ladder's load rating and of the weight it is supporting, including the weight of any tools or equipment.

For more information:

 ® **Occupational Safety and Health Administration**
U.S. Department of Labor
www.osha.gov   (800) 321-OSHA (6742)

OSHA 3246-10N-05

OSHA® FactSheet

Reducing Falls in Construction:
Safe Use of Stepladders

Workers who use ladders in construction risk permanent injury or death from falls and electrocutions. These hazards can be eliminated or substantially reduced by following good safety practices. This fact sheet examines some of the hazards workers may encounter while working on **stepladders** and explains what employers and workers can do to reduce injuries. OSHA's requirements for stepladders are in Subpart X—Stairways and Ladders of OSHA's Construction standards.

What is a Stepladder?

A **stepladder** is a portable, self-supporting, A-frame ladder. It has two front side rails and two rear side rails. Generally, there are steps mounted between the front side rails and bracing between the rear side rails. (See Figure 1, below.)

Top Cap

Top Step

Front Side Rails

Rear Side Rails

Step

Spreaders

Anti-Slip Safety Shoes/Feet

Figure 1: Stepladder

PLAN Ahead to Get the Job Done Safely.

A competent person must visually inspect stepladders for visible defects on a periodic basis and after any occurrence that could affect their safe use. Defects include, but are not limited to:

• Structural damage, split/bent side rails, broken or missing rungs/steps/cleats and missing or damaged safety devices.

• Grease, dirt or other contaminants that could cause slips or falls.
• Paint or stickers (except warning or safety labels) that could hide possible defects.

PROVIDE the Right Stepladder for the Job with the Proper Load Capacity.

• Use a ladder that can sustain at least four times the maximum intended load, except that each extra-heavy duty type 1A metal or plastic ladder shall sustain at least 3.3 times the maximum intended load. Also acceptable are ladders that meet the requirements set forth in Appendix A of Subpart X. Follow the manufacturer's instructions and labels on the ladder. To determine the correct ladder, consider your weight plus the weight of your load. Do not exceed the load rating and always include the weight of all tools, materials and equipment.

Type	Duty Rating	Use	Load
1AA	Special Duty	Rugged	375 lbs.
1A	Extra Heavy Duty	Industrial	300 lbs.
1	Heavy Duty	Industrial	250 lbs.
II	Medium Duty	Commercial	225 lbs.
III	Light Duty	Household	200 lbs.

Source for Types IA, I, II, III: Subpart X—Stairways and Ladders, Appendix A (American National Standards Institute (ANSI) 14.1, 14.2, 14.5 (1982)) of OSHA's Construction standards. Source for Type IAA: ANSI 14.1, 14.2, 14.5 (2009), which are non-mandatory guidelines.

137

TRAIN Workers to Use Stepladders Safely.

Employers must train each worker to recognize and minimize ladder-related hazards.

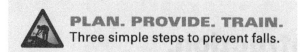

PLAN. PROVIDE. TRAIN.
Three simple steps to prevent falls.

Common Stepladder Hazards

- Damaged stepladder
- Ladders on slippery or unstable surface
- Unlocked ladder spreaders
- Standing on the top step or top cap
- Loading ladder beyond rated load
- Ladders in high-traffic location
- Reaching outside ladder side rails
- Ladders in close proximity to electrical wiring/equipment

Safe Stepladder Use—DO:

Read and follow all the manufacturer's instructions and labels on the ladder.

- Look for overhead power lines before handling or climbing a ladder.
- Maintain a 3-point contact (two hands and a foot, or two feet and a hand) when climbing/descending a ladder.
- Stay near the middle of the ladder and face the ladder while climbing up/down.
- Use a barricade to keep traffic away from the ladder.
- Keep ladders free of any slippery materials.
- Only put ladders on a stable and level surface that is not slippery.

Safe Stepladder Use—DO NOT:

- Use ladders for a purpose other than that for which they were designed. For example, do not use a folded stepladder as a single ladder.
- Use a stepladder with spreaders unlocked.
- Use the top step or cap as a step.
- Place a ladder on boxes, barrels or other unstable bases.
- Move or shift a ladder with a person or equipment on the ladder.
- Use cross bracing on the rear of stepladders for climbing.
- Paint a ladder with opaque coatings.
- Use a damaged ladder.
- Leave tools/materials/equipment on stepladder.
- Use a stepladder horizontally like a platform.
- Use a metal stepladder near power lines or electrical equipment.

OSHA standard: **29 CFR 1926 Subpart X**—Stairways and Ladders

American National Standards Institute standard: **ANSI A14.1, A14.2, A14.5—Ladder Safety Requirements** *(Not an OSHA standard, included to be used as guidance to meet OSHA's requirements)*

Employers using stepladders must follow the ladder requirements set forth in 29 CFR 1926 Subpart X. Per Appendix A to Subpart X of Part 1926—Ladders, ladders designed in accordance with the following ANSI standards will be considered in accordance with 29 CFR 1926.1053(a)(1): ANSI A14.1-1982—American National Standard for Ladders-Portable Wood-Safety Requirements, ANSI A14.2-1982—American National Standard for Ladders—Portable Metal—Safety Requirements, and ANSI A14.5-1982—American National Standard for Ladders—Portable Reinforced Plastic—Safety Requirements.

State plan guidance: States with OSHA-approved state plans may have additional requirements for avoiding falls from ladders. For more information on these requirements, please visit: www.osha.gov/dcsp/osp/statesstandards.html.

Most OSHA offices have compliance assistance specialists to help employers and workers comply with OSHA standards. For details call 1-800-321-OSHA (6742) or visit: www.osha.gov/htm/RAmap.html.

For assistance, contact us. We can help. It's confidential.

Occupational
Safety and Health
Administration

U.S. Department of Labor
www.osha.gov (800) 321-OSHA (6742)

DOC FS-3662 05/2013

OSHA FactSheet

Reducing Falls in Construction: Safe Use of Job-made Wooden Ladders

Workers who use job-made wooden ladders risk permanent injury or death from falls and electrocutions. These hazards can be eliminated or substantially reduced by following good safety practices. This fact sheet lists some of the hazards workers may encounter while working on **job-made wooden ladders** and explains what employers and workers can do to reduce injuries. OSHA's requirements for job-made ladders are in Subpart X—Stairways and Ladders of OSHA's Construction standards.

What is a Job-made Wooden Ladder?

A job-made wooden ladder is a ladder constructed at the construction site. It is not commercially-manufactured. A job-made wooden ladder provides access to and from a work area. It is not intended to serve as a work platform. These ladders are temporary, and are used only until a particular phase of work is completed or until permanent stairways or fixed ladders are installed. A 24-ft. job-made ladder built to the American National Standards Institute (ANSI) A14.4-2009 non-mandatory guidelines is shown below.

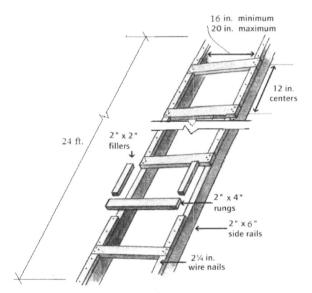

16 in. minimum
20 in. maximum

12 in. centers

24 ft.

2" x 2" fillers

2" x 4" rungs

2" x 6" side rails

2¼ in. wire nails

Figure 1: Single-Cleat Ladder

Training Requirements

Employers must provide a training program for employees using ladders and stairways. The training must enable each worker to recognize ladder-related hazards and to use ladders properly to minimize hazards.

Constructing a Safe Job-made Wooden Ladder

Side rails:

- Use construction-grade lumber for all components.
- Side rails of single-cleat ladders up to 24 ft. (7.3 m) long should be made with at least 2 in. (3.8 cm) x 6 in. (14 cm) nominal stock lumber.
- Side rails should be continuous, unless splices are the same strength as a continuous rail of equal length.
- The width of single-rung ladders should be at least 16 in. (41 cm), but not more than 20 in. (51 cm) between rails measured inside to inside.
- Rails should extend above the top landing between 36 in. (91.5 cm) and 42 in. (1.1 m) to provide a handhold for mounting and dismounting, and cleats must be eliminated above the landing level.
- Side rails of ladders which could contact energized electrical equipment should be made using nonconductive material. Keep ladders free of any slippery materials.
- Only put ladders on a stable and level surface that is not slippery.

Cleats:

- Cleats should be equally spaced 12 inches on center from the top of one cleat to the top of the next cleat.
- Cleats should be fastened to each rail with three 12d common wire nails which are nailed directly onto the smaller surfaces of the side rails.
- Making cuts in the side rails to receive the cleats is not advisable.
- Cleats should be at least 1 in. (2.5 cm) x 4 in. (8.9 cm) for ladders 16 ft. (41 cm) to 24 ft. (7.3 m) in length.

Filler Blocks:

- Filler should be 2 in. (3.8 cm) x 2 in. (3.8 cm) wood strips.
- Insert filler between cleats.
- Nail filler at the bottom of each side rail first. Nail the ends of a cleat to each side rail with three 12d common nails. One nail is placed 1-1/2 inch in from each end of the filler block.
- Nail the next two fillers and cleat, and then repeat. The ladder is complete when filler is nailed at the top of each rail.
- Make all side rails, rungs and fillers before the ladder is assembled.

Inspecting Ladders

- A competent person must visually inspect job-made ladders for defects on a periodic basis and after any occurrence that could affect their safe use.
- Defects to look for include: structural damage, broken/split side rails (front and back), missing cleats/steps, and parts/labels painted over.
- Ladders should be free of oil, grease and other slipping hazards.

PLAN. PROVIDE. TRAIN.

Three simple steps to prevent falls.

Safe Ladder Use—DO:

To prevent workers from being injured from falls from ladders, employers are encouraged to adopt the following practices:

- Secure the ladder's base so that it does not move.
- Smooth the wood surface of the ladder to reduce injuries to workers from punctures or lacerations and to prevent snagging of clothing.
- Use job-made wooden ladders with spliced side rails at an angle so that the horizontal distance from the top support to the foot of the ladder is one-eighth the working length of the ladder.
- Ensure that job-made wooden ladders can support at least four times the maximum intended load.
- Only use ladders for the purpose for which they were designed.
- Only put ladders on stable and level surfaces unless secured to prevent accidental movement.
- Ensure that the worker faces the ladder when climbing up and down.
- Maintain a 3-point contact (two hands and a foot, or two feet and a hand) when climbing a ladder.
- Keep ladders free of any slippery materials.
- Maintain good housekeeping in the areas around the top and bottom of ladders.

Safe Ladder Use—DO NOT:

- Paint a ladder with nontransparent coatings.
- Carry any object or load that could cause the worker to lose balance and fall.
- Subject a job-made wooden ladder to excessive loads or impact tests.

OSHA standard: **29 CFR 1926 Subpart X**—Stairways and Ladders

American National Standards Institute standard: **ANSI A14.4-1979, ANSI A14.4-2009**

Employers constructing job-made ladders must follow the ladder requirements set forth in 29 C.F.R. 1926 Subpart X. They are encouraged to consult the non-mandatory guidelines set forth in ANSI A.14.4-1979— Safety Requirements for Job-Made Ladders (referenced in Appendix A to Subpart X of Part 1926—Ladders) and ANSI A.14.4-2009—Safety Requirements for Job-Made Wooden Ladders.

State plan guidance: States with OSHA-approved state plans may have additional requirements for avoiding falls from ladders. For more information on these requirements, please visit: www.osha.gov/dcsp/ osp/statesstandards.html.

Most OSHA offices have compliance assistance specialists to help employers and workers comply with OSHA standards. For details call 1-800-321-OSHA (6742) or visit: www.osha.gov/htm/RAmap.html.

This is one in a series of informational fact sheets highlighting OSHA programs, policies or standards. It does not impose any new compliance requirements. For a comprehensive list of compliance requirements of OSHA standards or regulations, refer to Title 29 of the Code of Federal Regulations. This information will be made available to sensory-impaired individuals upon request. The voice phone is (202) 693-1999; teletypewriter (TTY) number: (877) 889-5627.

For assistance, contact us. We can help. It's confidential.

U.S. Department of Labor
www.osha.gov (800) 321-OSHA (6742)

DOC FS-3661 05/2013

Name: _____   Date: _____

Knowledge Check: Stairways and Ladders

1. When portable ladders are used for access to an upper landing surface, how many feet above the upper landing must the side rails extend?
   a. 2 feet
   b. 3 feet
   c. 4 feet
   d. 5 feet

2. You can use a metal ladder around power lines or exposed energized electrical equipment.
   a. True, but ONLY if there is no other option to get the work done.
   b. False, you should NEVER use a metal ladder in this circumstance.

3. Handrails must be able to withstand, without failure, how many pounds of weight applied within 2 inches of the top edge in any direction or outward direction?
   a. 300 pounds
   b. 250 pounds
   c. 200 pounds
   d. 175 pounds

4. Stairways that have four or more risers MUST have a stair rail.
   a. True
   b. False

5. A non-self-supporting ladder should be set up at _____ (horizontal distance/working length of ladder).
   a. 90 degree angle
   b. 30 degree angle
   c. 1:2 angle
   d. 1:4 angle

Tools – hand and power

Restraint Device on Power Press

What are the sources of amputations in the workplace?

Amputations are some of the most serious and debilitating workplace injuries. They are widespread and involve a variety of activities and equipment. Amputations occur most often when workers operate unguarded or inadequately safeguarded mechanical power presses, power press brakes, powered and non-powered conveyors, printing presses, roll-forming and roll-bending machines, food slicers, meat grinders, meat-cutting band saws, drill presses, and milling machines as well as shears, grinders, and slitters. These injuries also happen during materials handling activities and when using forklifts and doors as well as trash compactors and powered and non-powered hand tools. Besides normal operation, the following activities involving stationary machines also expose workers to potential amputation hazards: setting-up, threading, preparing, adjusting, cleaning, lubricating, and maintaining machines as well as clearing jams.

What types of machine components are hazardous?

The following types of mechanical components present amputation hazards:

- **Point of operation**—the area of a machine where it performs work on material.

- **Power-transmission apparatuses**—flywheels, pulleys, belts, chains, couplings, spindles, cams, and gears in addition to connecting rods and other machine components that transmit energy.

- **Other moving parts**—machine components that move during machine operation such as reciprocating, rotating, and transverse moving parts as well as auxiliary machine parts.

What kinds of mechanical motion are hazardous?

All mechanical motion is potentially hazardous. In addition to in-running nip points ("pinch points")—which occur when two parts move together and at least one moves in a rotary or circular motion that gears, rollers, belt drives,

and pulleys generate—the following are the most common types of hazardous mechanical motion:

- **Rotating**—circular movement of couplings, cams, clutches, flywheels, and spindles as well as shaft ends and rotating collars that may grip clothing or otherwise force a body part into a dangerous location.

- **Reciprocating**—back-and-forth or up-and-down action that may strike or entrap a worker between a moving part and a fixed object.

- **Transversing**—movement in a straight, continuous line that may strike or catch a worker in a pinch or shear point created between the moving part and a fixed object.

- **Cutting**—action generated during sawing, boring, drilling, milling, slicing, and slitting.

- **Punching**—motion resulting when a machine moves a slide (ram) to stamp or blank metal or other material.

- **Shearing**—movement of a powered slide or knife during metal trimming or shearing.

- **Bending**—action occurring when power is applied to a slide to draw or form metal or other materials.

Are there any OSHA standards that cover amputation hazards in the workplace?

Yes. The Occupational Safety and Health Administration (OSHA) has the following standards in *Title 29 of the Code of Federal Regulations (CFR)* to protect workers from amputations in the workplace:

- 29 *CFR* Part 1910 Subparts O and P cover machinery and machine guarding.

- 29 *CFR* 1926 Subpart I covers hand tools and powered tools.

- 29 *CFR* Part 1928 Subpart D covers agricultural equipment.

- 29 *CFR* Part 1915 Subparts C, H, and J; 29 *CFR* Part 1917 Subparts B, C, and G; and 29 *CFR* Part 1918 Subparts F, G, and H cover maritime operations.

144

What can employers do to help protect workers from amputations?

You should be able to recognize, identify, manage, and control amputation hazards commonly found in the workplace such as those caused by mechanical components of machinery, the mechanical motion that occurs in or near these components, and the activities that workers perform during mechanical operation.

Work practices, employee training, and administrative controls can help prevent and control amputation hazards. Machine safeguarding with the following equipment is the best way to control amputations caused by stationary machinery:

- **Guards** provide physical barriers that prevent access to hazardous areas. They should be secure and strong, and workers should not be able to bypass, remove, or tamper with them. Guards should not obstruct the operator's view or prevent employees from working.

- **Devices** help prevent contact with points of operation and may replace or supplement guards. Devices can interrupt the normal cycle of the machine when the operator's hands are at the point of operation, prevent the operator from reaching into the point of operation, or withdraw the operator's hands if they approach the point of operation when the machine cycles. They must allow safe lubrication and maintenance and not create hazards or interfere with normal machine operation. In addition, they should be secure, tamper-resistant, and durable.

You are responsible for safeguarding machines and should consider this need when purchasing machinery. New machinery is usually available with safeguards installed by the manufacturer. You can also purchase appropriate safeguards separately or build them in-house.

Are certain jobs particularly hazardous for some employees?

Yes. Under the *Fair Labor Standards Act*, the Secretary of Labor has designated certain non-farm jobs as especially hazardous for employees under the age of 18. These workers generally are prohibited from operating band saws, circular saws, guillotine shears, punching and shearing machines, meatpacking or meat-processing machines, paper products machines, woodworking machines, metal-forming machines, and meat slicers.

How can I get more information?

You can find more information about amputations, including the full text of OSHA's standards, on OSHA's website at **www.osha.gov**. In addition, publications explaining the subject of amputations in greater detail are available from OSHA. *Concepts and Techniques of Machine Safeguarding* (OSHA 3067) and *Control of Hazardous Energy (Lockout/Tagout)* (OSHA 3120) are available on OSHA's website. For other information about machine guarding see http://www.osha-slc.gov/SLTC/machineguarding/index.html.

A Guide for Protecting Workers from Woodworking Hazards (OSHA 3157) is available either on OSHA's website at **www.osha.gov** or from the Superintendent of Documents, P.O. Box 371954, Pittsburgh, PA 15250-7954, or phone (202) 512-1800, or online at http://bookstore.gpo.gov/index.html.

To file a complaint by phone, report an emergency, or get OSHA advice, assistance, or products, contact your nearest OSHA office under the "U.S. Department of Labor" listing in your phone book, or call us toll-free at **(800) 321-OSHA (6742)**; teletypewriter (TTY) number is (877) 889-5627. To file a complaint online or obtain more information on OSHA federal and state programs, visit OSHA's website at **www.osha.gov**.

U.S. Department of Labor
Occupational Safety and Health Administration
2002

Name: _____   Date: _____

Knowledge Check: Tools – Hand and Power

1. Which of the following is an example of an unsafe practice regarding the use of tools?
   a. Keeping cutting tools sharp
   b. Wearing eye and face protection while operating a grinder
   c. Using a screwdriver to carve or cut wood
   d. Following manufacturer's instructions when using a tool

2. Which term describes a tool that is powered by compressed air?
   a. Hydraulic
   b. Powder-actuated
   c. Electrical
   d. Pneumatic

3. Which of the following actions may expose workers to electrical shock hazards and should be avoided?
   a. Removing the grounding pin on a three-prong plug
   b. Using double-insulated tools
   c. Using a grounded adaptor to accommodate a two-prong receptacle
   d. Removing damaged tools from service and tagging them "Do Not Use"

4. Which of the following statements about guarding techniques is true?
   a. Guard the point of operation, in-running nip points, and rotating parts of tools.
   b. Remove guard from tool while it is in use, then replace when the job is completed.
   c. Adjust guard on abrasive wheel to allow maximum exposure of the wheel surface.
   d. Wear PPE because guards will not protect operator from flying chips and sparks or moving parts of tools.

5. Employers must satisfy all of the following requirements, except:
   a. Provide PPE necessary to protect employees who are operating hand and power tools and are exposed to hazards.
   b. Comply with OSHA training and inspection standards related to hand and power tools.
   c. Determine which manufacturer's requirements and recommendations for a tool shall be followed or ignored.
   d. Do not issue or permit the use of unsafe hand tools.

Concrete and masonry construction

Occupational Safety and Health Administration
www.osha.gov

Worker Safety Series
Concrete
Manufacturing

OSHA 3221-12N 2004

Concrete Manufacturing

- More than 250,000 people work in concrete manufacturing.

- Over 10 percent of those workers — 28,000 — experienced a job-related injury or illness and 42 died in just one year.

- Potential hazards for workers in concrete manufacturing:
    - Eye, skin and respiratory tract irritation from exposure to cement dust;
    - Inadequate safety guards on equipment;
    - Inadequate lockout/tagout systems on machinery;
    - Overexertion and awkward postures;
    - Slips, trips and falls; and
    - Chemical burns from wet concrete.

OSHA
Occupational Safety and
Health Administration

Hazards & Solutions

Manufacturing concrete can pose health and safety risks for the worker. For concrete manufacturing, the 10 OSHA standards most frequently included in the agency's citations were:

1. Hazard communication
2. Lockout/tagout
3. Confined spaces
4. Respiratory protection
5. Guarding floor & wall openings and holes
6. Electrical wiring methods
7. Noise exposure
8. Forklifts
9. Electrical systems design
10. Machine guarding

OSHA
Occupational Safety and
Health Administration

Cement Dust

Hazard: Exposure to cement dust can irritate eyes, nose, throat and the upper respiratory system. Skin contact may result in moderate irritation to thickening/cracking of skin to severe skin damage from chemical burns. Silica exposure can lead to lung injuries including silicosis and lung cancer.

Solutions:

• Rinse eyes with water if they come into contact with cement dust and consult a physician.

• Use soap and water to wash off dust to avoid skin damage.

• Wear a P-, N- or R-95 respirator to minimize inhalation of cement dust.

• Eat and drink only in dust-free areas to avoid ingesting cement dust.

OSHA
Occupational Safety and
Health Administration

Wet Concrete

Hazard: Exposure to wet concrete can result in skin irritation or even first-, second- or third-degree chemical burns. Compounds such as hexavalent chromium may also be harmful.

Solutions:

• Wear alkali-resistant gloves, coveralls with long sleeves and full-length pants, water-proof boots and eye protection.

• Wash contaminated skin areas with cold, running water as soon as possible.

• Rinse eyes splashed with wet concrete with water for at least 15 minutes and then go to the hospital for further treatment.

OSHA
Occupational Safety and
Health Administration

Machine Guarding

Hazard: Unguarded machinery used in the manufacturing process can lead to worker injuries.

Solutions:

- Maintain conveyor belt systems to avoid jamming and use care in clearing jams.

- Ensure that guards are in place to protect workers using mixers, block makers, cubers and metalworking machinery such as rebar benders, cutters and cage rollers.

- Establish and follow effective lockout/tagout procedures when servicing equipment.

- Be sure appropriate guards are in place on power tools before using them.

Falling Objects

Hazard: Workers may be hit by falling objects from conveyor belt systems, elevators or concrete block stacking equipment.

Solutions:

- Avoid working beneath cuber elevators, conveyor belts and stacker/destacker machinery.

- Stack and store materials properly to limit the risk of falling objects.

- Wear eye protection when chipping and cleaning forms, products or mixers.

OSHA
Occupational Safety and
Health Administration

Poor Ergonomics

Hazard: Improper lifting, awkward postures and repetitive motions can lead to sprains, strains and other musculoskeletal disorders.

Solutions:

- Use handtrucks or forklifts when possible.

- Lift properly and get a coworker to help if a product is too heavy.

- Avoid twisting while carrying a load. Shift your feet and take small steps in the direction you want to turn.

- Keep floors clear to avoid slipping and tripping hazards.

- Avoid working in awkward postures.

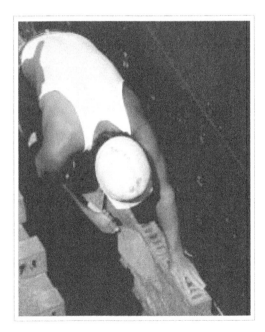

OSHA
Occupational Safety and
Health Administration

Confined Spaces

Hazard: Mixers and ready-mix trucks have confined spaces that pose safety risks for workers.

Solutions:

- Follow established procedures for confined space entry and work to assure safety.

- Guard against heat stress when cleaning truck mixer drums.

- Wear appropriate protective equipment to avoid silica exposure when removing concrete residues from inside truck mixer drums.

OSHA
Occupational Safety and
Health Administration

Vehicles

Hazard: Poorly maintained or improperly handled vehicles can lead to crushing injuries at the plant site or other injuries for truck drivers.

Solutions:

- Make sure back-up alarms on all vehicles are functioning.

- Avoid overloading cranes and hoists.

- Use care with the load out chute on concrete mixers to avoid injuries to hands and fingers.

- Beware of hot surfaces on equipment and truck components.

- Guard eyes against splashes of aggregate materials during loading and unloading.

- Use hearing protection if needed to guard against excessive noise exposure during cement loading/unloading and while using pneumatic chippers inside truck mixer drums.

OSHA
Occupational Safety and
Health Administration

Other Hazards

- Welding operations can lead to flash burns.

- Makeshift ladders, platforms and stairs with improper or no guardrails make falls more likely.

- Workers can also be injured by falling concrete forms if the forms are improperly chocked, braced or cribbed.

Worker Safety Tips

General Precautions

- Be sure you understand how to perform all your tasks and how to use tools and equipment safely.

- Follow confined space procedures when cleaning and working in mixer drums, hoppers, tanks and other places with potentially serious mechanical hazards, such as blades or sloping sides which may entrap employees, or atmospheric hazards, such as oxygen deficiency.

- Wear appropriate personal protective equipment to avoid being injured by flying or falling objects.

Vehicle Safety

- Be sure that trucks and other vehicles are in good working order, including audible back-up warning signals, before operating them.

- Avoid overloading hoists, cranes and forklifts.

Machine Safety

- Use lockout/tagout procedures to de-energize conveyors and other machinery before attempting to free any jams.

- Secure chutes and hatches to reduce injuries from swinging parts.

- Make sure guards are in place to protect you from moving parts of machinery and tools before you operate the equipment.

Overhead Hazards

- Be sure that form work, casting and stressing operations are adequately braced and chocked to avoid sudden release of materials.

- Make certain that rigging is in place to protect against falling objects and materials during hoisting and stacking procedures.

- Do not walk or work under overhead loads.

OSHA
Occupational Safety and
Health Administration

Think Safety Checklists

The following checklists may help you take steps to avoid hazards that cause injuries, illnesses and fatalities. As always, be cautious and seek help if you are concerned about a potential hazard.

General Safety

☐ Implement a comprehensive safety and health management system to find and fix all hazards at the worksite.

☐ Establish a written hazard communication program to inform all employees about chemical hazards and hazardous substances, reporting of hazards, appropriate personal protective equipment and what to do in emergency situations.

☐ Train workers in safe work practices and methods for all work activities, procedures and equipment as well as how to recognize and respond to potential workplace hazards, including rendering first aid.

☐ Put in place personal protective equipment programs. Train workers in selecting, cleaning and maintaining equipment such as respirators, protective clothing and goggles.

☐ Use safe work practices and appropriate personal protective equipment for all welding, cutting and burning; handling of chemicals (e.g., moist concrete, epoxies, form release agents); and during grinding, chipping, wire brushing, scraping and cleaning.

OSHA
Occupational Safety and
Health Administration

☐ Ensure that all tools and equipment – including forklifts, cranes, hoists and rigging – are maintained in good working condition, are inspected regularly and are operated by thoroughly trained, tested and competent workers.

Physical Hazards

☐ Set up a noise control program to reduce noise sources. Include sound-level measurements, audiometric testing, training and/or hearing protection equipment.

☐ Implement machine guarding and lockout/tagout procedures for all equipment and machinery servicing and/or maintenance work to prevent workers from being injured.

☐ Establish a confined-space entry program to protect workers cleaning the inside of mixer drums, storage bins, hoppers and other confined spaces.

Health Hazards

☐ Avoid exposure to cement dust to prevent bronchitis and silicosis.

☐ Prevent burns and skin and eye irritation by avoiding skin contact and eye contact with cement dust or wet cement.

☐ Wear the appropriate personal protective equipment, such as gloves, boots, goggles or HEPA-filter respirators.

☐ Avoid dusty areas and wet down work areas, as appropriate, to reduce or eliminate dust.

OSHA
Occupational Safety and
Health Administration

☐ Use special HEPA vacuums to clean up dust instead of dry sweeping.

☐ Reduce silica exposures during chipping, drilling and sawing of concrete materials with engineering controls, such as wet methods and local exhaust ventilation.

Fall Hazards

☐ Identify and fix fall hazards, such as slippery surfaces, damaged ladders and walkways, and any loose or unsteady hand- or footholds used to climb up and down on trucks and other equipment.

☐ Make sure all portable ladders have safety feet and are the proper length for the specific task. Secure them or tie them off to prevent movement.

☐ Ensure scaffolding and walking/working surfaces have adequate guardrails, safe accessibility and no tripping hazards or holes.

Ergonomics

☐ Implement appropriate work practices and/or controls to help reduce or eliminate potential back injuries from twisting, turning, lifting, awkward postures and whole body vibration.

☐ Train workers in appropriate mechanical and manual materials handling techniques and safety procedures to help reduce or eliminate musculoskeletal injuries.

☐ Provide dollies, handtrucks and conveyors to help minimize, reduce or eliminate the need to bend and lift.

OSHA
Occupational Safety and
Health Administration

Confined space entry

OSHA® FactSheet

Confined Spaces in Residential Construction

OSHA has developed a standard for Confined Spaces in Construction (29 CFR 1926 Subpart AA) that applies to spaces such as attics, basements, and crawl spaces. This Fact Sheet, developed after consultation with the National Association of Home Builders (NAHB), and a detailed **Frequently Asked Questions (FAQs)** document, clarify some of the standard's provisions and their application to residential construction work.

OSHA has developed a construction standard for Confined Spaces (29 CFR 1926 Subpart AA) — that applies to any space that meets the following three criteria:

- Is large enough for a worker to enter it;
- Has limited or restricted means of entry or exit; and
- Is not designed for continuous occupancy.

A confined space that contains certain hazardous conditions may be considered a *permit-required* confined space under the standard. *Permit-required* confined spaces can be immediately dangerous to workers' lives if not properly identified, evaluated, tested and controlled. A *permit-required* confined space means a confined space that has one or more of the following characteristics:

- Contains or has the potential to contain a hazardous atmosphere;
- Contains a material that has the potential for engulfing an entrant;
- Has an internal configuration such that an entrant could be trapped or asphyxiated by inwardly converging walls or by a floor which slopes downward and tapers to a smaller cross-section;
- Contains any other recognized serious safety or health hazard.

How Employers Can Determine if Confined Spaces or Permit-required Confined Spaces Exist

Before beginning work on a residential homebuilding project, each employer must ensure that a competent person identifies all confined spaces in which one or more employees it directs may work, and identifies each space that is a permit-required confined space. The competent person does not have to physically examine each attic, basement or crawl space, provided that the competent person can reliably determine whether the spaces with the same or similar configuration contain a hazard or potential hazard that would require the permit-space classification. The initial evaluation may be done using existing experience and knowledge of the space by the competent person and does not need to be documented. For example, a competent person responsible for inspecting new homes being built to identical specifications with the same materials need not physically inspect each attic separately to determine if it is a permit-required confined space.

How Common Spaces in Residential Construction are Impacted by the Standard

Spaces in a residential home may be considered confined spaces or permit-required confined spaces during the construction or remodeling process. However, the vast majority of the standard's requirements only apply to *permit-required* confined spaces, and attics, basements, and crawl spaces in a residential home — three common spaces – will not typically trigger these requirements.

Attics: In many instances, an attic will not be considered a confined space because there is not limited or restricted means for entry and exit. For example, an attic that can be accessed via pull down stairs that resemble the structure of a stationary stairway and do not require an employee to ascend /descend hand-over-hand would not be considered a confined space if there are no impediments to egress.

Attics that are determined to be confined spaces would generally not be **permit-required** confined spaces because they typically do not contain the types of hazards or potential hazards that make a confined space a permit-required confined space (those that could impair an entrant's ability to exist the space without assistance).

However, extreme heat in an attic can be considered a serious physical hazard such that the attic could be considered permit-required confined space. OSHA has not quantified how hot it must be to trigger the permit-required confined spaces requirements. However, heat that is extreme enough to cause heat exhaustion (e.g., dizziness, headaches, severe sweating, cramps) may impede an entrant's ability to exit the attic without assistance and would make a confined space permit-required.

Basements: Basements in a residential home that are designed for continuous occupancy by a homeowner are not considered confined spaces under the standard, provided the basement is configured as designed (e.g., has permanent stairs, a walk-out entry/exit, or an egress window installed).

Crawl Spaces: Crawl spaces in a residential home will not typically trigger the majority of the requirements of the standard unless they contain a physical hazard such as an exposed active electric wire.

For Employers

Regardless of the area, the competent person needs to pay particular attention to acute health hazards that may be present when assessing confined spaces, such as toxic (carbon monoxide), flammable, or explosive atmospheres. Safety Data Sheets (SDSs) must be maintained and reviewed to fully assess potential hazards prior to worker entry into a confined space to determine whether it is a permit-required space.

Employers' obligations under the standard will depend, in part, on what "type" of employer they are. However, most of the obligations in the standard apply to *entry* employers.

Host employer: The employer who owns or manages the property where the construction work is taking place.

Controlling contractor: The employer who has overall responsibility for construction at the worksite (note that if the controlling contractor owns or manages the property, then it is both a controlling employer and a host employer).

Entry employer (Sub Contractor): Any employer who decides that an employee it directs will enter a **permit-required** confined space.

The standard makes the controlling contractor the primary point of contact for information about permit-required confined spaces at the work site. The controlling contractor passes information it has about permit-required confined spaces at the work site on to the employers whose workers will enter the spaces (entry employers).

Likewise, entry employers must give the controlling contractor information about their entry program and hazards they encounter in the space, and the controlling contractor passes that information on to other entry employers. The controlling contractor is also responsible for making sure that employers outside a space know not to create hazards in the space, and that workers from different entry employers working in a space at the same time do not create hazards for each other.

Host/Controlling Employer Obligations

Before entry operations begin, a host employer with the following information must provide it to the controlling contractor:

- Location of each known permit-required confined space;
- Hazards or potential hazards in each space or the reason it is a permit-required confined space; and
- Any precautions that the host employer or any previous controlling contractor/entry employer implemented for the protection of workers in the permit-required confined space.

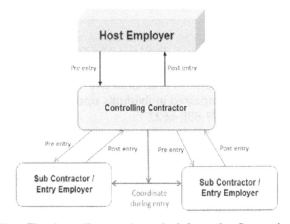

Note: The above diagram shows the information flow and coordination between these employers

159

The multi-employer communication requirements only apply to host employers with employees who work at the worksite, regardless of when those workers are at the site and only apply to *permit-required* confined spaces. In addition, beyond this duties discussed above, host employers and controlling contractors are not responsible for compliance with the *permit-required* confined space program provisions of the standard if they have no reason to anticipate that the employees they direct will enter a permit-required confined space.

Entry Employer Obligations

Inform employees: If a workplace contains a permit-required confined space, the entry employer must inform workers in the vicinity of each space of the location and danger posed by that space. This can be done by posting and positioning warning signs at each possible point of entry, or by other equally effective means. The employer must also either take steps to prevent its employees from entering that space or ensure that entry only occurs through a permit program or as otherwise allowed by the standard (alternative entry procedures).

Personal Protective Equipment: Entry employers allowing an employee to enter a permit space must attempt to eliminate or isolate the hazards in the space. When engineering and work-practice controls do not adequately protect employees, they must assess the space to determine what personal protective equipment (PPE) is needed to protect workers. Entry employers must provide workers with the required PPE and proper training on its use and about any related hazards before the work starts.

Training: The standard requires employers to ensure that their workers know about the existence and location of, and dangers posed by, each permit-required confined space, and that they may not enter such spaces without authorization. Entry employers must train workers involved in permit-required confined space operations so that they can perform their duties safely and understand the hazards in permit spaces and the methods used to isolate, control or protect workers. Workers not authorized to perform entry rescues must be trained on the dangers of attempting such rescues.

Written permit-required confined space entry program: The permit-required confined space program must establish a system for preparing, using, and canceling entry permits, which are written or printed documents that allow and control entry into permit spaces.

Rescue: Entry employers must ensure that properly trained rescue and emergency services are available before entry into permit-required confined spaces. For a full discussion of an entry employer's obligations to provide rescue, see OSHA's Fact Sheet entitled: Is 911 your Confined Space Rescue Plan?

Resources

For additional information see OSHA's Confined Spaces in Construction webpage at www.osha.gov/confinedspaces.

How to Contact OSHA

For questions or to get information or advice, to find out how to contact OSHA's free on-site consultation program, order publications, report a fatality or severe injury, or to file a confidential complaint, visit www.osha.gov or call 1-800-321-OSHA (6742).

For assistance, contact us. We can help. It's confidential.

www.osha.gov (800) 321-OSHA (6742)

U.S. Department of Labor

DOC FS-3914 06/2017

Lockout/Tagout

What is the OSHA standard for control of hazardous energy sources?

The OSHA standard for *The Control of Hazardous Energy (Lockout/Tagout), Title 29 Code of Federal Regulations (CFR)* Part 1910.147, addresses the practices and procedures necessary to disable machinery or equipment, thereby preventing the release of hazardous energy while employees perform servicing and maintenance activities. The standard outlines measures for controlling hazardous energies—electrical, mechanical, hydraulic, pneumatic, chemical, thermal, and other energy sources.

In addition, *29 CFR* 1910.333 sets forth requirements to protect employees working on electric circuits and equipment. This section requires workers to use safe work practices, including lockout and tagging procedures. These provisions apply when employees are exposed to electrical hazards while working on, near, or with conductors or systems that use electric energy.

Why is controlling hazardous energy sources important?

Employees servicing or maintaining machines or equipment may be exposed to serious physical harm or death if hazardous energy is not properly controlled. Craft workers, machine operators, and laborers are among the 3 million workers who service equipment and face the greatest risk. Compliance with the lockout/tagout standard prevents an estimated 120 fatalities and 50,000 injuries each year. Workers injured on the job from exposure to hazardous energy lose an average of 24 workdays for recuperation.

How can you protect workers?

The lockout/tagout standard establishes the employer's responsibility to protect employees from hazardous energy sources on machines and equipment during service and maintenance.

The standard gives each employer the flexibility to develop an energy control program suited to the needs of the particular workplace and the types of machines and equipment being maintained or serviced. This is generally done by affixing the appropriate lockout or tagout devices to energy-isolating devices and by deenergizing machines and equipment. The standard outlines the steps required to do this.

What do employees need to know?

Employees need to be trained to ensure that they know, understand, and follow the applicable provisions of the hazardous energy control procedures. The training must cover at least three areas: aspects of the employer's energy control program; elements of the energy control procedure relevant to the employee's duties or assignment; and the various requirements of the OSHA standards related to lockout/tagout.

What must employers do to protect employees?

The standards establish requirements that employers must follow when employees are exposed to hazardous energy while servicing and maintaining equipment and machinery. Some of the most critical requirements from these standards are outlined below:

- Develop, implement, and enforce an energy control program.

- Use lockout devices for equipment that can be locked out. Tagout devices may be used in lieu of lockout devices only if the tagout program provides employee protection equivalent to that provided through a lockout program.

- Ensure that new or overhauled equipment is capable of being locked out.

- Develop, implement, and enforce an effective tagout program if machines or equipment are not capable of being locked out.

- Develop, document, implement, and enforce energy control procedures. [See the note to *29 CFR* 1910.147(c)(4)(i) for an exception to the documentation requirements.]

- Use only lockout/tagout devices authorized for the particular equipment or machinery and ensure that they are durable, standardized, and substantial.

- Ensure that lockout/tagout devices identify the individual users.

- Establish a policy that permits only the employee who applied a lockout/tagout device to remove it. [See *29 CFR* 1910.147(e)(3) for exception.]

- Inspect energy control procedures at least annually.

- Provide effective training as mandated for all employees covered by the standard.

- Comply with the additional energy control provisions in OSHA standards when machines or equipment must be tested or repositioned, when outside contractors work at the site, in group lockout situations, and during shift or personnel changes.

How can you get more information?

OSHA has various publications, standards, technical assistance, and compliance tools to help you, and offers extensive assistance through its many safety and health programs: workplace consultation, voluntary protection programs, grants, strategic partnerships, state plans, training, and education. Guidance such as OSHA's *Safety and Health Management Program Guidelines* identify elements that are critical to the development of a successful safety and health management system. This and other information are available on OSHA's website at **www.osha.gov**.

- For a free copy of OSHA publications, send a self-addressed mailing label to this address: OSHA Publications Office, P.O. Box 37535, Washington, DC 20013-7535; or send a request to our fax at (202) 693-2498, or call us at (202) 693-1888.

- To file a complaint by phone, report an emergency, or get OSHA advice, assistance, or products, contact your nearest OSHA office under the "U.S. Department of Labor" listing in your phone book, or call us toll-free at **(800) 321-OSHA (6742)**. The tele-typewriter (TTY) number is (877) 889-5627.

- To file a complaint online or obtain more information on OSHA federal and state programs, visit OSHA's website.

This is one in a series of informational fact sheets highlighting OSHA programs, policies, or standards. It does not impose any new compliance requirements or carry the force of legal opinion. For compliance requirements of OSHA standards or regulations, refer to *Title 29 of the Code of Federal Regulations*. This information will be made available to sensory-impaired individuals upon request. Voice phone: (202) 693-1999. See also OSHA's website at **www.osha.gov**.

U.S. Department of Labor
Occupational Safety and Health Administration
2002

OSHA FactSheet

Procedures for Atmospheric Testing in Confined Spaces[1]

Atmospheric testing is required for two distinct purposes: evaluation of the hazards of the permit space and verification that acceptable conditions exist for entry into that space.

A confined space is one that is large enough to enter and perform assigned work in; it has limited or restricted ways to enter or exit the space; and it was not designed to be occupied continuously by a worker.

Evaluation testing

The atmosphere within a confined space must be tested using equipment that is designed to detect the chemicals that may be present at levels that are well below the defined exposure limits. Evaluation testing is done to:

- determine what chemical hazards are or may become present in the space's atmosphere, and
- identify what steps must be followed and what conditions must be met to ensure that atmospheric conditions are safe for a worker to enter the space.

The testing results and the decisions about what steps must be followed before entry must be evaluated by, or reviewed by, a technically qualified professional like an OSHA consultation service, a certified industrial hygienist, a registered safety engineer, or a certified safety professional. The technically qualified professional must consider all of the serious hazards in his/her evaluation or review.

A permit space is a confined space that has one or more of the following features: it has or may contain a hazardous atmosphere; it contains a material that can engulf a person who enters; it has an inside design that could trap or asphyxiate a person who

enters (inwardly converging walls, or a floor that slopes downward to a smaller section); or it has any other serious safety or health hazards.

Verification Testing

Before a permit space that may have a hazardous atmosphere can be entered, the atmosphere must be tested using the steps identified on the permit (developed during evaluation testing). Verification testing is done to make sure that the chemical hazards that may be present are below the levels necessary for safe entry, and that they meet the conditions identified on the permit. Test the atmosphere in the following order: (1) for oxygen, (2) for combustible gases, and then (3) for toxic gases and vapors.[2] The testing results -- the actual test concentrations -- must be recorded on the permit near the levels identified for safe entry.

Duration of Testing

For each test required on the permit, you must allow enough time for the air from the space to be drawn into the equipment and for the sensor (or other detection device) to react to the chemical if it is present. This is considered the "minimum response time" and it will be noted by the manufacturer in the operator's manual. Be aware that you will need to add time to this "minimum response time" if you have attached hosing or a probe extension to the inlet. The additional time is needed to allow the air from the different depths of the space to be pulled into the equipment inlet.

Testing Conditions in Spaces that May Have Layered Atmospheres

For permit spaces that are deep or have areas leading away from the entry point, the atmosphere may be layered or may be different in remote areas. For these spaces, testing must be done in the area surrounding the worker, which is considered four (4) feet in the direction of travel and to each side. If a sample probe is used to do the testing, then the worker must move slowly enough so that testing is completed, keeping the equipment "response time" in mind, before he/she moves into the new area.

Retesting the Space During Entry or Before Re-Entry

Test the permit space routinely to make sure that the atmospheric conditions continue to be safe for entry.[3]

[1] Title 29 Code of Federal Regulations 1910.146, Appendix B.
[2] 29 CFR 1910.146(c)(5)(ii)(C) and (d)(5)(iii).
[3] 29 CFR 1910.146(c)(5)(ii)(F) and (d)(5)(ii).

For more complete information:

OSHA Occupational Safety and Health Administration

U.S. Department of Labor
www.osha.gov
(800) 321-OSHA

DSTM 9/2005

OSHA® FactSheet

Is 911 your Confined Space Rescue Plan?

Permit-required confined spaces can present conditions that are immediately dangerous to workers' lives or health if not properly identified, evaluated, tested and controlled.

OSHA has developed a standard for Confined Spaces in Construction (29 CFR 1926 Subpart AA) for any space that meets all of the following criteria:

- Is large enough for a worker to enter;
- Has limited means of entry or exit; and
- Is not designed for continuous occupancy.

One provision of the standard requires employers to develop and implement procedures for summoning rescue or emergency services in permit-required confined spaces. An employer who relies on local emergency services for assistance is required to meet the requirements of §1926.1211 — *Rescue and emergency services*.

OSHA recognizes that not all rescue services or emergency responders are trained and equipped to conduct confined space rescues. When employers identify an off-site rescue service, it is critical that the rescuers can protect their employees. The emergency services should be familiar with the exact site location, types of permit-required confined spaces and the necessary rescue equipment.

For Employers

Calling emergency responders to provide rescue services can be a suitable way of providing for rescues in a permit-required confined space. Pre-planning will ensure that the emergency service is capable, available and prepared.

Prior to the start of the rescue work operation, employers must evaluate prospective emergency responders and select one that has:

- Adequate equipment for rescues, such as: atmospheric monitors, fall protection, extraction equipment, and self-contained breathing apparatus (SCBA) for the particular permit-required confined spaces.

Emergency service workers perform a practice rescue inside a manhole.

Photo: Oregon OSHA

- The ability to respond and conduct a rescue in a timely manner based on the site conditions and is capable of conducting a rescue if faced with potential hazards specific to the space. Such hazards may include:

  - Atmospheric hazards (e.g., flammable vapors, low oxygen)
  - Electrocution (e.g., unprotected, energized wires)
  - Flooding or engulfment potential
  - Poor lighting
  - Fall hazards
  - Chemical hazards

- Agreed to notify the employer in the event that the rescue team becomes unavailable.

Employers must also:

- Inform the emergency responders of potential hazards when they are called to perform a rescue at the worksite; and

165

- Provide emergency responders with access to all permit-required confined spaces. Such access may include:

  o Information on access routes, gates or landmarks
  o A project site plan if necessary
  o GPS coordinates if in a remote location

Additionally, employers should ensure that:

- The most efficient means to contact emergency responders is available;

- Any changes to the project site conditions are communicated to the rescue service; and

- Emergency responders are willing to visit the site and conduct a joint training exercise with the employer.

For Emergency Service Providers

Permit-required confined space emergencies can threaten workers' safety and health. Talking with the employer about the hazards they might encounter will assist in preparing for the situation. The following are some questions responders should be able to answer when an employer requests their services:

- Are you able to respond and conduct a rescue in a timely manner based on the site conditions?

- Do you have the appropriate equipment for response and rescue, such as: atmospheric monitors, fall protection, extraction equipment, and self-contained breathing apparatus (SCBA) for the particular permit-required confined spaces?

- Are you prepared for the hazards the employer has identified?

  o Atmospheric hazards (e.g., flammable vapors, low oxygen)
  o Electrocution (e.g., unprotected, energized wires)
  o Flooding or engulfment potential
  o Poor lighting
  o Fall hazards
  o Chemical hazards

- Are you trained for the hazards identified by the employer?

  o Hazard Communication training (HAZCOM)
  o Respiratory Protection training
  o Hazardous Material training
  o HAZWOPER training
  o Hazard recognition
  o Can you cope with other hazards the company may have identified on the site?
  o Do you need to develop a new procedure for these hazards/conditions?

- Has the employer provided you with the **exact** location of the work site?

  o Information on access routes, gates or landmarks
  o A project site plan if necessary
  o GPS coordinates if in a remote location

- Can you visit the site and hold a practice rescue?

- Does the company know the best way to contact you?

- How would the company communicate any changes to site conditions throughout the project?

- Could other emergencies or group training preclude you from responding and how will that be communicated?

OSHA encourages all emergency service providers to work closely with employers who request their services for permit-required confined space rescues. Pre-rescue planning, communication, and effective coordination of rescue activities are critical in the event that a life-threatening incident should occur.

Private sector commercial emergency service providers are covered by Federal OSHA and must comply with the provisions of §1926.1211. Similarly, state and local government emergency service providers in a state with an OSHA approved state plan must comply with these requirements. See www.osha.gov/dcsp/osp for information on state-plan requirements.

For more information on confined spaces in construction, visit OSHA's website at: www.osha.gov/confinedspaces.

Workers' Rights

Workers have the right to:

- Working conditions that do not pose a risk of serious harm.
- Receive information and training (in a language and vocabulary the worker understands) about workplace hazards, methods to prevent them, and the OSHA standards that apply to their workplace.
- Review records of work-related injuries and illnesses.
- File a complaint asking OSHA to inspect their workplace if they believe there is a serious hazard or that their employer is not following OSHA's rules. OSHA will keep all identities confidential.

- Exercise their rights under the law without retaliation, including reporting an injury or raising health and safety concerns with their employer or OSHA. If a worker has been retaliated against for using their rights, they must file a complaint with OSHA as soon as possible, but no later than 30 days.

For more information, see OSHA's Workers page.

How to Contact OSHA

For questions or to get information or advice, to report an emergency, fatality, inpatient hospitalization, amputation, or loss of an eye, or to file a confidential complaint, contact your nearest OSHA office, visit www.osha.gov or call OSHA at 1-800-321-OSHA (6742), TTY 1-877-889-5627.

For assistance, contact us. We can help. It's confidential.

www.osha.gov (800) 321-OSHA (6742)

U.S. Department of Labor

DOC FS-3849 04/2016

Motor vehicles, mechanized equipment and marine operations; rollover protective structures and overhead protection; and signs, signals and barricades

OSHA® FATALFacts

No. 1 – 2012

Oil Patch

U.S. Department of Labor   Occupational Safety and Health Administration   www.osha.gov   (800) 321-OSHA (6742)

ACCIDENT SUMMARY

Accident Type: ....Vehicle, Highway
Weather Conditions/Time of Day: .... Wet/Night
Type of Operation:.................................... Rig crew driving home after shift
Size of Work Crew: 4
Worksite Inspection Conducted by Employer: .... N/A
Competent Safety Monitoring on Site: .... N/A
Safety and Health Program in Effect: .... Yes
Training and Education for Employees: .... Yes
Job Title of Deceased Employees: .... Not reported
Age/Sex of Deceased Workers: (Worker 1; Worker 2) 34/M; 32/M
Time on Job: .... 8 years; Not reported
Short Service Employee (< 1 year): .... No; Not reported
Time at Task: 12-hour shift + 1 hour driving; 12-hour shift + 1 hour riding

Photo by Robert Falcione © 2009 HopNews.com

BRIEF DESCRIPTION OF ACCIDENT

Four workers were in a six-passenger pickup truck driving on a two-lane blacktop paved road. These workers were traveling home after their shift. It was night and the road was wet. The driver approached a left-hand curve at an unsafe speed and failed to negotiate the curve. The truck went into a skid and onto the unimproved shoulder, rolled over five times, and came to rest in an upright position off the roadway. The driver and one of the rear passengers were ejected as the truck rolled over and they were killed. The two coworkers that remained in the vehicle during the rollover sustained minor injuries. Only one person out of the four was wearing a seat belt. The speed limit on the curve was 40 mph (dry conditions), and the truck was determined to have been traveling at 47 mph.

ACCIDENT PREVENTION

1. Require employees to wear seat belts when they are traveling in company vehicles.
2. Develop and implement a company vehicle safety program for all employees, e.g., supervisors, crew members, sales personnel, etc.
3. Instruct employees to comply with all highway safety regulations and to reduce driving speed during inclement weather and when road conditions have deteriorated.
4. Stress to employees that operating vehicles while fatigued is dangerous to themselves, their passengers, and others that may encounter their vehicle. Make sure that employees understand that management does not want them driving if they are too fatigued to drive safely.
5. Ensure vehicles are properly maintained, e.g., brakes, tire pressure, etc.

Note: The described case was selected as being representative of improper work practices which likely contributed to a fatality from an accident. The accident prevention recommendations do not necessarily reflect the outcome of any legal aspects of the incident case. OSHA encourages your company or organization to duplicate and share this information.

You Have a Voice in the Workplace

The *Occupational Safety and Health Act of 1970* affords workers the right to a safe workplace (see OSHA's **Worker Rights** page, www.osha.gov/workers.html). Workers also have the right to file a complaint with OSHA if they believe that there are either violations of OSHA standards or serious workplace hazards.

How OSHA Can Help

For questions or to get information or advice, to report an emergency, report a fatality or catastrophe, or to file a confidential complaint, contact your nearest OSHA office, visit www.osha.gov or call our toll-free number at 1-800-321-OSHA (6742), TTY 1-877-889-5627. It's confidential.

More Information

Upstream oil and gas safety and health:
www.osha.gov/SLTC/oilgaswell drilling/index.html

OSHA standards and regulations:
www.osha.gov/law-regs.html

OSHA publications:
www.osha.gov/publications

OSHA's free On-site Consultation services:
www.osha.gov/consultation

Training resources:
www.osha.gov/dte/index.html

DEP-FF-3614   12/2012

OSHA® FactSheet

Traffic Lanes and Personnel Safety Zones

Workers involved in marine cargo handling are often exposed to being struck by moving vehicles or equipment.

When longshore workers are coning, signaling or performing other tasks on foot near cranes, employers should take measures to ensure a safe work environment by providing traffic lanes and personnel safety zones.

The traffic lanes and personnel safety zones should be clearly marked, and wide enough to protect longshore workers, accommodate the equipment being used and, in general, conform to the following guidance:

- Traffic lanes should be wide enough to allow for the widest piece of equipment (e.g., bomb carts, straddle carriers, etc.) expected to be driven within the lanes.

- Personnel safety zones should be provided on both sides of a traffic lane.

- All personnel safety zones should be wide enough to accommodate cone boxes and should provide adequate space for longshore workers to walk around cone boxes without stepping into traffic lanes.

- Provisions should be made to guide drivers so that haulage equipment does not extend into traffic lanes and drivers can align equipment under the crane.

- Semi-tractors should be driven within traffic lanes so that haulage equipment does not extend into personnel safety zones where longshore workers are positioned.

- Special safety provisions should be made to accommodate specialty or project cargo that might be transported under the

Striped lanes are personnel safety zones.

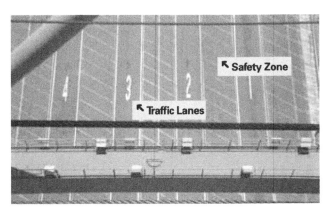

Unmarked lanes are traffic lanes.

crane on flatbeds, "mafis" or low boys, and which may extend into personnel safety zones.

- The traffic pattern under the crane should be well established and understood by the drivers and longshore workers on foot. Precautions should be taken if deviations from the traffic pattern must be made – for example, if reefers need to be turned or if equipment turn-outs are planned.

- Hatch covers should not extend into traffic lanes or personnel safety zones.

- During bomb cart operations, cone bins and coning operations should be relocated from under the crane's activity area.

Striped traffic lanes and personnel safety zones under the crane.

This is one in a series of informational fact sheets highlighting OSHA programs, policies or standards. It does not impose any new compliance requirements. For a comprehensive list of compliance requirements of OSHA standards or regulations, refer to Title 29 of the Code of Federal Regulations. This information will be made available to sensory-impaired individuals upon request. The voice phone is (202) 693-1999; teletypewriter (TTY) number: (877) 889-5627.

For assistance, contact us. We can help. It's confidential.

U.S. Department of Labor
www.osha.gov (800) 321-OSHA (6742)

DSG FS-3540 05/2012

U. S. Department of Labor
Occupational Safety and Health Administration
Directorate of Science, Technology and Medicine
Office of Science and Technology Assessment

Safety and Health Information Bulletin: Compactor Rollover Hazard

Safety and Health Information Bulletin

SHIB 09/29/2008

Preface

Between 2000 and 2006, OSHA investigated over 50 rollover incidents that involved a variety of roller/compactor makes and models. Of the rollover accidents investigated:

- 5 involved roller/compactors with rollover protective structures (ROPS) where operators used the seatbelts provided. None of these accidents resulted in a fatality.

- 19 involved roller/compactors with ROPS, but seatbelts were not used. In some cases, seatbelts were not provided. In other cases, the seatbelts provided were not used by the operators. Fourteen of these accidents resulted in fatalities. In a number of these cases, the operator was either ejected or jumped from the equipment, and was pinned under or crushed by the ROPS.

- 1 case involved a pneumatic rubber-tired roller/compactor where the ROPS and seatbelt had been removed prior to the accident. The operator involved was fatally injured in the accident. This accident is described below (Accident #1)>

*Safety and Health Information Bulletin (SHIB) is not a standard or regulation, and it creates no **new** legal obligations. The SHIB is advisory in nature, informational in content, and is intended to assist employers in providing a safe and healthful workplace. The Occupational Safety and Health Act requires employers to comply with safety and health standards promulgated by OSHA or by a state with an OSHA-approved state plan. In addition, pursuant to Section 5(a)(1), the General Duty Clause of the Act, employers must provide their employees with a workplace free from recognized hazards likely to cause death or serious physical harm. Employers can be cited for violating the General Duty Clause if there is a recognized hazard and they do not take reasonable steps to prevent or abate the hazard. However, failure to implement any recommendations in this SHIB is not, in itself, a violation of the General Duty Clause. Citations can only be based on standards, regulations, and the General Duty Clause.*

- 6 cases involved pneumatic rubber-tired roller/compactors without ROPS. In all of these cases, the accident resulted in a fatality. One such accident is described below (Accident #2).

The fatal accidents in the last two bullets above are the focus of this Safety and Health Information Bulletin (SHIB), and are described in detail below.

Purpose

The purpose of this Safety and Health Information Bulletin is:

- to remind employers and employees of the rollover hazard when operating roller/compactor machines, and that ROPS and seatbelts can reduce the risk;
- to alert users and operators that, when they operate roller/compactors on uneven surfaces, the likelihood of a rollover is significantly increased; and
- to encourage employers to carefully evaluate roadways and work surfaces where roller/compactors are operated for dangerous inclines/declines.

Background

The OSHA Englewood Area Office investigated two fatal accidents in 2005 in southern Colorado involving the rollover of pneumatic rubber-tired roller/compactors. The machines involved in these fatal accidents were produced by different manufacturers, but they were very similar in nature. Each machine had pneumatic rubber tires and a low center of gravity. These machines are often used in the compacting process during road construction and paving operations.

In both cases, OSHA concluded that if the machine had been equipped with a ROPS system, and if the operator had been wearing a seatbelt, the likelihood of the operator's survival would have increased significantly.

Roller/Compactor Involved in Accident #1
(ROPS and seatbelts were removed prior to the accident)

Pneumatic Tired Roller/Compactor
Figure 1

Roller/Compactor Involved in Accident #2
(ROPS was not provided and the operator was not wearing a seatbelt)

Self-Propelled Pneumatic Tired Roller/ Compactor
Figure 2

Accident Description

- Accident #1 – In May 2005, an employee was fatally injured while operating a pneumatic rubber- tired roller/compactor on a roadway during asphalt compacting. The roller/compactor ran off the road and traveled down a 22-degree sloping embankment. It rolled over 1½ times, coming to a stop on its top. The operator was thrown from the machine and was fatally crushed between the machine and the ground. Although the roller/compactor was originally equipped and sold with a ROPS and a seatbelt, the ROPS and seatbelt had been removed prior to the accident.

- Accident #2 – In August 2005, an employee was operating a pneumatic rubber-tired roller/compactor on a gravel road, rolling magnesium chloride into the gravel. The roller/compactor ran off the road and traveled down a 28-degree sloping embankment. It rolled onto its side and came to a stop. As the machine traveled down the embankment, the operator was thrown from the machine and fatally crushed. The roller/compactor was not provided with a ROPS and the operator was not wearing a seatbelt.

Other Information

A ROPS is a protective frame that is mounted on the machine and extends above the operator's seat (see Figure 1). In addition to bearing the weight of the machine during a rollover event, ROPS are designed to minimize the likelihood that the machine will overturn completely, thereby reducing the possibility that the operator will be crushed as a result of rollover or upset. A principle applied in ROPS design is to restrict the overturn to no more than 90 degrees. [1] A ROPS may be designed with one, two, or four posts, and it may have a canopy overhead; the canopy may be designed as part of the ROPS. Some machines have a single-post ROPS with a canopy that extends to the sides which is designed to absorb the impact of a rollover.

ROPS need to be used in combination with a seatbelt. As discussed in the Preface, operators who do not use seatbelts may be ejected from the machine and then crushed between the machine and the ground. The operator can even strike the ROPS as the operator is thrown from the equipment. A ROPS only provides protection if the operator remains in the seat. In some investigations, OSHA noted that operators had removed their seatbelts and jumped from the equipment, negating the protection offered by a ROPS.

During the investigation of Accidents #1 and #2, it was determined that ROPS were available for both machines. In Accident #1, the ROPS had been removed by the employer for convenience during a previous project and had not been replaced. In Accident #2, the machine had initially been sold without ROPS, but an aftermarket ROPS had been developed, tested and was available.

The Center to Protect Workers Rights (CPWR), through a cooperative agreement with the National Institute for Occupational Safety and Health (NIOSH), evaluated 58 roller/compactor overturn accidents and summarized the results in a report titled *Compactor Overturns and Rollover Protective Structures (M. Meyers, April 2004)*. This report highlighted a number of hazards associated with rollovers, including:

- Working near the edge of a road or an embankment was the most hazardous situation in the 58 rollover accidents studied. The second most significant factors were steep slopes and roadway curves, where problems with gear-shifting and brakes resulted in runaways.
- Compacting soil appeared to be more hazardous than other operations. Hazards included the soil edges and soft soil pockets that could drop under the weight of the unit.
- Loading and unloading roller/compactors onto and off of trailers posed a potential overturn hazard. Hazards were caused by skidding on the ramps, using wood blocks or planks as ramps, or loading/unloading a machine that was too narrow to span both units of the ramp.

Conclusions

During the course of OSHA's investigations, it was determined that if the machines involved in these accidents had been equipped with ROPS, and if the operators had been wearing seatbelts, the likelihood of the operator's survival would have increased significantly.

OSHA Requirements

While OSHA does not have a standard requiring employers to use ROPS or seatbelts for this type of roller/compactor equipment, it is important for employers to understand that under the General Duty Clause of the OSH Act (section 5(a)(1) of the Act), employers must provide their employees with a workplace that is free from recognized hazards likely to cause death or serious physical harm. It is OSHA's position that the hazard of equipment rollover is a "recognized hazard" within the meaning of the General Duty Clause of the OSH Act. [3, 4]

In cases where the employer chooses to operate these types of machines in areas where the potential for rollover is present (e.g., loading or unloading, operating on slopes or near slope edges, etc.) and the equipment is not equipped with ROPS and seatbelts, a General Duty Clause violation may exist.

In addition, OSHA's Construction Standard "General safety and health provisions," 29 CFR 1926.20(b)(4), states "the employer shall permit only those employees qualified by training or experience to operate equipment and machinery." Section 1926.21(b)(2), "Safety training and education," states further that "the employer shall instruct each employee in the recognition and avoidance of unsafe conditions...."

Therefore, employers performing construction work are required to ensure that roller/compactor operators are trained to use the equipment properly and to understand how to recognize those situations and conditions that pose a rollover hazard. For example, operators need to understand that:

- soft edges can cause one side of the equipment to sink and therefore may pose a risk of rollover;
- turning away from a slope with articulated steering can destabilize the compactor;
- improperly inflated tires can destabilize roller/compactors; and
- rain or wet conditions can pose a hazard during unloading and can increase the possibility of rollovers

near embankments as soil conditions become unstable.

Although OSHA does not have a standard that requires ROPS for roller/compactor equipment, OSHA does have construction and agriculture standards that have requirements for ROPS involving other types of equipment. Specifically, OSHA's Construction Standard 29 CFR 1926.1001 sets minimum performance criteria for ROPS for certain scrapers, loaders, dozers and graders, and crawler tractors, and 29 CFR 1926.1002 sets requirements for ROPS frames for the protection of operators of wheel-type agricultural and industrial tractors used in construction. OSHA's Agriculture Standard 29 CFR 1928.51(b)(2)(i)(A) requires ROPS for tractors used in agricultural operations, as well as seatbelts where ROPS are required. 29 CFR 1928.52 and 1928.53 establishes test and performance requirements for protective frames and protective enclosures designed for wheel-type agricultural tractors to minimize the frequency and severity of operator injury. These standards are beyond the scope of this SHIB, but noted for informational purposes. However, to ensure that ROPS used by the construction industry will protect roller/compactor operators, OSHA recommends that construction employers use ROPS on these machines that comply with the testing requirements specified by these standards.

Recommendations

Employers using roller/compactors should evaluate their worksites and operations to identify potential rollover hazards. Although the conditions that cause such hazards may not be present at one construction site, they may be present at the next one. Therefore, OSHA recommends that as a matter of practice in all cases,

employers should institute the following measures:

- equip roller/compactors with a ROPS and seatbelt;
- instruct operators to always wear seatbelts whenever operating the equipment;
- consider using a warning system such as barricades, hand or mechanical signals, or stop logs when the equipment is operated near sloped edges, such as an embankment and roadway edges, to alert equipment operators of their proximity to the hazard; and
- conduct pre-shift inspections to make sure all equipment systems, including the braking system, the tires, and operator controls, are in proper working condition.

References

1. CPWR. Compactor Overturns and Rollover Protective Structures, 2004. Available online at: http://www.cdc.gov/eLCOSH/docs/d0600/d000656/d000656.html

2. NIOSH. Preventing Injuries When Working with Ride-on Roller/Compactors, 2005. http://www.cdc.gov/elcosh/docs/d0600/d000678/d000678.html

3. OSHA. *ROPS/seatbelts for roller compactors; lockout/tagout in construction.* Letter of Interpretation dated March 16, 1998 and addressed to Mr. Brian McQuade. http://www.osha.gov/pls/oshaweb/owadisp.show_document?p_table=INTERPRETATIONS&p_id=22547

4. OSHA. *Guidelines for ROPS on
    pneumatic compactors and "skid
    steer" equipment.* Letter of
    Interpretation dated March 16, 1998
    and addressed to Mr. Robert S.
    Beisel.
    http://www.osha.gov/pls/oshaweb/owadi
    sp.show_document?p_table=INTERPRE
    TATIONS&p_id_=22546

Edwin G. Foulke, Jr.
Assistant Secretary for
Occupational Safety and Health

OSHA FactSheet

Work Zone Traffic Safety

Transportation incidents and workers struck by vehicles or mobile equipment account for the highest number of fatal work injuries, according to the Bureau of Labor Statistics. Workers such as emergency responders, clean-up, utility, demolition, construction, and others in areas where there are moving vehicles and traffic are exposed to being struck-by moving vehicles. Work zones are used to move traffic in an approved direction and are typically identified by signs, cones, barrels, and barriers.

General

There must be a traffic control plan for the movement of vehicles in areas where there are also workers conducting other tasks. Drivers, workers on foot, and pedestrians must be able to see and understand the routes they are to follow. The authority in charge, Federal, state, or local, will determine the configuration of the temporary traffic control zone for motorists and pedestrians. The construction project manager will determine the internal traffic control plan within the construction/demolition worksite. When there are several projects, coordinated vehicle routes and communication between contractors will reduce vehicular struck-by incidents.

Signs

Standard highway signs for information, speed limits, and work zones will assist drivers in identifying, in designated traffic paths, such directives as: EVACUATION ROUTE; DO NOT ENTER; REDUCED SPEED AHEAD; ROAD CLOSED; and NO OUTLET. Using standard highway signs for internal construction worksite traffic control will assist workers in recognizing the route they are to use at the construction site.

Traffic Control Devices

Standard traffic control devices, signals, and message boards will instruct drivers to follow a path away from where work is being done. The authority in charge will determine the approved traffic control devices such as cones, barrels, barricades, and delineator posts that will be used as part of the traffic control plan. These standard devices should also be used inside the work zone.

Work Zone Protections

Various styles of concrete, water, sand, collapsible barriers, crash cushions, and truck-mounted attenuators are available to limit motorist intrusions into the construction work zone.

Flagging

Flaggers and others providing temporary traffic control should wear high visibility clothing with a background of fluorescent orange-red or yellow-green and retroreflective material of orange, yellow, white, silver, or yellow-green. In areas of traffic movement, this personal protective equipment will make the worker visible for at least 1,000 feet, so that the worker can be seen from any direction, and make the worker stand out from the background. Check the label or packaging to ensure that the garments are performance class 2 or 3.

Drivers should be warned in advance with signs that there will be a flagger ahead. Flaggers should use STOP/SLOW paddles, paddles with lights, or flags (flags should be used only in emergencies.) The STOP sign should be octagonal with a red background and white letters and border. The SLOW sign is the same shape, with an orange background and black letters and a border.

Lighting

Flagger stations should be illuminated. Lighting for workers on foot and equipment operators is to be at least 5 foot-candles or greater. Where available lighting is not sufficient, flares or chemical lighting should be used. Glare affecting workers and motorists should be controlled or eliminated.

Training

Flaggers should be trained/certified and use the signaling methods required by the authority in charge. Workers on foot, equipment operators, and drivers in internal work zones need to know the routes that construction vehicles will use. Equipment operators and signal persons need to know the hand signals used on the worksite. Operators and workers on foot need to know the visibility limits and the "blind spots" for each vehicle on site. Workers on foot should wear high visibility safety garments designated as class 1, 2, or 3. Workers should be made aware of the ways in which shiftwork and nightwork may affect their performance.

Driving

Seat belts and rollover protection should be used on equipment and vehicles as stated by the manufacturer.

This is one in a series of informational fact sheets highlighting OSHA programs, policies or standards. It does not impose any new compliance requirements. For a comprehensive list of compliance requirements of OSHA standards or regulations, refer to Title 29 of the Code of Federal Regulations. This information will be made available to sensory impaired individuals upon request. The voice phone is (202) 693-1999; teletypewriter (TTY) number: (877) 889-5627.

For more complete information:

OSHA Occupational Safety and Health Administration

U.S. Department of Labor
www.osha.gov
(800) 321-OSHA

DOC 9/2005

Powered industrial vehicles

Preventing Injuries and Deaths of Workers Who Operate or Work Near Forklifts

WARNING!

Workers who operate or work near forklifts may be struck or crushed by the machine or the load being handled.

The National Institute for Occupational Safety and Health (NIOSH) requests assistance in preventing injuries and deaths of workers who operate or work near forklifts. Most fatalities occur when a worker is crushed by a forklift that has overturned or fallen from a loading dock.

NIOSH investigations of forklift-related deaths indicate that many workers and employers (1) may not be aware of the risks of operating or working near forklifts and (2) are not following the procedures set forth in the Occupational Safety and Health Administration (OSHA) standards, consensus standards, or equipment manufacturer's guidelines.

This Alert describes seven incidents resulting in the deaths of seven workers who were either operating or working near forklifts. In each incident, the deaths could have been prevented by using proper safety procedures and equipment and by following the provisions of the OSHA standards.

NIOSH requests that editors of trade journals, safety and health officials, industry associations, unions, and employers in all industries bring the recommendations in this Alert to the attention of all workers who are at risk.

BACKGROUND

Forklifts, also known as powered industrial trucks, are used in numerous work settings, primarily to move materials. Each year in the United States, nearly 100 workers are killed and another 20,000 are seriously injured in forklift-related incidents [BLS 1997, 1998].

Typical sit-down type forklift.

Forklift overturns are the leading cause of fatalities involving forklifts; they represent about 25% of all forklift-related deaths.

FATALITY DATA

The following paragraphs summarize information about fatalities involving forklifts. The information is from databases that identify work-related fatalities in the United States.

National Traumatic Occupational Fatalities (NTOF) Surveillance System

In the United States, 1,021 workers died from traumatic injuries suffered in forklift-related incidents from 1980 to 1994. The NTOF Surveillance System uses death certificates to identify work-related deaths. These fatalities resulted from the following types of incidents:

Type of incident	% total victims
Forklift overturns	22
Worker on foot struck by forklift . .	20
Victim crushed by forklift	16
Fall from forklift	9

Census of Fatal Occupational Injuries (CFOI)

The Bureau of Labor Statistics CFOI identified 94 fatal injuries associated with forklifts in 1995 [BLS 1997].

CURRENT STANDARDS

Occupational Safety and Health Administration (OSHA)

OSHA has developed standards for powered industrial trucks (such as low- and high-lift trucks and forklift trucks) [29 CFR[*] 1910.178] and for forklifts used in the construction industry [29 CFR 1926.600; 1926.602].

Training

OSHA has promulgated the *Final Rule for Powered Industrial Truck Operator Training* [29 CFR 1910.178(l)], which became effective March 1, 1999. The standard requires operator training and licensing as well as periodic evaluations of operator performance. The standard also addresses specific training requirements for truck operation, loading, seat belts, overhead protective structures, alarms, and maintenance of industrial trucks. Refresher training is required if the operator is observed operating the truck in an unsafe manner, is involved in an accident or near miss, or is assigned a different type of truck.

Forklift Maintenance

OSHA requires that industrial trucks be examined before being placed in service. They shall not be placed in service if the examination shows any condition adversely affecting the safety of the vehicle. Such examination shall be made at least daily. When industrial trucks are used around the clock, they shall be examined after each shift. When defects are found, they shall be immediately reported and corrected [29 CFR 1910.178(q)(7)].

Forklift Operation

OSHA requirements for forklift operation are as follows:

* On all grades, the load and load-engaging means shall be tilted back, if applicable, and raised only as far as

---

[*]*Code of Federal Regulations*. See CFR in references.

needed to clear the road surface. The forks shall not be raised or lowered while the forklift is moving [29 CFR 1910.178 (n)(7)(iii)].

- Under all travel conditions, the truck shall be operated at a speed that will permit it to be brought safely to a stop [29 CFR 1910.178 (n)(8)].

- The operator shall slow down and sound the horn at cross aisles and other locations where vision is obstructed [29 CFR 1910.178 (n)(4)].

- The operator is required to look toward and keep a clear view of the travel path [29 CFR 1910.178(n)(6)].

- Unauthorized personnel shall not be permitted to ride on powered industrial trucks. A safe place to ride shall be provided where the riding of trucks is authorized [29 CFR 1910.178 (m)(3)].

- Forklift trucks shall not be driven up to anyone standing in front of a bench or other fixed object [29 1910.178 (m)(1)].

Fair Labor Standards Act (FLSA) and Youth Employment

The FLSA [29 USC† 201 et seq.] (the primary law governing the employment of youth under age 18) includes work declared hazardous for youth by the Secretary of Labor. Hazardous Order No. 7, *Power-Driven Hoisting Apparatus Occupations*, prohibits workers under age 18 from using forklifts and similar equipment in nonagricultural industries [29 CFR 570.58]. In agricultural industries, minors

---

†*United States Code.*

under age 16 are prohibited from using forklifts [29 CFR 570.71 (a)(3)(ii)].

Not all working minors are covered by the FLSA. The regulations in agriculture do not apply to minors working on their parents' farms. Also exempted are youths aged 14 and 15 who are working under carefully regulated conditions in a bona fide vocational agriculture program.

American Society of Mechanical Engineers (ASME)/American National Standards Institute (ANSI)

ASME/ANSI B56.1–1993 requires the following [ASME 1993].

Maintenance and Safety Equipment

- Brakes, steering mechanisms, control mechanisms, warning devices, lights, governors, lift overload devices, guard and safety devices, lift and tilt mechanisms, articulating axle stops, and frame members shall be carefully and regularly inspected and maintained in a safe condition (ASME/ANSI B56.1–1993m 6.2.7) [ASME 1993].

- When work is being performed from an elevated platform, a restraining means such as rails, chains, etc., shall be in place, or a body belt with lanyard or deceleration device shall be worn by the person(s) on the platform (ASME/ANSI B56.1, §4.17.1[b]) [ASME 1993].

Operation

- An operator should avoid turning, if possible, and should use extreme caution on grades, ramps, or inclines. Normally the operator should travel straight up and down (ASME/ANSI B56.1, §5.3.8[d]) [ASME 1993].

• The operator of a sit-down type forklift should stay with the truck if lateral or longitudinal tipover occurs. The operator should hold on firmly and lean away from the point of impact (ASME/ANSI B56.1, §5.3.18[d]) [ASME 1993].

In addition to the above regulations, employers and workers should follow operator's manuals, which are supplied by all equipment manufacturers and describe the safe operation and maintenance of forklifts.

CASE REPORTS

The cases presented here were investigated by the NIOSH Fatality Assessment and Control Evaluation (FACE) Program. The case reports were selected to represent the most common types of fatal forklift incidents: (1) forklift overturns, (2) workers struck, crushed, or pinned by a forklift, and (3) falls from a forklift.

Case 1—Forklift Overturn

On September 18, 1996, the 43-year-old president of an advertising sign company was killed while using a sit-down type forklift to unload steel tubing from a flatbed trailer. He was driving the forklift about 5 miles per hour beside the trailer on a concrete driveway with a 3% grade. The victim turned the forklift behind the trailer, and the forklift began to tip over on its side. The victim jumped from the operator's seat to the driveway. When the forklift overturned, the victim's head and neck became pinned to the concrete driveway under the falling-object protective structure (overhead guard). An inspection of the forklift revealed that the right-side rear axle stop was damaged before the incident and was not restricting the lateral sway of the forklift when it turned. Also,

slack in the steering mechanism required the operator to turn the steering wheel slightly more than half a revolution before the wheels started to turn. The forklift was not equipped with a seat belt [NIOSH 1996b].

Case 2—Forklift Overturn

On April 25, 1995, a 37-year-old shop foreman was fatally injured after the sit-down type forklift he was operating overturned. The victim was turning while backing down an incline with a 4% grade. The forklift was transporting a 3-foot-high, 150-pound stack of cardboard with the forks raised approximately 60 inches off the ground. No one witnessed the incident. The victim was found with his head pinned under the overhead guard. The forklift was not equipped with a seat belt [California Department of Health Services 1996].

Case 3—Forklift Overturn

On November 25, 1996, a 41-year-old male laborer was fatally injured when the sit-down type forklift he was operating fell off a loading dock and pinned him under the overhead guard. The forklift was not equipped with a seat belt. The loading dock had large cracks in the surface and was in need of extensive repair. It was raining when the victim left the storage building to lift a load from the back of a pickup truck. Evidence indicates that either the victim's forklift was too close to the outer edge of the loading dock (which crumbled) or the right front tire was caught in a large crack in the loading dock, causing the forklift to overturn [Indiana State Department of Health 1996].

Case 4—Worker Struck by Forklift

On October 19, 1995, a 39-year-old female punch press operator at a computer components manufacturer was fatally injured while performing normal work tasks at her station. A forklift was traveling in reverse at high speed toward the victim's work station. A witness observed the forklift strike a metal scrap bin (about 3 by 5 by 3½ feet), propelling it toward the punch press station. The bin hit the press and rebounded toward the forklift. There it was hit once again and shoved back against the corner of the press, striking and crushing the victim against the press [NIOSH 1996c].

Case 5—Fall from Forklift

On July 21, 1997, a 36-year-old male electric-line technician was fatally injured after falling from and being run over by a forklift. While the operator was driving the forklift, the victim was riding on the forks. As the operator approached an intersection, he slowed down and turned his head to check for oncoming traffic. When he turned his head back, he could not see the victim. He stopped the forklift, dismounted, and found the victim underneath the right side of the forklift [NIOSH 1997a].

Case 6—Fall from Forklift

On September 24, 1997, a 61-year-old male maintenance manager of a shelter for the homeless died after falling 7 feet from a safety platform that had been elevated by a forklift. The victim had been raised in a steel-framed, cage-type safety platform that had not been secured to the forklift. The victim removed a fluorescent light bulb from its fixture and stepped to one side of the safety platform. When the victim shifted his weight from the center of the platform to the outer edge, the safety platform toppled off the forks. The victim fell about 7 feet, struck his head on a concrete floor, and was subsequently struck by the steel safety platform [NIOSH 1997b].

Case 7—Fall from Forklift

On September 6, 1995, a 47-year-old male assistant warehouse manager was fatally injured while working with a forklift operator to pull tires from a storage rack. The two workers had placed a wooden pallet on the forks of the forklift, and the victim then stood on the pallet. The operator raised the forks and victim 16 feet above a concrete floor to the top of the storage rack. The victim had placed a few tires on the pallet when the operator noticed that the pallet was becoming unstable. The victim lost his balance and fell, striking his head on the floor [NIOSH 1996a].

CONCLUSIONS

National fatality data indicate that the three most common forklift-related fatalities involve forklift overturns, workers on foot being struck by forklifts, and workers falling from forklifts. The case studies indicate that the forklift, the factory environment, and actions of the operator can all contribute to fatal incidents involving forklifts. In addition, these fatalities indicate that many workers and employers are not using or may be unaware of safety procedures and the proper use of forklifts to reduce the risk of injury and death.

RECOMMENDATIONS

Reducing the risk of forklift incidents requires a safe work environment, a safe forklift, comprehensive worker training, safe work practices, and systematic traffic management.

NIOSH recommends that employers and workers comply with OSHA regulations and consensus standards, maintain equipment, and take the following measures to prevent injury when operating or working near forklifts.

Employers

Worker Training

- Make sure that workers do not operate a forklift unless they have been trained and licensed.

- Develop, implement, and enforce a comprehensive written safety program that includes worker training, operator licensure, and a timetable for reviewing and revising the program. A comprehensive training program is important for preventing injury and death. Operator training should address factors that affect the stability of a forklift—such as the weight and symmetry of the load, the speed at which the forklift is traveling, operating surface, tire pressure, and driving behavior.

- Inform operators of sit-down type forklifts that they can be crushed by the overhead guard or another part of the truck after jumping from the overturning forklift. The operator of a sit-down type forklift should stay with the truck if lateral or longitudinal tipover occurs. The operator should hold on firmly and lean away from the point of impact.

- Train operators of stand-up type forklifts with rear-entry access to exit from the truck by stepping backward if a lateral tipover occurs.

- Ensure that operator restraint systems are being used on sit-down type forklifts. Since 1992, forklift manufacturers have been required to equip new sit-down type forklifts with operator restraint systems. Many manufacturers of these forklifts offer restraint systems that can be retrofitted on older forklifts. Many of the fatalities resulting from overturns of sit-down type forklifts might have been prevented if the operator had been restrained. The overhead guard of the forklift is generally the part that crushes the operator's head or torso after he or she falls or jumps outside of the operator's compartment. The risk of being crushed by the overhead guard or another rigid part of the forklift is greatly reduced if the operator of a sit-down type forklift remains inside the operator's compartment. Because many forklifts are not equipped with a restraint system and operator compliance is less than 100% on forklifts equipped with a restraint system, *operators of sit-down type forklifts should be instructed not to jump from the operator's compartment but to stay inside by leaning in the opposite direction of the overturn*.

- Train operators to handle asymmetrical loads when their work includes this activity.

Forklift Inspection and Maintenance

- Establish a vehicle inspection and maintenance program.

- Retrofit old sit-down type forklifts with an operator restraint system if possible.

Lifting

- Ensure that operators use only an approved lifting cage and adhere to general safety practices for elevating personnel with a forklift. Also, secure the platform to the lifting carriage or forks.

- Provide means for personnel on the platform to shut off power to the truck whenever the truck is equipped with vertical only or vertical and horizontal controls for lifting personnel.

Workers on Foot

- Separate forklift traffic and other workers where possible.

- Limit some aisles to *workers on foot only* or *forklifts only*.

- Restrict the use of forklifts near time clocks, break rooms, cafeterias, and main exits, particularly when the flow of workers on foot is at a peak (such as at the end of a shift or during breaks).

- Install physical barriers where practical to ensure that workstations are isolated from aisles traveled by forklifts.

- Evaluate intersections and other blind corners to determine whether overhead dome mirrors could improve the visibility of forklift operators or workers on foot.

- Make every effort to alert workers when a forklift is nearby. Use horns, audible backup alarms, and flashing lights to warn workers and other forklift operators in the area. Flashing lights are especially important in areas where the ambient noise level is high.

Work Environment

- Ensure that workplace safety inspections are routinely conducted by a person who can identify hazards and conditions that are dangerous to workers. Hazards include obstructions in the aisle, blind corners and intersections,

and forklifts that come too close to workers on foot. The person who conducts the inspections should have the authority to implement prompt corrective measures.

- Install the workstations, control panel, and equipment away from the aisle when possible. Do not store bins, racks, or other materials at corners, intersections, or other locations that obstruct the view of operators or workers at workstations.

- Enforce safe driving practices such as obeying speed limits, stopping at stop signs, and slowing down and blowing the horn at intersections.

- Repair and maintain cracks, crumbling edges, and other defects on loading docks, aisles, and other operating surfaces.

Workers

- Do not operate a forklift unless you have been trained and licensed.

- Use seatbelts if they are available.

- Report to your supervisor any damage or problems that occur with a forklift during your shift.

- Do not jump from an overturning, sit-down type forklift. Stay with the truck if lateral or longitudinal tipover occurs. Hold on firmly and lean in the opposite direction of the overturn.

- Exit from a stand-up type forklift with rear-entry access by stepping backward if a lateral tipover occurs.

- Use extreme caution on grades, ramps, or inclines. Normally you should travel only straight up and down.

- On all grades, tilt the load back if applicable, and raise it only as far as needed to clear the road surface.

- Do not raise or lower the forks while the forklift is moving.

- Do not handle loads that are heavier than the rated weight capacity of the forklift.

- Operate the forklift at a speed that will permit it to be stopped safely.

- Slow down and sound the horn at intersections and other locations where vision is obstructed.

- Look toward the path of travel and keep a clear view of it.

- Do not allow passengers to ride on forklift trucks unless a seat is provided.

- When dismounting from a forklift, always set the parking brake, lower the forks, and neutralize the controls.

- Do not drive up to anyone standing in front of a bench or other fixed object.

- Do not use a forklift to elevate workers who are standing on the forks.

- Do not elevate a worker on a platform unless the vehicle is directly below the work area.

- Whenever a truck is used to elevate personnel, secure the elevating platform to the lifting carriage or forks of the forklift.

- Use a restraining means such as rails, chains, or a body belt with a lanyard or deceleration device for the person(s) on the platform.

- Do not drive to another location with the work platform elevated.

ACKNOWLEDGMENTS

The principal contributors to this Alert were Richard Braddee and James Collins, Ph.D., of the Division of Safety Research. Please direct any comments, questions, or requests for additional information to the following:

Dr. Nancy Stout
Director
Division of Safety Research
National Institute for Occupational Safety
 and Health
1095 Willowdale Road
Morgantown, WV 26505–2888

Telephone: 304–285–5894; or call 1–800–35–NIOSH (1–800–356–4674).

We greatly appreciate your assistance in protecting the health of U.S. workers.

Lawrence J. Fine, M.D., Dr.P.H.
Acting Director, National Institute for
 Occupational Safety and Health
Centers for Disease Control and
 Prevention

REFERENCES

ASME [1993]. Safety standard for low lift and high lift trucks. New York: American Society of Mechanical Engineers and

189

American National Standards Institute, ASME B56.1–1993.

BLS [1997]. Fatal workplace injuries in 1995: a collection of data and analysis. Washington, DC: U.S. Department of Labor, Bureau of Labor Statistics, Report 913.

BLS [1998]. Occupational injuries and illnesses: counts, rates, and characteristics, 1995. Washington, DC: U.S. Department of Labor, Bureau of Labor Statistics, Bulletin 2493.

California Department of Health Services [1996]. Shop foreman dies after being crushed by a forklift in California. Berkeley, CA: California Department of Health Services, California Fatality and Control Evaluation Program (CA FACE) Report No. 95CA00801.

CFR. Code of Federal regulations. Washington, DC: U.S. Government Printing Office, Office of the Federal Register.

Indiana State Department of Health [1996]. Laborer killed when forklift falls off loading dock. Indianapolis, IN: Indiana State Department of Health, Indiana Fatality Assessment and Control Evaluation Program, (IN FACE) Report No. 96IN14901.

NIOSH [1996a]. Assistant manager dies after 15-foot fall from forklift-suspended pallet—South Carolina. Morgantown, WV: U.S. Department of Health and Human Services, Public Health Service, Centers for Disease Control and Prevention, National Institute for Occupational Safety and Health, Fatality Assessment and Control Evaluation (FACE) Report No. 95–20.

NIOSH [1996b]. Company president killed when forklift overturns—North Carolina. Morgantown, WV: U.S. Department of Health and Human Services, Public Health Service, Centers for Disease Control and Prevention, National Institute for Occupational Safety and Health, Fatality Assessment and Control Evaluation (FACE) Report No. 97–01.

NIOSH [1996c]. Press operator dies after forklift rams scrap bin—North Carolina. Morgantown, WV: U.S. Department of Health and Human Services, Public Health Service, Centers for Disease Control and Prevention, National Institute for Occupational Safety and Health, Fatality Assessment and Control Evaluation (FACE) Report No. 96–04.

NIOSH [1997a]. Electric line technician dies after falling from forklift—North Carolina. Morgantown, WV: U.S. Department of Health and Human Services, Public Health Service, Centers for Disease Control and Prevention, National Institute for Occupational Safety and Health, Fatality Assessment and Control Evaluation (FACE) Report No. 97–19.

NIOSH [1997b]. Maintenance manager dies after falling 7 feet from an elevated forklift safety platform—North Carolina. Morgantown, WV: U.S. Department of Health and Human Services, Public Health Service, Centers for Disease Control and Prevention, National Institute for Occupational Safety and Health, Fatality Assessment and Control Evaluation (FACE) Report No. 98–01.

USC. United States code. Washington, DC: US Government Printing Office.

Steel erection

Steel Erection: Inspection Guide
OSHA eTool

This section provides a summary of standards that address activities requiring approval or inspection by a responsible person, i.e., employer, controlling contractor, engineer of record, qualified rigger, qualified person, competent person, or crane operator.

- Controlling Contractor
- Cranes and Rigging
- Metal Buildings
- Structural Steel Assembly
- Open Web Steel Joists
- Landing and Placing Loads
- Training

Controlling Contractor

Approval to Begin Steel Erection:

Before authorizing the commencement of steel erection, the controlling contractor must provide written notification to the steel erector ensuring that [29 CFR 1926.752(a)]:

- Concrete in footings, piers, and walls has been cured to a level that will provide adequate strength to support any forces imposed during steel erection. [29 CFR 1926.752(a)(1)]

- Anchor bolt repairs, replacements and modifications were done with the approval of the project Structural Engineer of Record (SER). [29 CFR 1926.752(a)(2) and 29 CFR 1926.755(b)(1)]

Site Layout:

The controlling contractor must ensure that the following is provided and maintained [29 CFR 1926.752(c)]:

- Adequate access roads into and through the site for the safe delivery and movement of:
  - Derricks
  - Cranes
  - Trucks
  - Other necessary equipment
  - Material to be erected [29 CFR 1926.752(c)(1)]

- Means and methods for pedestrian and vehicular control. [29 CFR 1926.752(c)(1)] EXCEPTION: This requirement does not apply to roads outside of the construction site.

- Adequate space for the safe storage of materials and the safe operation of the erector's equipment. This space must be:
  - Firm
  - Properly graded
  - Drained
  - Readily accessible to the work [29 CFR 1926.752(c)(2)]

Column Anchorage:

Before the erection of a column, the controlling contractor must provide written notification to the steel erector if there has been any repair, replacement, or modification of the anchor rods (anchor bolts) of that column. [29 CFR 1926.755(b)(2)]

(Non-hoist) Falling Object Protection:

The controlling contractor must bar other construction processes below steel erection unless overhead protection for the employees below is provided. [29 CFR 1926.759(b)]

For additional information, see reference to suspended loads.

Fall Protection:

Fall protection provided by the steel erector shall remain in the area where steel erection activity has been completed, to be used by other trades, only if the controlling contractor or its authorized representative [29 CFR 1926.760(e)]:

- Has directed the steel erector to leave the fall protection in place. [29 CFR 1926.760(e)(1)]

- And has inspected and accepted control and responsibility of the fall protection before authorizing persons other than steel erectors to work in the area. [29 CFR 1926.760(e)(2)]

Site-specific Erection Plan

Employers may elect, because of conditions specific to the worksite, to develop alternate means of providing for employee protection. If a site-specific erection plan is used, it must:

- Be developed by a qualified person.

- And be available at the worksite. [29 CFR 1926.752(e)]

A site-specific erection plan may be developed during one or more pre-construction conferences and site inspections involving the erector, the controlling contractor, and others, such as the project engineer and the fabricator. If a site-specific erection plan is developed, the following elements are to be considered [Non-mandatory Appendix A]:

- The sequence of erection activity, developed in coordination with the controlling contractor, including the following:

- Material deliveries
- Material staging and storage
- Coordination with other trades and construction activities

■ A description of the crane and derrick selection and placement procedures, including the following:

- Site preparation
- Path for overhead loads
- Critical lifts, including rigging supplies and equipment

■ A description of steel erection activities and procedures, including the following:

- Stability considerations requiring temporary bracing and guying
- Erection bridging terminus point
- Notifications regarding repair, replacement and modifications of anchor rods (anchor bolts)
- Columns and beams (including joists and purlins)
- Connections
- Decking
- Ornamental and miscellaneous iron

■ A description of the fall protection procedures that will be used.

■ A description of the procedures that will be used to prevent falling object hazards.

■ A description of the special procedures required for hazardous non-routine tasks.

■ A certification for each employee who has received training for performing steel erection operations as required.

■ A list of the qualified and competent persons.

■ A description of the procedures that will be used in the event of rescue or emergency response.

In addition, the plan should include identification of the site and project and be signed and dated by the qualified person(s) responsible for its preparation and modification.

Cranes and Rigging

Crane operators must be responsible for operations under their direct control. Whenever there is any doubt as to safety, the operator must have the authority to [29 CFR 1926.753(c)(1)(iv)]:

■ Stop all hoisting activities.

■ Refuse to handle loads until safety has been assured.

Safety latches on hooks must not be deactivated or made inoperable, except [29 CFR 1926.753(c)(5)]:

- When a qualified rigger has determined that the hoisting and placing of purlins and single joists can be performed more safely by doing so. [29 CFR 1926.753(c)(5)(i)]

- When equivalent protection is provided in a site-specific erection plan. [29 CFR 1926.753(c)(5)(ii)]

Prior to each shift, cranes being used in steel erection activities must be visually inspected by a competent person. The inspection must include observation for deficiencies during operation, including, at a minimum [29 CFR 1926.753(c)(1)(i)]:

- All control mechanisms for maladjustments. [29 CFR 1926.753(c)(1)(i)(A)]

- Control and drive mechanism for excessive wear of components and contamination by [29 CFR 1926.753(c)(1)(i)(B)]:
  - Lubricants
  - Water
  - Other foreign matter

- Safety devices, including, but not limited to [29 CFR 1926.753(c)(1)(i)(C)]:
  - Boom-angle indicators
  - Boom stops
  - Boom kick-out devices
  - Anti-two block devices
  - Load moment indicators where required

- Air, hydraulic, and other pressurized lines, especially those that flex during operation, for:
  - Deterioration
  - Leakage, [29 CFR 1926.753(c)(1)(i)(D)]

- Hooks and latches for [29 CFR 1926.753(c)(1)(i)(E)]:
  - Deformation
  - Chemical damage
  - Cracks
  - Wear

- Wire-rope reeving for compliance with hoisting equipment manufacturer's specifications. [29 CFR 1926.753(c)(1)(i)(F)]

- Electrical apparatus for [29 CFR 1926.753(c)(1)(i)(G)]:
  - Malfunctioning
  - Signs of excessive deterioration
  - Dirt

- ○ Moisture accumulation
- ■ Hydraulic system for proper fluid level. [29 CFR 1926.753(c)(1)(i)(H)]
- ■ Tires for proper inflation and condition. [29 CFR 1926.753(c)(1)(i)(I)]
- ■ Ground conditions around the hoisting equipment for [29 CFR 1926.753(c)(1)(i)(J)]:
  - ○ Proper support, including ground settling under and around outriggers.
  - ○ Ground water accumulationSimilar conditions
  - ○ The hoisting equipment for level position, including after each move and setup. [29 CFR 1926.753(c)(1)(i)(K) and 29 CFR 1926.753(c) (1)(i)(L)]

If any deficiency is identified, an immediate determination must be made by the competent person as to whether the deficiency constitutes a hazard. [29 CFR 1926.753(c)(1)(ii)]

- ■ If the deficiency is determined to constitute a hazard, the hoisting equipment must be removed from service until the deficiency has been corrected. [29 CFR 1926.753(c)(1)(iii)]
- ■ A qualified rigger (a rigger who is also a qualified person) must inspect the rigging before each shift. [29 CFR 1926.753(c)(2)]

All hoisting operations in steel erection must be pre-planned to ensure that where employees must work under the load, the materials being hoisted are rigged by a qualified rigger. [29 CFR 1926.753(d)(2)(iii)]

When employees work under suspended loads, all loads must be rigged by a qualified rigger. [29 CFR 1926.753(d)(2)(iii)]

Multiple-lift rigging assembly capacity must be certified by the manufacturer or a qualified rigger. [29 CFR 1926.753(e)(2)]

Metal Buildings

Purlins and girts are prohibited from being used as an anchorage point for a fall arrest system, unless written approval is obtained from a qualified person. [29 CFR 1926.758(g)]

Structural Steel Assembly

Plumbing Up:

- ■ Plumbing-up equipment must be installed during the steel erection process, when deemed necessary by a competent person to ensure the stability of the structure. [29 CFR 1926.754(d)(1)]
- ■ When plumbing-up equipment is used, it must be in place and properly installed before the structure is loaded with construction material such as loads of joists, bundles of decking or bundles of bridging. [29 CFR 1926.754(d)(2)]
- ■ Plumbing-up equipment may be removed only with the approval of a competent person. [29 CFR 1926.754(d)(3)]

Columns:

All columns must be evaluated by a competent person to determine whether guying or bracing is needed; if needed, it must be installed. [29 CFR 1926.755(a)(4)]

Anchor Rods (Anchor Bolts):

- Approval by the project structural engineer of record is required before anchor rods (anchor bolts) can be [29 CFR 1926.755(b)(1)]:
  - Repaired
  - Replaced
  - Field-modified

- Before the erection of a column, the controlling contractor must provide written notification to the steel erector if there has been any [29 CFR 1926.755(b)(2)]:
  - Repair
  - Replacement
  - Modification of the anchor rods (anchor bolts) of that column

Beams and Columns:

- During the final placing of solid web structural members, the load must not be released from the hoisting line until [29 CFR 1926.756(a)(1)]:
  - The members are secured with at least two bolts per connection, of the same size and strength as shown in the erection drawings.
  - These bolts are drawn up wrench-tight.
  - The equivalent, as specified by the project structural engineer of record.

- A competent person must determine if more than two bolts are necessary to ensure the stability of cantilevered members. If additional bolts are needed, they must be installed. [29 CFR 1926.756(a)(2)]

Diagonal Bracing:

Solid web structural members used as diagonal bracing must be secured by [29 CFR 1926.756(b)]:

- At least one bolt per connection drawn up wrench-tight.
- The equivalent, as specified by the project structural engineer of record.

Open Web Steel Joists

Where constructability does not allow a steel joist to be installed at the column:

- An alternate means of stabilizing joists must be installed on both sides near the column and it must [29 CFR 1926.757(a)(2)(i)]:

- Provide equivalent stability to a steel joist field-bolted at the column. [29 CFR 1926.757(a)(2)(i)(A)]

- Be designed by a qualified person. [29 CFR 1926.757(a)(2)(i)(B)]

- Be shop-installed. [29 CFR 1926.757(a)(2)(i)(C)]

- Be included in the erection drawings. [29 CFR 1926.757(a)(2)(i)(D)]

■ Where steel joists at or near columns span more than 60 feet:

- The joists need to be set in tandem with all bridging installed. [29 CFR 1926.757(a)(4)]

- An alternative method of erection may be used, provided it [29 CFR 1926.757(a)(4)]:

    ▪ Provides equivalent stability to the steel joist.

    ▪ Is designed by a qualified person.

    ▪ Is included in the site-specific erection plan.

Any modification that affects the strength of a steel joist or steel-joist girder must be made with the approval of the project structural engineer of record. [29 CFR 1926.757(a)(7)]

Steel joists and steel-joist girders must not be used as anchorage points for a fall-arrest system unless written approval to do so is obtained from a qualified person. [29 CFR 1926.757(a)(9)]

When bolted diagonal erection bridging is required, the following will apply:

■ The bridging must be indicated on the erection drawing. [29 CFR 1926.757(d)(6)(i)]

■ The erection drawing must be the exclusive indicator of the proper placement of this bridging. [29 CFR 1926.757(d)(6)(ii)]

Landing and Placing Loads

During the construction period, the employer placing a load on steel joists must ensure that the load is distributed so as not to exceed the carrying capacity of any steel joist. [29 CFR 1926.757(e)(1)] No bundle of decking may be placed on steel joists until [29 CFR 1926.757(e)(4)]:

■ All bridging has been installed and anchored.

■ All joist bearing ends are attached.

■ All of the following conditions are met:

- The employer has first determined that the structure or portion of the structure is capable of supporting the load. This determination must be [29 CFR 1926.757(e)(4)(i)]:

    ▪ Made by a qualified person.

    ▪ Documented in a site-specific erection plan.

- The bundle of decking is placed on a minimum of three steel joists. [29 CFR 1926.757(e)(4)(ii)]

- The joists supporting the bundle of decking are attached at both ends. [29 CFR 1926.757(e)(4)(iii)]

- At least one row of bridging is installed and anchored. [29 CFR 1926.757(e)(4)(iv)]

- The total weight of the bundle of decking does not exceed 4,000 pounds. [29 CFR 1926.757(e)(4)(v)]

- Placement of the bundle of decking is within 1 foot of the bearing surface of the joist end. [29 CFR 1926.757(e)(4)(vi)]

Training

Fall Hazards:

- Employee training must be provided by a qualified person. [29 CFR 1926.761(a)]

- All employees exposed to fall hazards must be trained and instructed in the following areas [29 CFR 1926.761(b)]:

  - The recognition and identification of fall hazards in the work area. [29 CFR 1926.761(b)(1)]

  - The use and operation of protective systems such as guardrail systems, personal fall-arrest systems, positioning- device systems, fall-restraint systems, safety net systems, and other protection to be used. [29 CFR 1926.761(b)(2)]

  - The correct procedures for erecting, maintaining, disassembling, and inspecting the fall protection systems to be used. [29 CFR 1926.761(b)(3)]

  - Procedures for protection from falls to lower levels and into holes and openings in walking/working surfaces and walls. [29 CFR 1926.761(b)(4)]

  - All the fall protection requirements of this subpart. [29 CFR 1926.761(b)(5)]

Special Training:

The employer must also provide special training to employees involved in the following activities:

- Multiple-lift rigging operations, including [29 CFR 1926.753(e)(1)(iv)]:

  - Multiple lift hazards

  - Proper procedures and equipment required to perform multiple lifts. [29 CFR 1926.753(e)]

- Connecting, including [29 CFR 1926.761(c)(2)]:

  - Connecting hazards

  - The establishment, access, proper connecting techniques, and required work practices.

- Work in Controlled Decking Zones, including [29 CFR 1926.760(c)(4)]:

  - Hazards of working in a Controlled Decking Zone.

  - The establishment, access, proper installation techniques, and required work practices.

Welding and cutting

Welding with Arc-Welding Equipment
Self-Inspection Checklist
NIOSH

Guidelines

This checklist covers regulations issued by the U.S. Department of Labor, Occupational Safety and Health Administration (OSHA) under the general industry standards 29 CFR 1910.254 and 1910.306, and the construction standards 1926.351 and 1926.353. It applies to the use of arc-welding and cutting equipment. This checklist must be used with the Welding, Cutting, and Brazing--General Requirements checklist. The regulations cited apply only to private employers and their employees, unless adopted by a State agency and applied to other groups such as public employees. A yes answer to a question indicates that this portion of the inspection complies with the OSHA or U.S. Environmental Protection Agency (EPA) standard, or with a nonregulatory recommendation.

General

2. Are employees and students properly instructed and qualified to operate arc-welding equipment? [29 CFR 1910.254(a)(3) and 1926.351(d)]

Application of Arc-Welding Equipment

3. Does arc-welding equipment comply with the Requirements for Electric Arc-Welding Apparatus (NEMA EW-1-1962, National Electric Manufacturers Association), or the Safety Standard for Transformer-Type Arc-Welding Machines (ANSI C33-2-1956, Underwriters Laboratories)? [29 CFR 1910.254(b)(1)]

4. Are arc-welding machines designed and constructed to operate under their anticipated environmental conditions including unusual altitude, temperature, corrosive chemicals, steam, humidity, oil vapors, flammable liquids, vibration/shock, dust, or weather? [29 CFR 1910.254(b)(2)]

5. Are alternating-current manual arc-welding and cutting machines limited to 80 volts? [29 CFR 1910.254(b)(3)(i)(A)]

6. Are alternating-current automatic arc-welding and cutting machines limited to 100 volts? [29 CFR 1910.254(b)(3)(i)(B)]

7. Are manual or automatic direct-current (DC) arc-welding and cutting machines limited to 100 volts? [29 CFR 1910.254(b)(3)(ii)(A)]

8. Are terminals for welding leads protected from contact? [29 CFR 1910.254(b)(4)(iv)]

9. When manual electrode holders are used, are they designed specifically for arc welding and cutting? [29 CFR 1926.351(a)(1)]

10. Are manual electrode holders of a capacity capable of safely handling the maximum rated current required by the electrodes? [29 CFR 1926.351(a)(1)]

11. Are the outer surfaces of the jaws of the holder and all current-carrying parts passing through the portion of the holder that the arc welder or cutter grips fully insulated against the maximum voltage to ground? [29 CFR 1926.351(a)(2)]

12. Are arc-welding and cutting cables completely insulated, flexible, and capable of handling the maximum current requirement of the work in progress? [29 CFR 1926.351(b)(1)]

Installation of Arc-Welding Equipment

13. Are arc-welding machine frames or cases electrically grounded? [29 CFR 1910.254(c)(2)(i)]

14. Does the circuit between the ground and the grounded power conductor have resistance low enough to permit sufficient current to flow to cause the fuse or circuit breaker to interrupt the current? [29 CFR 1926.351(c)(5)]

15. Do ground return cables have a safe current-carrying capacity equal to or greater than the maximum output capacity of the arc-welding or cutting unit that it services? [29 CFR 1926.351(c)(1)]

16. Are chains, wire ropes, cranes, hoists, elevators, and conduits containing electrical conductors prohibited from being used to complete work-lead circuits? [29 CFR 1910.254(c)(2)(ii) and (iii) and 1926.351(c)(2)]

17. If pipelines are temporarily used to complete work-lead circuits, are they free from threaded joints, flange-bolted joints, or caulked joints? [29 CFR 1910.254(c)(2)(ii)]

   Note: Special precautions must also be used to avoid sparking at connection of the work-lead current.

18. If a structure or pipeline is used as a ground-return circuit, are periodic inspections performed to determine that the required electrical contact exists at all joints? [29 CFR 1926.351(c)(3)]

   Note: The generation of an arc, sparks, or heat at any point shall cause rejection of the structures as a ground circuit. If the structure or pipelines are used continuously, all joints should be bonded and periodic inspections conducted to ensure that no condition of electrolysis or fire hazard exists because of such use.

19. Are all grounding connections checked to determine that they are mechanically strong and electrically adequate for the required current? [29 CFR 1910.254(c)(2)(v) and 1926.351(c)(6)]

20. Is a disconnecting switch with overcurrent protection located at or near each arc-welding machine that does not have such a switch? [29 CFR 1910.254(c)(3)(i) and 29 CFR 1910.306(d)(1)]

21. Is a disconnecting switch with overcurrent protection provided for each outlet intended for connection to a portable welding machine? [29 CFR 1910.254(c)(3)(i)]

22. For individual welding machines, is the rated current-carrying capacity of the supply conductors not less than the rated primary current of the welding machine? [29 CFR 1910.254(c)(3)(ii)]

23. Are all DC arc-welding machines connected with the same polarity? [29 CFR 1910.254(c)(3)(iv)(A)]

24. Are all AC arc-welding machines connected to the same phase of the supply circuit and with the same instantaneous polarity? [29 CFR 1910.254(c)(3)(iv)(B)]

Operation and Maintenance

25. Are employees and students assigned to operate or maintain arc-welding equipment acquainted with the requirements of 29 CFR 1910.252 and 1910.254? [29 CFR 1910.254(d)(1)]

26. Are employees and students engaged in gas-shielded arc-welding acquainted with Recommended Safe Practices for Gas-Shielded Arc-Welding (A6.1-1966, American Welding Society)? [29 CFR 1910.254(d)(1)]

27. Are arc-welding machine hookups checked before starting operations? [29 CFR 1910.254(d)(2)]

28. Is coiled welding cable spread out before use to avoid serious overheating and damage to insulation? [29 CFR 1910.254(d)(2)]

29. Is the grounding of the welding machine frame checked before operations are started? [29 CFR 1910.254(d)(3)]

30. Are arc-welding machines checked for leaks of cooling water, shielding gas, or engine fuel before operations are started? [29 CFR 1910.254(d)(4)]

31. Is proper switching equipment provided for shutting down the machine? [29 CFR 1910.254(d)(5)]

32. Are the manufacturer's printed rules and instructions covering operation of the equipment supplied strictly followed? [29 CFR 1910.254(d)(6)]

33. When not in use for any substantial period of time (such as during lunch hour or overnight) are (a) electrodes removed from the holders; (b) the holders safely placed so they cannot make contact with people, conductive objects, fuel or compressed gas tanks; and (c) the machines disconnected form the power source? [29 CFR 1910.254(d)(7) and 1926.351(d)(1) and (d)(3)]

34. Are electrode cables free from splices within 10 feet from holders? [29 CFR 1910.254(d)(8) and 1926.351(b)(1)]

> Note: The general industry standard 1910.254(d)(9)(iii) and the construction standard 1926.351(b)(1) permit joining lengths of cable by standard insulated connectors specifically designed for that purpose. The construction standard, however, also permits splices that are insulated as well as the original cable.

35. Is the operator required to report any equipment defects or safety hazards and to discontinue use until safety has been assured? [29 CFR 1910.254(d)(9)(i) and 1926.351(d)(4)]

36. Are arc-welding machines repaired only by qualified personnel? [29 CFR 1910.254(d)(9)(i)]

37. If arc-welding machines become wet, are they thoroughly dried and tested before use? [29 CFR 1910.254(d)(9)(ii)]

38. Is dipping hot electrode holders into water prohibited? [29 CFR 1926.351(d)(2)]

39. Are cables with damaged insulation or exposed bare conductors replaced? [29 CFR 1910.254(d)(9)(iii)]

> Note: The construction standard 1926.351(b)(4) permits repair of cables with rubber and friction tape or other equivalent means as long as the areas are protected by sufficient insulation.

40. When metal-arc welding with inert gas, are special precautions taken for hazards associated with chlorinated solvents? [29 CFR 1926.353(d)(1)(i)]

> Note: Inert-gas metal-arc welding produces 5 to 30 times more ultraviolet radiation then shielded metal-arc welding. The ultraviolet rays cause the decomposition of chlorinated solvents, liberating toxic fumes and gases. When in use, chlorinated solvents must be kept at least 200 feet away from the exposed arc (unless shielded) and surfaces prepared with chlorinated solvents must be thoroughly dry before welding is permitted. In addition, the shading density for filter lenses must be increased. All skin must be covered to protect against flashes and radiant energy.

OSHA® FactSheet

Controlling Hazardous Fume and Gases during Welding

Welding joins materials together by melting a metal work piece along with a filler metal to form a strong joint. The welding process produces visible smoke that contains harmful metal fume and gas by-products. This fact sheet discusses welding operations, applicable OSHA standards, and suggestions for protecting welders and coworkers from exposures to the many hazardous substances in welding fume.

Types of welding

Welding is classified into two groups: fusion (heat alone) or pressure (heat and pressure) welding. There are three types of fusion welding: electric arc, gas and thermit. Electric arc welding is the most widely used type of fusion welding. It employs an electric arc to melt the base and filler metals. Arc welding types in order of decreasing fume production include:

Flux Core Arc Welding (FCAW) filler metal electrode; flux shield

Shielded Metal Arc (SMAW) electrode provides both flux and filler material

Gas Metal Arc (GMAW or MIG) widely used; consumable electrode for filler metal, external gas shield

Tungsten Inert Gas (GTAW or TIG) superior finish; non-consumable electrode; externally-supplied inert gas shield

Gas or oxy-fuel welding uses a flame from burning a gas (usually acetylene) to melt metal at a joint to be welded, and is a common method for welding iron, steel, cast iron, and copper. Thermit welding uses a chemical reaction to produce intense heat instead of using gas fuel or electric current. Pressure welding uses heat along with impact-type pressure to join the pieces.

Oxy-fuel and plasma cutting, along with brazing, are related to welding as they all involve the melting of metal and the generation of airborne metal fume. Brazing is a metal-joining process where only the filler metal is melted.

Welder using local exhaust ventilation to remove fume from breathing zone. (Photo courtesy of the Lincoln Electric Company).

What is in welding fume?

Metals

Aluminum, Antimony, Arsenic, Beryllium, Cadmium, Chromium, Cobalt, Copper, Iron, Lead, Manganese, Molybdenum, Nickel, Silver, Tin, Titanium, Vanadium, Zinc.

Gases

- **Shielding**—Argon, Helium, Nitrogen, Carbon Dioxide.
- **Process**—Nitric Oxide, Nitrogen Dioxide, Carbon Monoxide, Ozone, Phosgene, Hydrogen Fluoride, Carbon Dioxide.

Factors that affect worker exposure to welding fume

- Type of welding process
- Base metal and filler metals used
- Welding rod composition
- Location (outside, enclosed space)
- Welder work practices
- Air movement
- Use of ventilation controls

Health effects of breathing welding fume

- Acute exposure to welding fume and gases can result in eye, nose and throat irritation, dizziness and nausea. Workers in the area who experience these symptoms should leave the area immediately, seek fresh air and obtain medical attention.
- Prolonged exposure to welding fume may cause lung damage and various types of cancer, including lung, larynx and urinary tract.
- Health effects from certain fumes may include metal fume fever, stomach ulcers, kidney damage and nervous system damage. Prolonged exposure to manganese fume can cause Parkinson's–like symptoms.
- Gases such as helium, argon, and carbon dioxide displace oxygen in the air and can lead to suffocation, particularly when welding in confined or enclosed spaces. Carbon monoxide gas can form, posing a serious asphyxiation hazard.

Welding and Hexavalent Chromium

- Chromium is a component in stainless steel, nonferrous alloys, chromate coatings and some welding consumables.
- Chromium is converted to its hexavalent state, Cr(VI), during the welding process.
- Cr(VI) fume is highly toxic and can damage the eyes, skin, nose, throat, and lungs and cause cancer.
- OSHA regulates worker exposure to Cr(VI) under its Chromium (VI) standard, 29 CFR 1910.1026 and 1926.1126.
- OSHA's Permissible Exposure Limit (PEL) for Cr(VI) is 5 µg/m3 as an 8-hour time-weighted average.

Reducing exposure to welding fume

- Welders should understand the hazards of the materials they are working with. OSHA's Hazard Communication standard requires employers to provide information and training for workers on hazardous materials in the workplace.
- Welding surfaces should be cleaned of any coating that could potentially create toxic exposure, such as solvent residue and paint.
- Workers should position themselves to avoid breathing welding fume and gases. For example, workers should stay upwind when welding in open or outdoor environments.

- General ventilation, the natural or forced movement of fresh air, can reduce fume and gas levels in the work area. Welding outdoors or in open work spaces does not guarantee adequate ventilation. In work areas without ventilation and exhaust systems, welders should use natural drafts along with proper positioning to keep fume and gases away from themselves and other workers.
- Local exhaust ventilation systems can be used to remove fume and gases from the welder's breathing zone. Keep fume hoods, fume extractor guns and vacuum nozzles close to the plume source to remove the maximum amount of fume and gases. Portable or flexible exhaust systems can be positioned so that fume and gases are drawn away from the welder. Keep exhaust ports away from other workers.
- Consider substituting a lower fume-generating or less toxic welding type or consumable.
- Do not weld in confined spaces without ventilation. Refer to applicable OSHA regulations (see list below).
- Respiratory protection may be required if work practices and ventilation do not reduce exposures to safe levels.

Some OSHA standards applicable to welding:
- **Welding, Cutting & Brazing**—29 CFR 1910 Subpart Q
- **Welding & Cutting**—29 CFR 1926 Subpart J
- **Welding, Cutting & Heating**—29 CFR 1915 Subpart D
- **Permit-required confined spaces**—29 CFR 1910.146
- **Confined & Enclosed Spaces & Other Dangerous Atmospheres in Shipyard Employment**—29 CFR 1915 Subpart B
- **Hazard Communication**—29 CFR 1910.1200
- **Respiratory Protection**—29 CFR 1910.134
- **Air Contaminants**—29 CFR 1910.1000 **(general industry)**, 29 CFR 1915.1000 **(shipyards)**, 29 CFR 1926.55 **(construction)**

More Information

For more information on hexavalent chromium exposure, visit OSHA's website at www.osha.gov.

This is one in a series of informational fact sheets highlighting OSHA programs, policies or standards. It does not impose any new compliance requirements. For a comprehensive list of compliance requirements of OSHA standards or regulations, refer to Title 29 of the Code of Federal Regulations. This information will be made available to sensory-impaired individuals upon request. The voice phone is (202) 693-1999; teletypewriter (TTY) number: (877) 889-5627.

For assistance, contact us. We can help. It's confidential.

U.S. Department of Labor
www.osha.gov (800) 321-OSHA (6742)

DSG FS-3647 03/2013

Fire protection and prevention

OSHA **FACT** *Sheet*

Fire Safety in the Workplace

What should employers do to protect workers from fire hazards?

Employers should train workers about fire hazards in the workplace and about what to do in a fire emergency. If you want your workers to evacuate, you should train them on how to escape. If you expect your workers to use firefighting equipment, you should give them appropriate equipment and train them to use the equipment safely. (See Title 29 of the *Code of Federal Regulations* Part 1910 Subparts E and L; and Part 1926 Subparts C and F.)

What does OSHA require for emergency fire exits?

Every workplace must have enough exits suitably located to enable everyone to get out of the facility quickly. Considerations include the type of structure, the number of persons exposed, the fire protection available, the type of industry involved, and the height and type of construction of the building or structure. In addition, fire doors must not be blocked or locked when employees are inside. Delayed opening of fire doors, however, is permitted when an approved alarm system is integrated into the fire door design. Exit routes from buildings must be free of obstructions and properly marked with exit signs. See 29 *CFR* Part 1910.36 for details about all requirements.

Do employers have to provide portable fire extinguishers?

No. But if you do, you must establish an educational program to familiarize your workers with the *general principles* of fire extinguisher use. If you expect your workers to use portable fire extinguishers, you must provide *hands-on training* in using this equipment. For details, see 29 *CFR* Part 1910 Subpart L.

Must employers develop emergency action plans?

Not every employer is required to have an emergency action plan. OSHA standards that require such plans include the following:

- Process Safety Management of Highly Hazardous Chemicals, 1910.119

- Fixed Extinguishing Systems, General, 1910.160
- Fire Detection Systems, 1910.164
- Grain Handling, 1910.272
- Ethylene Oxide, 1910.1047
- Methylenedianiline, 1910.1050
- 1,3 Butadiene, 1910.1051

When required, employers must develop emergency action plans that:

- Describe the routes for workers to use and procedures to follow.
- Account for all evacuated employees.
- Remain available for employee review.
- Include procedures for evacuating disabled employees.
- Address evacuation of employees who stay behind to shut down critical plant equipment.
- Include preferred means of alerting employees to a fire emergency.
- Provide for an employee alarm system throughout the workplace.
- Require an alarm system that includes voice communication or sound signals such as bells, whistles, or horns.
- Make the evacuation signal known to employees.
- Ensure emergency training.
- Require employer review of the plan with new employees and with all employees whenever the plan is changed.

Must employers have a fire prevention plan?

OSHA standards that require fire prevention plans include the following:

- Ethylene Oxide, 1910.1047
- Methylenedianiline, 1910.1050
- 1,3 Butadiene, 1910.1051

Employers covered by these standards must implement plans to minimize the frequency of evacuations. All fire prevention plans must:

- Be available for employee review.

- Include housekeeping procedures for storage and cleanup of flammable materials and flammable waste.
- Address handling and packaging of flammable waste. (Recycling of flammable waste such as paper is encouraged.)
- Cover procedures for controlling workplace ignition sources such as smoking, welding, and burning.
- Provide for proper cleaning and maintenance of heat producing equipment such as burners, heat exchangers, boilers, ovens, stoves, and fryers and require storage of flammables away from this equipment.
- Inform workers of the potential fire hazards of their jobs and plan procedures.
- Require plan review with all new employees and with all employees whenever the plan is changed.

What are the rules for fixed extinguishing systems?

Fixed extinguishing systems throughout the workplace are among the most reliable fire fighting tools. These systems detect fires, sound an alarm, and send water to the fire and heat. To meet OSHA standards employers who have these systems must:

- Substitute (temporarily) a fire watch of trained employees to respond to fire emergencies when a fire suppression system is out of service.
- Ensure that the watch is included in the fire prevention plan and the emergency action plan.
- Post signs for systems that use agents (e.g., carbon dioxide, Halon 1211, etc.) posing a serious health hazard.

How can you get more information on safety and health?

OSHA has various publications, standards, technical assistance, and compliance tools to help you, and offers extensive assistance through workplace consultation, voluntary protection programs, strategic partnerships, alliances, state plans, grants, training, and education. OSHA's *Safety and Health Program Management Guidelines* (*Federal Register* 54:3904–3916, January 26, 1989) detail elements critical to the development of a successful safety and health management system. This and other information are available on OSHA's website.

- For one free copy of OSHA publications, send a self-addressed mailing label to OSHA Publications Office, 200 Constitution Avenue, N.W., N-3101, Washington, DC 20210; or send a request to our fax at (202) 693–2498, or call us at (202) 693–1888.

- To order OSHA publications online at **www.osha.gov**, go to **Publications** and follow the instructions for ordering.

- To file a complaint by phone, report an emergency, or get OSHA advice, assistance, or products, contact your nearest OSHA office under the U.S. Department of Labor listing in your phone book, or call toll-free at **(800) 321–OSHA (6742)**. The teletypewriter (TTY) number is (877) 889–5627.

- To file a complaint online or obtain more information on OSHA federal and state programs, visit OSHA's website.

This is one in a series of informational fact sheets highlighting OSHA programs, policies, or standards. It does not impose any new compliance requirements. For a comprehensive list of compliance requirements of OSHA standards or regulations, refer to *Title 29 of the Code of Federal Regulations*. This information will be made available to sensory-impaired individuals upon request. The voice phone is (202) 693–1999. See also OSHA's website at **www.osha.gov**.

2002

OSHA® FATALFacts

No. 5 – 2012

Oil Patch

U.S. Department of Labor   Occupational Safety and Health Administration

www.osha.gov (800) 321-OSHA (6742)

ACCIDENT SUMMARY

Accident Type: .... Flash fire from crude oil vapors
Weather Conditions: ....Clear, sunny
Type of Operation: ....Oil well servicing/Production
Size of Work Crew: 3
Worksite Inspection Conducted by Employer: .... No
Competent Safety Monitoring on Site:... No
Safety and Health Program In Effect: ....Minimal
Training and Education for Employees: ....Minimal
Job Title of Deceased Employee: ....Laborer
Age/Sex of Deceased Employee: 26/M
Time on Job: .... 1 day
Time at Task: .... 2 hours
Short Service Employee (<1 Year): .... Yes
Time Employed: ....2 months

Cut end of pipe in trench.

BRIEF DESCRIPTION OF ACCIDENT

Three employees were working on a leaking crude oil flow line that connected a production well to its tank battery. They dug a trench to access the leaking flow line and cut out a 6-ft. long section from the pipe using a cold cutter. Two of the employees attempted to thread the cut on the flow line with a manual pipe threading machine (threader) but the dies on the threader were dull. Therefore, the workers asked the office to have new dies for the machine delivered to the site. Instead of installing the new dies in the manual pipe threader that was used earlier, the dies were installed in an electric pipe threader. Two of the employees got in the trench with the electric pipe threader and started to thread the exposed pipe when flammable vapors were ignited by the electric pipe threader. As a result, a flash fire engulfed the trench in flames. The third employee discharged two fire extinguishers to extinguish the fire. The two employees that were in the trench were hospitalized with second- and third-degree burns to their arms, neck and faces. One of these employees died at the hospital. The other burned employee was hospitalized and released at a later date.

ACCIDENT PREVENTION

1. Perform job hazard analyses (JHAs) prior to beginning work to determine potential hazards of the job and their controls such as leaking flammable vapors from equipment that had previously contained hydrocarbons, control of ignition sources, working in excavations, and lockout/tagout.
2. Do not use electrical tools and equipment that are not approved for the hazardous location where the work is to be performed, i.e., do not allow unapproved electrical tools and equipment to be an ignition source for flammable vapors.
3. Develop and implement a hot work permitting program that includes atmospheric monitoring for concentrations of flammable vapors and provide ventilation to limit the concentration of flammable vapors to below 10% of their LEL.

You Have a Voice in the Workplace

The *Occupational Safety and Health Act of 1970* affords workers the right to a safe workplace (see OSHA's **Worker Rights** page, www.osha.gov/workers.html). Workers also have the right to file a complaint with OSHA if they believe that there are either violations of OSHA standards or serious workplace hazards.

How OSHA Can Help

For questions or to get information or advice, to report an emergency, report a fatality or catastrophe, or to file a confidential complaint, contact your nearest OSHA office, visit www.osha.gov or call our toll-free number at 1-800-321-OSHA (6742), TTY 1-877-889-5627. It's confidential.

More Information

Upstream oil and gas safety and health: www.osha.gov/SLTC/oilgaswell drilling/index.html

OSHA standards and regulations: www.osha.gov/law-regs.html

OSHA publications: www.osha.gov/publications

OSHA's free On-site Consultation services: www.osha.gov/consultation

Training resources: www.osha.gov/dte/index.html

4. Provide and require the use of flame-resistant clothing (FRC) for workers who are exposed to flash-fire hazards.
5. Provide worker training emphasizing the following:
    a. hazards related to working with piping and other equipment that has contained hydrocarbons;
    b. the use of electrically approved tools and equipment for locations where flammable vapors might be present, i.e., hazardous atmospheres; and
    c. hazards of working in trenches, for example, engulfment hazards and fire/explosion hazards due to the fact that flammable vapors accumulate and do not readily dissipate from trenches and other low-lying areas.

Note: The described case was selected as being representative of improper work practices which likely contributed to a fatality from an accident. The accident prevention recommendations do not necessarily reflect the outcome of any legal aspects of the incident case. OSHA encourages your company or organization to duplicate and share this information.

OSHA® Occupational Safety and Health Administration

U.S. Department of Labor
www.osha.gov (800) 321-OSHA (6742)

DEP FF-3618 12/2012

Ergonomics

What Are Musculoskeletal Disorders?

Our bodies normally recover from the wear and tear of work after a period of rest. But if the stresses continue day after day without time to recover, the damage can lead to ergonomic injuries.

Many different terms are used to describe these ergonomic injuries. For example:

- **Cumulative trauma disorders (CTDs).** Ergonomic injuries involve strain that may develop, or accumulate, over time.

- **Repetitive strain injuries (RSIs).** Ergonomic injuries are often caused by repeating the same motions over and over.

- **Musculoskeletal disorders (MSDs).** Ergonomic injuries affect the muscles, bones, tendons, nerves, and tissues.

These terms do not necessarily refer to different conditions. Many ergonomic injuries can be described in all three ways.

These disorders include a number of specific diseases such as carpal tunnel syndrome, bursitis, and tendinitis. Back injuries are the most common and most costly MSD.

Symptoms of these disorders are most common in the back, hands, arms, wrists, elbows, neck, and shoulders. They include:

- Soreness or pain (aching or sharp)
- Stiffness
- Swelling
- Loss of coordination
- Numbness
- Tingling (as though the area is "asleep")
- Unexplained weakness

If your work exposes you to any of the ergonomic risk factors described in Factsheet B, these symptoms may be signs that you have an MSD.

It is important to seek medical care if these symptoms:

- Last for more than a week
- Bother you so much that you restrict activities or take time off to recover.

If You Believe You Have an MSD

- Seek early treatment. The longer you have symptoms without getting help, the harder they can be to treat successfully.

- Find a doctor who understands work-related health problems. Don't be afraid to educate your doctor about the possible causes of MSDs at your workplace.

- If your problem is work-related, file a workers' compensation claim to cover lost work time and/or medical costs.

- Don't return to the same working conditions that caused your problem. Work with others at your workplace to ensure that the equipment or activities that contributed to your injury are changed.

- Above all, don't let your condition get you down. Finding the right doctor, getting effective treatment, and improving your work environment take persistence and energy. Don't hesitate to ask for help and don't give up until the problem is solved.

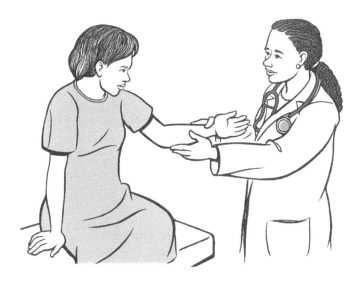

Risk Factors for Ergonomic Injuries

The field of ergonomics examines the fit between workers and their jobs. It looks at:

● What body movements and positions people use when they work.

● What tools and equipment they use.

● The physical environment (temperature, noise, lighting, etc.).

● The organizational environment (deadlines, teamwork, supervision).

● Whether any of these factors may place a worker at risk of injuries or illnesses.

The goal of ergonomics is to fit workplace conditions and job demands to the capabilities of the individual worker, instead of making the worker fit the job.

To prevent injuries, *ergonomic risk factors* must be identified. Ergonomic risk factors are workplace situations that cause wear and tear on the body and can cause injury. Once these have been identified, you can work on finding ways to eliminate them.

Ergonomic Risk Factors

RISK FACTORS	DEFINITION	POSSIBLE SOLUTIONS
Repetition	Making the same motion over and over.	Redesign task to reduce repetitions; increase rest time between repetitions; rotate among tasks with different motions.
Awkward Posture	Prolonged bending, reaching, kneeling, squatting, or twisting any part of your body.	Redesign tasks and equipment to keep the body in more "neutral" positions.
Forceful Motion	Excessive effort needed to do tasks such as pulling, pounding, pushing, and lifting.	Redesign task to reduce the exertion needed; assign more staff; use mechanical assists.
Stationary Position	Staying in one position too long, causing fatigue in muscles and joints.	Redesign task to avoid stationary positions; provide opportunities to change position.
Direct Pressure	Prolonged contact of the body with a hard surface or edge.	Improve tool and equipment design or layout to eliminate pressure; provide cushioning material.
Vibration	Using vibrating tools or equipment.	Insulate the hand or body from vibration; keep tools or equipment in good condition to reduce excessive vibration.
Extreme Temperature	Working where it is too hot or too cold. Cold reduces feeling, blood flow, and strength. Heat increases fatigue.	Control temperature where possible; insulate the body against cold by wearing gloves and warm clothing; provide breaks and fresh water in hot environments.
Work Stress	Includes machine-paced work, inadequate breaks, monotonous tasks, multiple deadlines, poor work organization, or poor supervision.	Establish reasonable workload, sufficient breaks, task variety, individual autonomy.

- The more risk factors you face, the greater your chance of injury.

- The longer you are exposed to a risk factor, the greater your chance of injury.

- By reducing or eliminating risk factors, the chance of injury can be decreased.

Identifying Risk Factors

Below are some ways to identify ergonomic risk factors.

TALK TO WORKERS: SURVEYS OR INTERVIEWS

Workers are often the best source of information on the potential problems posed by their jobs. You can conduct a written survey or talk to people individually. Factsheet C is a sample worker health survey.

LOOK AT JOBS: INSPECTIONS AND JOB EVALUATIONS

Conduct a walkaround inspection of the workplace to see which jobs or tasks may pose ergonomic problems. Those jobs can then be evaluated to identify specific risk factors. When evaluating a job, break the work down into the smallest pieces possible so that you can be specific and detailed.

Once you have watched people do their work and asked them about it, use a checklist or similar form to record risk factors as well as to track your progress in resolving a problem. Factsheet D is a sample ergonomics inspection checklist.

Below are some tips for conducting job evaluations.

A job evaluation should include three parts:

- **Discussion.** Talk to the people doing the job. Ask whether they experience pain or discomfort while performing the job and what specific activities seem to trigger that pain. Understanding the relationship between pain and specific activities can help you pinpoint tasks, workstations, equipment, or tools which may be causing or aggravating injuries.

- **Job description.** Collect information that fully describes each specific task, job, workstation, tool, and/or piece of equipment that you evaluate. Include information about speed, production requirements, and work schedule, including break times. See if there is a written job description available and supplement it with your own notes.

- **Observation and measurement.** Use direct observation, videotapes, photos, and sketches to identify risk factors. Use a checklist to record specific risk factors, including the weights of objects, how long they are held, or how far they are moved.

Health hazards in construction

OSHA FactSheet

Protecting Workers from Asbestos Hazards

Cleaning up after a flood requires hundreds of workers to renovate and repair, or tear down and dispose of, damaged or destroyed structures and materials. However, repair, renovation, and demolition operations often generate airborne asbestos, a mineral fiber that can cause chronic lung disease or cancer. The Occupational Safety and Health Administration (OSHA) has developed regulations designed to protect cleanup workers from asbestos hazards.

How You Can Become Exposed to Asbestos

Before it was known that inhalation of asbestos fibers causes several deadly diseases—including asbestosis, a progressive and often fatal lung disease, and lung and other cancers—asbestos was used in a large number of building materials and other products because of its strength, flame resistance, and insulating properties. Asbestos was used in asbestos-cement pipe and sheeting, floor and roofing felts, dry wall, floor tiles, spray on ceiling coatings, and packing materials. When buildings containing these materials are renovated or torn down, or when the asbestos- containing materials themselves are disturbed, minute asbestos fibers may be released into the air. The fibers are so small that they often cannot be seen with the naked eye; the fact that you can inhale these fibers without knowing it makes asbestos an even more dangerous hazard.

OSHA's Standards for Asbestos

The work of flood cleanup personnel involves the repair, renovation, removal, demolition, or salvage of flood-damaged structures and materials. Such materials may contain or be covered with asbestos, and cleanup personnel are protected by OSHA's construction industry asbestos standard (Title 29 Code of Federal Regulations (CFR), Part 1926.1101). This standard requires employers to follow various procedures to protect their employees from inhaling

asbestos fibers. The standard contains many requirements that vary depending on the kind of work being undertaken, the amount of asbestos in the air, and other factors. You and your employer can obtain a copy of this standard and the booklet, Asbestos Standards for Construction (OSHA 3096) describing how to comply with it, from OSHA Publications, P.O. Box 37535, Washington, DC 20013-7535, (202) 693- 1888(phone), or (202) 693-2498(fax); or visit OSHA's website at www.osha.gov.

Major Elements of OSHA's Asbestos Standard

The following include some of the major requirements of the asbestos standard. For complete information on all requirements, see 29 CFR 1926.1101.

- A permissible exposure limit (PEL) of 0.1 fiber of asbestos per cubic centimeter of air as averaged over an 8-hour period, with an excursion limit of 1.0 asbestos fibers per cubic centimeter over a 30-minute period.
- Requirements for an initial exposure assessment to ascertain expected exposures during that work operation, and periodic expo-sure monitoring in certain instances.
- Use of engineering controls, to the extent feasible, to meet the PEL. Where this is not possible, engineering controls must be used to reduce exposures to the lowest levels possible and then supplemented by the use of appropriate respiratory protection.

- Use of regulated areas to limit access to locations where asbestos concentrations may be dangerously high.
- No smoking, eating, or drinking in asbestos-regulated areas.
- Requirements for warning signs and caution labels to identify and communicate the presence of hazards and hazardous materials; recordkeeping; and medical surveillance.

Additional Information

For more information on this, and other health-related issues impacting workers, visit OSHA's Web site at www.osha.gov.

This is one in a series of informational fact sheets highlighting OSHA programs, policies or standards. It does not impose any new compliance requirements. For a comprehensive list of compliance requirements of OSHA standards or regulations, refer to Title 29 of the Code of Federal Regulations. This information will be made available to sensory impaired individuals upon request. The voice phone is (202) 693-1999; teletypewriter (TTY) number: (877) 889-5627.

For more complete information:

OSHA Occupational Safety and Health Administration

U.S. Department of Labor
www.osha.gov
(800) 321-OSHA

DSTM 9/2005

Crystalline Silica Exposure
Health Hazard Information

What is crystalline silica?

Crystalline silica is a basic component of soil, sand, granite, and many other minerals. Quartz is the most common form of crystalline silica. Cristobalite and tridymite are two other forms of crystalline silica. All three forms may become respirable size particles when workers chip, cut, drill, or grind objects that contain crystalline silica.

What are the hazards of crystalline silica?

Silica exposure remains a serious threat to nearly 2 million U.S. workers, including more than 100,000 workers in high risk jobs such as abrasive blasting, foundry work, stonecutting, rock drilling, quarry work and tunneling. The seriousness of the health hazards associated with silica exposure is demonstrated by the fatalities and disabling illnesses that continue to occur in sandblasters and rockdrillers. Crystalline silica has been classified as a human lung carcinogen. Additionally, breathing crystalline silica dust can cause **silicosis**, which in severe cases can be disabling, or even fatal. The respirable silica dust enters the lungs and causes the formation of scar tissue, thus reducing the lungs' ability to take in oxygen. There is no cure for silicosis. Since silicosis affects lung function, it makes one more susceptible to lung infections like **tuberculosis.** In addition, smoking causes lung damage and adds to the damage caused by breathing silica dust.

What are the symptoms of silicosis?

Silicosis is classified into three types: chronic/classic, accelerated, and acute.

Chronic/classic silicosis, the most common, occurs after 15–20 years of moderate to low exposures to respirable crystalline silica. Symptoms associated with chronic silicosis may or may not be obvious; therefore, workers need to have a chest x-ray to determine if there is lung damage. As the disease progresses, the worker may experience shortness of breath upon exercising and have clinical signs of poor oxygen/carbon dioxide exchange. In the later stages, the worker may experience fatigue, extreme shortness of breath, chest pain, or respiratory failure.

Accelerated silicosis can occur after 5–10 years of high exposures to respirable crystalline silica. Symptoms include severe shortness of breath, weakness, and weight loss. The onset of symptoms takes longer than in acute silicosis.

Acute silicosis occurs after a few months or as long as 2 years following exposures to extremely high concentrations of respirable crystalline silica. Symptoms of acute silicosis include severe disabling shortness of breath, weakness, and weight loss, which often leads to death.

Where are construction workers exposed to crystalline silica?

Exposure occurs during many different construction activities. The most severe exposures generally occur during abrasive blasting with sand to remove paint and rust from bridges, tanks, concrete structures, and other surfaces. Other construction activities that may result in severe exposure include: jack hammering, rock/well drilling, concrete mixing, concrete drilling, brick and concrete block cutting and sawing, tuck pointing, tunneling operations.

Where are general industry employees exposed to crystalline silica dust?

The most severe exposures to crystalline silica result from abrasive blasting, which is done to clean and smooth irregularities from molds, jewelry, and foundry castings, finish tombstones, etch or frost glass, or remove paint, oils, rust, or dirt form objects needing to be repainted or treated. Other exposures to silica dust occur in cement and brick manufacturing, asphalt pavement manufacturing, china and ceramic manufacturing and the tool and die, steel and foundry industries. Crystalline silica is used in manufacturing, household abrasives, adhesives, paints, soaps, and glass. Additionally, crystalline silica exposures occur in the maintenance, repair and replacement of refractory brick furnace linings.

In the maritime industry, shipyard employees are exposed to silica primarily in abrasive blasting operations to remove paint and clean and prepare steel hulls, bulkheads, decks, and tanks for paints and coatings.

How is OSHA addressing exposure to crystalline silica?

OSHA has an established Permissible Exposure Limit, or PEL, which is the maximum amount of crystalline silica to which workers may be exposed during an 8-hour work shift (29 *CFR* 1926.55, 1910.1000). OSHA also requires hazard communication training for workers exposed to crystalline silica, and requires a respirator protection program until engineering controls are implemented. Additionally, OSHA has a National Emphasis Program (NEP) for Crystalline Silica exposure to identify, reduce, and eliminate health hazards associated with occupational exposures.

What can employers/employees do to protect against exposures to crystalline silica?

- Replace crystalline silica materials with safer substitutes, whenever possible.

- Provide engineering or administrative controls, where feasible, such as local exhaust ventilation, and blasting cabinets. Where necessary to reduce exposures below the PEL, use protective equipment or other protective measures.

- Use all available work practices to control dust exposures, such as water sprays.

- Wear only a N95 NIOSH certified respirator, if respirator protection is required. Do not alter the respirator. Do not wear a tight-fitting respirator with a beard or mustache that prevents a good seal between the respirator and the face.

- Wear only a Type CE abrasive-blast supplied-air respirator for abrasive blasting.

- Wear disposable or washable work clothes and shower if facilities are available. Vacuum the dust from your clothes or change into clean clothing before leaving the work site.

- Participate in training, exposure monitoring, and health screening and surveillance programs to monitor any adverse health effects caused by crystalline silica exposures.

- Be aware of the operations and job tasks creating crystalline silica exposures in your workplace environment and know how to protect yourself.

- Be aware of the health hazards related to exposures to crystalline silica. Smoking adds to the lung damage caused by silica exposures.

- Do not eat, drink, smoke, or apply cosmetics in areas where crystalline silica dust is present. Wash your hands and face outside of dusty areas before performing any of these activities.

- Remember: If it's silica, it's not just dust.

How can I get more information on safety and health?

OSHA has various publications, standards, technical assistance, and compliance tools to help you, and offers extensive assistance through workplace consultation, voluntary protection programs, strategic partnerships, alliances, state plans, grants, training, and education. OSHA's *Safety and Health Program Management Guidelines* (*Federal Register* 54:3904-3916, January 26, 1989) detail elements critical to the development of a successful safety and health management system. This and other information are available on OSHA's website.

- For one free copy of OSHA publications, send a self-addressed mailing label to OSHA Publications Office, 200 Constitution Avenue N.W., N-3101, Washington, DC 20210; or send a request to our fax at (202) 693–2498, or call us toll-free at (800) 321–OSHA.

- To order OSHA publications online at **www.osha.gov**, go to **Publications** and follow the instructions for ordering.

- To file a complaint by phone, report an emergency, or get OSHA advice, assistance, or products, contact your nearest OSHA office under the U.S. Department of Labor listing in your phone book, or call toll-free at **(800) 321– OSHA (6742)**. The teletypewriter (TTY) number is (877) 889–5627.

- To file a complaint online or obtain more information on OSHA federal and state programs, visit OSHA's website.

OSHA
Occupational Safety
and Health Administration
U.S. Department of Labor

2002

OSHA FactSheet

Protecting Workers from Lead Hazards

Cleaning up after a flood requires hundreds of workers to renovate and repair, or tear down and dispose of, damaged or destroyed structures and materials. Repair, renovation and demolition operations often generate dangerous airborne concentrations of lead, a metal that can cause damage to the nervous system, kidneys, blood forming organs, and reproductive system if inhaled or ingested in danger-ous quantities. The Occupational Safety and Health Administration (OSHA) has developed regulations designed to protect workers involved in construction activities from the hazards of lead exposure.

How You Can Become Exposed to Lead

Lead is an ingredient in thousands of products widely used throughout industry, including lead-based paints, lead solder, electrical fittings and conduits, tank linings, plumbing fixtures, and many metal alloys. Although many uses of lead have been banned, lead-based paints continue to be used on bridges, railways, ships, and other steel structures because of its rust- and corrosion-inhibiting properties. Also, many homes were painted with lead-containing paints. Significant lead exposures can also occur when paint is removed from surfaces previously covered with lead-based paint.

Operations that can generate lead dust and fumes include:
- Demolition of structures;
- Flame-torch cutting;
- Welding;
- Use of heat guns, sanders, scrapers, or grinders to remove lead paint; and
- Abrasive blasting of steel structures

OSHA has regulations governing construc-tion worker exposure to lead. Employers of construction workers engaged in the repair, renovation, removal, demolition, and salvage of flood-damaged structures and materials are responsible for the development and implementation of a worker protection program in accordance with Title 29 Code of Federal Regulations (CFR), Part 1926.62. This program is essential to minimize worker risk of lead exposure. Construction projects vary in their scope and potential for exposing workers to lead and other hazards. Many projects involve only limited exposure, such as the removal of paint from a few interior residential surfaces, while others may involve substantial exposures. Employers must be in compliance with OSHA's lead standard at all times. A copy of the standard and a brochure— Lead in Construction (OSHA 3142) —describing how to comply with it, are avail-able from OSHA Publications, P.O. Box 37535, Washington, D.C. 20013-7535, (202) 693-1888(phone), or (202) 693-2498(fax); or visit OSHA's website at www.osha.gov.

Major Elements of OSHA's Lead Standard
- A permissible exposure limit (PEL) of 50 micrograms of lead per cubic meter of air, as averaged over an 8-hour period.
- Requirements that employers use engineering controls and work practices, where feasible, to reduce worker exposure.
- Requirements that employees observe good personal hygiene practices, such as washing hands before eating and taking a shower before leaving the worksite.
- Requirements that employees be provided with protective clothing and, where necessary, with respiratory protection accordance with 29 CFR 1910.134.

- A requirement that employees exposed to high levels of lead be enrolled in a medical surveillance program.

Name: _____   Date: _____

Knowledge Check: Health Hazards in Construction

1. Which of the following is a common type of health hazard?
   a. Chemical hazards
   b. Economic hazards
   c. Electrical hazards
   d. Fall hazards

2. Which of the following is an example of a physical health hazard?
   a. Asbestos
   b. Noise
   c. Silica
   d. Lead

3. Which is an appropriate engineering control for protection against noise exposures?
   a. Audiograms
   b. Earplugs
   c. Increasing distance between source
   d. Constructing sound barriers

4. Which is a requirement of the employer?
   a. Determine if workers exposures exceed OSHA PELs
   b. Perform medical evaluations on all employees
   c. Develop silica training programs for all employees
   d. Provide workers with steel-toed boots

Managing safety and health

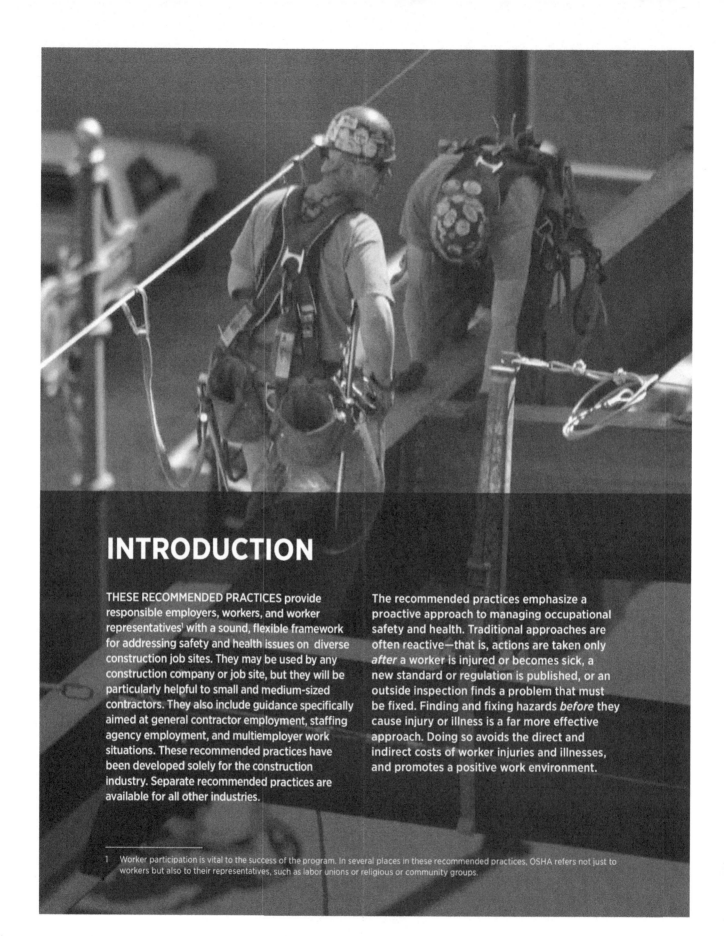

INTRODUCTION

THESE RECOMMENDED PRACTICES provide responsible employers, workers, and worker representatives[1] with a sound, flexible framework for addressing safety and health issues on diverse construction job sites. They may be used by any construction company or job site, but they will be particularly helpful to small and medium-sized contractors. They also include guidance specifically aimed at general contractor employment, staffing agency employment, and multiemployer work situations. These recommended practices have been developed solely for the construction industry. Separate recommended practices are available for all other industries.

The recommended practices emphasize a proactive approach to managing occupational safety and health. Traditional approaches are often reactive—that is, actions are taken only *after* a worker is injured or becomes sick, a new standard or regulation is published, or an outside inspection finds a problem that must be fixed. Finding and fixing hazards *before* they cause injury or illness is a far more effective approach. Doing so avoids the direct and indirect costs of worker injuries and illnesses, and promotes a positive work environment.

1   Worker participation is vital to the success of the program. In several places in these recommended practices, OSHA refers not just to workers but also to their representatives, such as labor unions or religious or community groups.

These best practices present principles and approaches to implementing and maintaining a safety and health program for the entire construction company. OSHA recognizes that a wide variety of small and large construction job sites exist. Some are short-duration, while others may take years to complete; some sites are characterized by frequently changing conditions, while other sites' conditions may change less often. An effective program emphasizes top-level ownership, participation by employees, and a "find and fix" approach to workplace hazards.

The "find and fix" approach to workplace hazards refers to the "Hazard Identification" and "Hazard Prevention and Control" core elements. Because of the wide variety of site conditions, these two core elements should be implemented on a site-specific basis in order to effectively detect and correct hazards.

The concept of continuous improvement is central to these recommended practices. As with any journey, the first step is often the most challenging. The idea is to begin with a basic program and grow from there. By initially focusing on achieving modest goals, monitoring performance, and evaluating outcomes, you can help your company progress over time along the path to higher levels of safety and health.

THE BENEFITS OF IMPLEMENTING THESE RECOMMENDED PRACTICES

Responsible employers know that the main goal of a safety and health program is to prevent work-related injuries, illnesses, and deaths, as well as the suffering and financial hardship these events can cause for workers, their families, and their employers.

Employers may find that implementing these recommended practices brings other benefits as well. The renewed or enhanced commitment to safety and health and the cooperative atmosphere between employers and workers have been linked to:

- Improvements in production and quality.
- Better employee morale.
- Improved employee recruiting and retention.
- A more favorable image and reputation (among customers, suppliers, and the community).

A study of small employers in Ohio found that workers' compensation claims fell dramatically after working with OSHA's SHARP program to adopt programs similar to those described in these recommended practices.

average number of claims
DECREASED
52%

cost per claim
DECREASED
80%

average lost time per claim
DECREASED
87%

claims
(per million dollars of payroll)
DECREASED
88%

Source: Ohio Bureau of Workers' Compensation (2011), Ohio 21(d) SHARP Program Performance Assessment.

IMPLEMENTING
a safety & health program

can help employers avoid the

INDIRECT
COSTS
that result from

WORKPLACE
INCIDENTS

such as

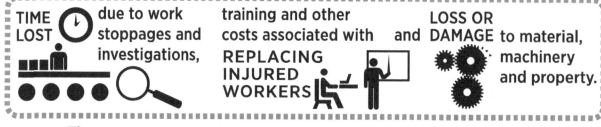

TIME LOST due to work stoppages and investigations,

training and other costs associated with **REPLACING INJURED WORKERS**

and **LOSS OR DAMAGE** to material, machinery and property.

These **INDIRECT COSTS** have been estimated to be at least **2.7** times the **DIRECT COSTS**

Source: Leigh, J.P. (2011), Economic Burden of Occupational Injury and Illness in the United States. Milbank Quarterly, 89:728-772.[2]

HOW TO USE THE RECOMMENDED PRACTICES

Each section of the recommended practices describes a core program element (see page 7), followed by several action items. Each action item is an example of steps that general contractors, subcontractors, managers, supervisors, and workers can take to establish, implement, maintain, and improve safety and health programs. A general self-evaluation tool can be found on the recommended practices Web page. It can be tailored to your construction site to track your progress and document how you have implemented (or will implement) each action item.

Seven interrelated elements

The seven core elements are interrelated and are best viewed as part of an integrated system. Actions taken under one core element can

---

2   The 2.7 multiplier for indirect costs includes some social costs, such as workers' compensation costs not covered by insurance.

(and likely will) affect actions needed under one or more other elements. For example, workers must be trained in reporting procedures and hazard identification techniques in order to be effective participants. Thus, the "Education and Training" core element supports the "Worker Participation" core element. Similarly, setting goals (as described under "Management Leadership") will be more effective if you routinely evaluate your progress in meeting those goals (see "Program Evaluation and Improvement"). Progress in each core element is important to achieve maximum benefit from the program.

One size does not fit all

While the action items under each core element are specific, they are not prescriptive. The process described in these recommended practices can, and should, be tailored to the needs of each construction company and/or job site. Likewise, your safety and health program can and should evolve. Experimentation, evaluation, and program modification are all part of the process. You may also experience setbacks from time to time. What is important is that you learn from setbacks, remain committed to finding out what works best for you, and continue to try different approaches.

Injuries and illnesses occur in all construction trades. The preventive approaches described in these recommended practices work equally well for small and large organizations in the construction industry. Small employers may find that they can best accomplish the actions outlined in these recommended practices using informal communications and procedures. Larger employers, who have more complex work processes and hazards, may require a more formal and detailed program. They may also wish to integrate their safety and health program with other programs that they are using to manage production, quality control, and environmental protection or sustainability.

The importance of worker participation

Throughout these recommended practices, OSHA emphasizes the importance of worker participation in the safety and health program. For a program to succeed, workers (and, if applicable, their representatives) must participate in developing and implementing every element of the safety and health program. This emphasis on worker participation is consistent with the OSH Act, OSHA standards, and OSHA enforcement policies and procedures, which recognize the rights and roles of workers and their representatives in matters of workplace safety and health. Several action items described in these recommended practices rely on perspectives, expertise, and input that can come only from workers and their representatives.

When more than one employer is involved

Employers and workers on "multiemployer" worksites should pay particular attention to the "Coordination and Communication for Employers on Multiemployer Worksites" section. This section describes actions that controlling employers such as general contractors, prime contractors and construction managers, subcontractors, and temporary staffing agencies (and their workers) should take to ensure protection of everyone on the job site.

For tools and resources to help you implement these recommended practices, visit: **www.osha.gov/shpguidelines**

NINE EASY THINGS TO GET YOUR PROGRAM STARTED

If these recommended practices appear challenging, here are some simple steps you can take to get started. Completing these steps will give you a solid base from which to take on some of the more structured actions presented in the recommended practices.

1. ALWAYS SET SAFETY AND HEALTH AS THE TOP PRIORITY

Tell your workers that making sure they finish the day and go home safely is the way you do business. Assure them that you will work with them to find and fix any hazards that could injure them or make them sick.

2. LEAD BY EXAMPLE

Practice safe behaviors yourself and make safety part of your daily conversations with workers.

3. IMPLEMENT A REPORTING SYSTEM

Develop and communicate a simple procedure for workers to report any injuries, illnesses, incidents (including near misses/close calls), hazards, or safety and health concerns without fear of retaliation. Include an option for reporting hazards or concerns anonymously.

4. PROVIDE TRAINING

Train workers on how to identify and control hazards using, for example, OSHA's Hazard Identification Training Tool.

5. CONDUCT INSPECTIONS

Inspect the job site with workers and ask them to identify any activity, piece of equipment, or material that concerns them. Use checklists and other resources, such as OSHA's Construction Industry Digest, to help identify problems.

6. COLLECT HAZARD CONTROL IDEAS

Talk with workers about ideas on safety improvements throughout the project.

7. IMPLEMENT HAZARD CONTROLS

Assign workers the task of choosing, implementing, and evaluating the solutions.

8. ADDRESS EMERGENCIES

Identify foreseeable emergency scenarios and develop instructions on what to do in each case. Meet to discuss these procedures and post them in a visible location at the job site.

9. MAKE IMPROVEMENTS

Set aside a regular time to discuss safety and health issues, with the goal of identifying ways to improve the program.

Foundations for safety leadership

MANAGEMENT LEADERSHIP

MANAGEMENT PROVIDES the leadership, vision, and resources needed to implement an effective safety and health program. Management leadership means that business owners, managers, and supervisors:

- Make worker safety and health a core organizational value.

- Are fully committed to eliminating hazards, protecting workers, and continuously improving safety and health on job sites.

- Provide sufficient resources to implement and maintain the safety and health program.

- Visibly demonstrate and communicate their safety and health commitment to workers and others.

- Set an example through their own actions.

Action item 1: Communicate your commitment to a safety and health program

A clear, written policy helps you communicate that safety and health is a primary organizational value—as important as productivity, profitability, product or service quality, and customer satisfaction.

How to accomplish it

Establish a written policy signed by top management describing the organization's commitment to safety and health, and pledging to establish and maintain a safety and health program for all workers.

- Communicate the policy to all workers and, at appropriate times and places, to relevant parties, including:

  - Contractors, subcontractors, staffing agencies, and temporary workers at your worksite(s)

  - Suppliers and vendors

  - Other businesses in a multi-tenant building

  - Visitors

  - Customers

- Reinforce management commitment by considering safety and health in all business decisions, including estimating and bidding on projects, subcontractor and vendor selection, scheduling, and implementing safety designs into construction processes, drawings, and modifications.

- Be visible in operations and set an example by following the same safety and health procedures you expect workers to follow. Conduct weekly or daily toolbox talks on safety and health, and discuss/review safety and health indicators and/or open safety items on a "to do" list.

Action item 2: Define program goals

By establishing specific goals and objectives, management sets expectations for managers, supervisors, and workers, and for the program overall. The goals and objectives should focus on specific actions that will improve worker safety and health.

How to accomplish it

- Establish realistic, measurable goals for improving safety and health.

- Develop plans to achieve the goals by assigning tasks and responsibilities to particular people, setting timeframes, and determining resource needs.

Action item 3: Allocate resources

Management provides the resources needed to implement the safety and health program, pursue program goals, and address program shortcomings when they are identified.

How to accomplish it

- Estimate the resources needed to establish and implement the program. One example is ensuring safety equipment is included in the project budget.

- Allow time in workers' schedules for them to fully participate in the program. Safety can be built into the labor rates when estimating a project.

- Integrate safety and health into planning and budgeting processes, and align budgets with program needs.

- Provide and direct resources to operate and maintain the program, meet safety and health commitments, and pursue program goals.

Note: Resource needs will vary depending on your organization's size, complexity, hazard types, and program maturity and development. Resource needs may include capital equipment and supplies, staff time, training, access to information and tools (e.g., vendor information, Safety Data Sheets, injury/illness data, checklists, online databases) and access to safety and health experts, including OSHA's free and confidential On-site Consultation Program (see "For More Information" in the introduction to these recommended practices).

Action item 4: Expect performance

Management leads the program effort by establishing roles and responsibilities and providing an open, positive environment that encourages communication about safety and health.

How to accomplish it

- Identify a frontline person or persons who will lead the safety program effort, make plans, coordinate activities, and track progress. Define and regularly communicate responsibilities and authorities for implementing and maintaining the program, and hold people accountable for performance.

- Provide positive recognition for meeting or exceeding safety and health goals aimed at preventing injury and illness (e.g., reporting close calls/near misses, attending training, conducting inspections).

- Establish ways for management and all workers to communicate freely and often about safety and health issues, without fear of retaliation.

Note: Maintaining a positive and encouraging tone is important. Successful programs reward, rather than discipline, workers who identify problems or concerns, much like successful quality programs. Disciplinary measures should be reserved for situations in which an individual manager or worker is uncooperative or becomes an impediment to progress.

WORKER PARTICIPATION

TO BE EFFECTIVE, any safety and health program needs the meaningful participation of workers and their representatives. Workers have much to gain from a successful program, and the most to lose if the program fails. They also often know the most about potential hazards associated with their jobs. Successful programs tap into this knowledge base.

Worker participation means participation in establishing, operating, evaluating, and improving the safety and health program. All workers at a worksite should participate, including those employed by subcontractors and temporary staffing agencies (see "Coordination and Communication on Multiemployer Worksites").

IN AN EFFECTIVE safety and health program, all workers:

- Are encouraged to participate in the program and feel comfortable providing input and reporting safety or health concerns.

- Have access to information they need to participate effectively in the program.

- Have opportunities to participate in all phases of program design and implementation.

- Do not experience retaliation when they raise safety and health concerns; report injuries, illnesses, and hazards; participate in the program; or exercise safety and health rights.

Note: Worker participation is vital to the success of safety and health programs. Where workers are represented by a union, it is important that worker representatives also participate in the program, consistent with the rights provided to worker representatives under the Occupational Safety and Health Act of 1970 and the National Labor Relations Act.

RETALIATION AGAINST WORKERS IS ILLEGAL

Section 11(c) of the Occupational Safety and Health Act of 1970 prohibits employers from retaliating against employees for exercising a variety of rights guaranteed under the OSH Act, such as filing a safety and health complaint with OSHA, raising a health and safety concern with their employers, participating in an OSHA inspection, or reporting a work-related injury or illness. OSHA vigorously enforces the anti-retaliation protections provided under 11(c) of the OSH Act and other federal statutes. For more information, see www.whistleblowers.gov.

Action item 1: Encourage workers to participate in the program

By encouraging workers to participate in the program, management signals that it values their input into safety and health decisions.

How to accomplish it

- Give workers the necessary time and resources to participate in the program.

- Acknowledge and provide positive reinforcement to those who participate in the program.

- Maintain an open door policy that invites workers to talk to managers about safety and health and to make suggestions.

Action item 2: Encourage workers to report safety and health concerns

Workers are often best positioned to identify safety and health concerns and program shortcomings, such as emerging job site hazards, unsafe conditions, close calls/near misses, and actual incidents. By encouraging reporting and following up promptly on all reports, employers can address issues before someone gets hurt or becomes ill.

How to accomplish it

- Establish a simple process for workers to report injuries, illnesses, close calls/near misses, hazards, and other safety and health concerns, and respond to reports promptly. Include an option for anonymous reporting to reduce fear of reprisal.[3]

- Report back to workers routinely and frequently about action taken in response to their concerns and suggestions.

- Emphasize that management will use reported information only to improve job site safety and health, and that no worker will experience retaliation for bringing such information to management's attention (see Action item 5).

- Empower all workers to initiate or request a temporary suspension or shutdown of any work activity or operation they believe to be unsafe.

- Involve workers in finding solutions to reported issues.

---

3   Under OSHA's injury and illness recordkeeping rule (29 CFR 1904), employers are required to establish a "reasonable" procedure for employees to report work-related injuries and illnesses promptly and accurately. A reasonable procedure is defined as one that would not deter or discourage a reasonable employee from accurately reporting a workplace injury or illness.

Action item 3: Give workers access to safety and health information

Sharing relevant safety and health information with workers fosters trust and helps organizations make more informed safety and health decisions.

How to accomplish it

- Give workers the information they need to understand safety and health hazards and control measures on the job site. Some OSHA standards require employers to make specific types of information available to workers, such as:

  - Safety Data Sheets (SDSs)

  - Injury and illness data (prevent disclosure of sensitive and personal information as required)

  - Results of worker exposure monitoring conducted at job sites (prevent disclosure of sensitive and personal information as required)

- Other useful information for workers to review can include:

  - Chemical and equipment manufacturer safety recommendations

  - Job site equipment and vehicle inspection reports

  - Incident investigation reports (prevent disclosure of sensitive and personal information as required)

  - Job hazard analyses (JHAs) and/or job safety analyses (JSAs)

Action item 4: Involve workers in all aspects of the program

Including worker input at every step of program design and implementation improves your ability to identify the presence and causes of job site hazards, creates a sense of program ownership among workers, enhances their understanding of how the program works, and helps sustain the program over time.

How to accomplish it

- Provide opportunities for workers to participate in all aspects of the program, including, but not limited to helping:

  - Develop the program and set goals to reduce or eliminate injuries and illnesses.

  - Report hazards and develop solutions that improve safety and health.

  - Analyze hazards in each step of routine and nonroutine jobs, tasks, and processes.

  - Define and document safe work practices.

  - Conduct site inspections, including equipment and vehicles.

  - Develop and revise safety procedures.

  - Participate in incident and close call/near miss investigations.

  - Train current coworkers and new hires.

  - Develop, implement, and evaluate training programs.

  - Evaluate program performance and identify ways to improve it.

  - Take part in exposure monitoring and medical surveillance associated with health hazards.

- Conduct daily planning meetings, huddles, toolbox talks, or tailgate meetings to engage workers in the safety and health program.

Action item 5: Remove barriers to participation

To participate meaningfully in the program, workers must feel that their input is welcome, their voices will be heard, and they can access reporting mechanisms. Participation will be suppressed if language, education, or skill levels on the job site are not considered, or if workers fear retaliation or discrimination for speaking up (for example, if investigations focus on blaming individuals rather than the underlying conditions that led to the incident, or if reporting an incident or concern could jeopardize the award of incentive-based prizes, rewards, or bonuses).

How to accomplish it

- Ensure that workers from all levels of the organization can participate regardless of their skill level, education, or language.

- Provide frequent and regular feedback to show employees that their safety and health concerns are being heard and addressed.

- Authorize sufficient time and resources to facilitate worker participation; for example, hold safety and health meetings during regular working hours.

- Ensure that the program protects workers from being retaliated against for reporting injuries, illnesses, and hazards; participating in the program; or exercising their safety and health rights. Ensure that other policies and programs do not discourage worker participation.

- Post the Section 11(c) fact sheet (found at www.whistleblowers.gov) in the workplace or otherwise make it available for easy access by employees.

Note: Incentive programs (such as point systems, awards, and prizes) should be designed in a manner that does not discourage injury and illness reporting; otherwise, hazards may remain undetected. Although sometimes required by law or insurance providers, mandatory drug testing following injuries can also suppress reporting. Effective safety and health programs recognize positive safety and health activities, such as reporting hazardous conditions or suggesting safer work procedures. (See OSHA's "Employer Safety Incentive and Disincentive Policies and Practices" memorandum, dated March 12, 2012: www.osha.gov/as/opa/whistleblowermemo.html.)

Skills	Actions
Leads by Example	• Establishes safety expectations as a core value • Shares safety vision with team members • Demonstrates a positive attitude about safety • Walks the Talk • Leads up
Engages and Empowers Team Members	Engages, encourages, and empowers team members to identify and act upon unsafe situations by... • Reporting hazards and safety concerns • Providing solutions • Reporting near misses • Stopping work if necessary
Actively Listens and Practices 3-way Communication	• Actively listens to **hear** what team members are saying • Practices 3-way communication by having person repeat the message they heard
DEvelops Team Members Through Teaching, Coaching, and Feedback	• Respectfully teaches and coaches workers • Watches the learner fix the hazardous situation or perform the task to make sure it's done correctly • Focuses on potential consequences rather than on the team member • Uses the FIST principle: **F**acts, **I**mpact, **S**uggestions, **T**imely
Recognizes Team Members for a Job Well Done	• Privately and/or publicly acknowledges team members for going above and beyond when it comes to safety

Books in the OSHA Outreach Training Program Series

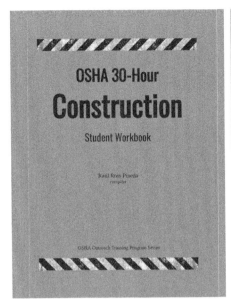

OSHA 30-Hour Construction Student Workbook (ISBN-13: 978-1975997830)

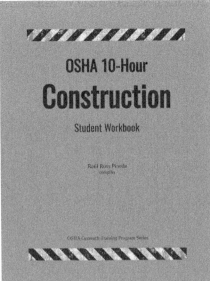

OSHA 10-Hour construction Student Workbook (ISBN-13: 978-1546484363)

OSHA 10-Hour General Industry; Student Workbook (ISBN-13: 978-1979408592)

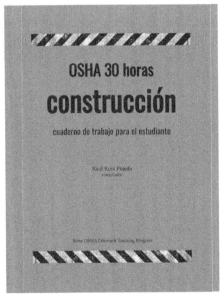

OSHA 30 horas construcción cuaderno de trabajo para el estudiante (ISBN-13: 978-1977837479)

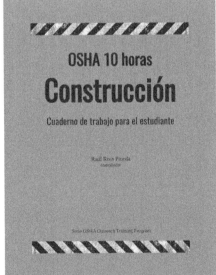

OSHA 10 horas construcción cuaderno de trabajo para el estudiante (ISBN-13: 978-1974103553)

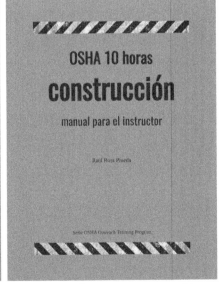

OSHA 10 horas construcción: manual para el instructor

(coming soon)

Search by author, title or ISBN in your favorite online bookstore

Made in the USA
Las Vegas, NV
25 September 2023

78064276R00142